The Gospel according to Bob Dylan

The Gospel according to Bob Dylan

The Old, Old Story for Modern Times

Michael J. Gilmour

WESTMINSTER
JOHN KNOX PRESS
LOUISVILLE • KENTUCKY

© 2011 Michael J. Gilmour

First edition
Published by Westminster John Knox Press
Louisville, Kentucky

11 12 13 14 15 16 17 18 19 20—10 9 8 7 6 5 4 3 2 1

Scripture quotations, unless otherwise indicated, are from the New Revised Standard Version of the Bible, copyright © 1989 by the Division of Christian Education of the National Council of the Churches of Christ in the U.S.A., and used by permission.

Excerpt from "Death Is Not the End: Artistic Collaboration and a Musical Resurrection in Bob Dylan's *Chronicles*," *Montague Street* 1 (Winter 2009). Reprinted by permission.

This book has not been prepared, approved, or licensed by any person or entity associated with Bob Dylan.

Book design by Sharon Adams
Cover design by designpointinc.com
Cover illustration: © Bettmann/Corbis Images

Library of Congress Cataloging-in-Publication Data

Gilmour, Michael J.
  The Gospel according to Bob Dylan : the old, old story for modern times / Michael J. Gilmour.
       p. cm.
  Includes bibliographical references.
  ISBN 978-0-664-23207-8 (alk. paper)
  1. Dylan, Bob, 1941—Criticism and interpretation. 2. Popular music—Religious aspects. 3. Bible in music. I. Title.
  ML420.D98G5516 2011
  782.42164092--dc22
                                                              2010034957

PRINTED IN THE UNITED STATES OF AMERICA

∞ The paper used in this publication meets the minimum requirements of the American National Standard for Information Sciences—Permanence of Paper for Printed Library Materials, ANSI Z39.48-1992.

Westminster John Knox Press advocates the responsible use of our natural resources. The text paper of this book is made from 30% post-consumer waste.

Most Westminster John Knox Press books are available at special quantity discounts when purchased in bulk by corporations, organizations, and special-interest groups. For more information, please e-mail SpecialSales@wjkbooks.com.

Contents

Preface

> Opinions are to the vast apparatus of social existence what oil is
> to machines: one does not go up to a turbine and pour machine
> oil over it; one applies a little to hidden spindles and joints that
> one has to know.
>
> Walter Benjamin[1]

A confession. I sometimes use the shuffle feature on my iPod
when listening to Bob Dylan. Another confession. I like Dylan
compilations and greatest-hits packages. Some purists might
cringe, preferring to experience and think about whole albums,
not a hodge-podge of individual songs. Better to spend seventy-
plus minutes with *Blonde on Blonde*, they say, enjoying each track
in its intended environment as it resonates with others lyrically
and musically. Every album is a unique mixture of inspiration,
musicianship, artistic vision, emotional headspace, influence, and
political and social moment. *Blonde on Blonde* is a product of
1965–1966, so don't mash it up with a live performance from
the 1970s, or with *"Love and Theft."* Greatest-hits packages and
compilations, they say, are mere money grabs by record labels,
artificial constructs intended to hook particular buyers wanting
only a few key songs, not the *real* fans who already own the complete works. Musicians often have little to do with such collections
anyway (though there are exceptions, like Dylan's 1985 *Biograph*
for which he provides extensive comments on the songs).

I have my purist moments, to be sure, and more times than
not play through whole albums, imagining they tell a single story

from opening to closing notes. Still, the jumble of shuffling and the quirky selections of "best of" CDs and compilations appeal to me. I like the surprising tastes generated by fifty-plus Dylan discs thrown together into some kind of folk-country-rock-gospel-blues-Americana musical stew. I also enjoy hearing the varying textures in his recorded voice over the span of a half century. I always discover or rediscover something—an unexpected intertext, a sentiment, or an idea forgotten or not previously noticed. The experience is a little like a Bob Dylan concert. No two shows are alike, and you never know what you will get from night to night.

Such an unsystematic, haphazard approach to the Bob Dylan canon temporarily disrupts the tendency to hear his music through some predetermined grid, some guiding concern like a biographical interpretation of songs or focus on religious, political, or literary dimensions of his work. It also limits a listener's habits of choice, since most gravitate to a few favorite CDs while ignoring others. When I waive this control every now and again, allowing the iPod to make selections for me, there is opportunity for a fresh hearing of songs, including ones usually passed over. What thrills me about this music is its ability to startle—those unexpected flashes of insight and beauty, those revelatory moments.

This subjective and idiosyncratic approach to analysis is appropriate for commentary on the spirituality of Bob Dylan's music. So much that is observed and experienced in this area is in the eye (or ear) of the beholder, as we regularly discover value and profundity in places where others see (or hear) nothing.

I take my lead from the essayist Walter Benjamin (1892–1940) who, writing in the late 1920s, claimed the construction of life "is at present in the power of facts far more than convictions."[2] He rejects a style of writing and discourse about literature and culture that he describes as sterile and pretentious (which, unfortunately for me, includes books!) and prefers instead forms of expression that are more spontaneous and in the moment, such as leaflets and placards. If Benjamin were with us today, I suspect he would add e-mail, tweets, and blogs to his list. He prizes participation in the subject matter.

Writing about music and religion in the pretentious and sterile medium of a book is problematic, to allow Benjamin's point, because in many ways the discovery of meaning in both categories depends on lived experience. Participation is necessary, and dwelling on facts alone apart from opinion and conviction limits possibilities for discourse considerably. Benjamin's distinction of fact and opinion is particularly useful for a discussion about perceived religious significance in music because it is a subject where "facts" are hard to come by. It is difficult to pinpoint why a song is spiritually consequential, and arguing such things rarely proves convincing to all. We must work with opinions and convictions that by their very nature are idiosyncratic and contingent on the one holding them.

Walter Benjamin resembles Bob Dylan in certain respects. They share habits of writing and ways of looking at the world that are evident despite differences in their preferred modes of expression. For both, much of their most important work occurs in the limited confines of their chosen mediums—essays and short articles for Benjamin; song lyrics for Dylan—resulting in compact expression and penetrating aphorisms. Both writers also explore an oddly eclectic range of subjects easily overlooked by others, taking an interest in the easily forgotten and overlooked, the inconspicuous miscellany, the quickly discarded, and the ephemera of the busy modern world. One need only compare section headings in Benjamin's *One-Way Street* with titles of Dylan's satellite program *Theme Time Radio Hour* to see what I mean:

Benjamin: Filling Station; Breakfast Room; Standard Clock; Manorially Furnished Ten-Room Apartment; Chinese Curios; Gloves; Mexican Embassy; Construction Site; First Aid; Antiques; Tax Advice

Dylan: Weather; Mother; Drinking; Baseball; Coffee; Jail; Father; Wedding; Divorce; Summer; Flowers; Cars; Rich Man, Poor Man; Devil; Eyes; Dogs; Friends & Neighbors; Radio; The Bible

It seems both men share an insatiable curiosity and ability to find caches of meaning in the simplest things.

Benjamin and Dylan constantly use citation as well. The singer admits he cannot list all the influences because "there's too many / to mention. . . . Open up yer eyes an' ears an' yer influenced."[3] His work is an intertextual web, composed of allusions to and quotations of songs, literature, films, cultural references past and present, and anything else that helps him spin a good yarn. So too for Walter Benjamin, whose most famous work is the incomplete and fragmentary *Arcades Project*,[4] composed largely of quotations and notes, rather than a systematic, flowing prose. Benjamin's magnum opus highlights yet another similarity between these writers. In the *Arcades Project*, Benjamin compiles information about nineteenth-century urban life as a way of better understanding the commoditization of modern times. He turns to history to see contemporary society more clearly. So too with Bob Dylan, who feeds constantly on the music and stories of bygone days and yet helps us make sense of our own time and place. Because of such shared habits of thought and writing, I return to Walter Benjamin periodically, looking to him for illuminations as we explore Dylan's work.

Though I employ "the pretentious, universal gesture of the book,"[5] I still hope to find a voice suitable for my subject and avoid the kind of writing Benjamin describes as sterile. To help achieve this, I try as much as possible to alternate "action and writing" as he prescribes, which I take to mean articulating a lived experience of my subject. What might this mean for understanding Dylan? For one thing, Benjamin prizes the "prompt language" of opinion and conviction, which provides some justification to include personal, purely subjective reactions to Bob Dylan's music. For another, I understand his references to "action and writing" and "active communities"[6] as indicating dialogue with like-minded souls. This dialogue can include texts, so I often introduce other writings—including literary and theoretical texts—as collaborators in this exploration of religious meaning and music. Of course, it can also include dialogue with Bob Dylan fans, and I am fortunate to have many in my circle of influence who are quick to share their ideas and listen to mine. However, there are too many to mention "an' I might leave one out" if I tried to list them all, "An' that wouldn't be fair."[7]

Introduction

I believe the songs.

Bob Dylan

There Was This Song I Heard One Time

In a recent novel, Salman Rushdie refers to a musician whose songs "could break open the seals of the universe and let divinity through into the everyday world" and a poet who "opened windows in the heart and mind through which both light and darkness could be seen."[1] Music can lift audiences out of the day-to-day, allowing them to "see" with new eyes that which is right in front of them and that which is beyond them—call it divinity, transcendence, spirituality, or whatever you choose. These words also describe the poet's ability to reveal the human condition in all its light and darkness, to allow glimpses into the self with all that is good about it and all that is not. Music and its poetry help those with ears to hear better understand their place in this world, and, on occasion, they permit something approaching spiritual insight. The narrator in the Tragically Hip's song "Bobcaygeon" *(Phantom Power,* 1998) has an epiphany of sorts when he sees "the constellations / Reveal themselves one star at a time." What triggers this revelation? Was it the one addressed by the singer (and therefore love and romance, presumably)? Maybe, but he entertains other possibilities too: "Coulda been the Willie Nelson, coulda been the wine."[2] Music might lie behind his newfound ability to pull patterns out of the night sky. And if music has the potential to do this, it might also provide comfort and a spiritual resource as it does for the singer in U2's *No Line On The Horizon* (2009): "Let me in the sound, now / God, I'm going down / I don't wanna drown now / Meet me in the sound"; "I've found grace inside a sound / I found grace, it's all that I found" ("Get on Your Boots" and "Breathe").[3]

Bob Dylan is a musician and poet fitting Rushdie's descriptions, and one who produces the kind of art celebrated by the Tragically Hip and U2—art that feeds both mind and spirit. I find divinity shining through his songs into my everyday life, hence the subtitle of this book: *The Old, Old Story for Modern Times*. I take these words from the A. Katherine Hankey poem "Tell Me the Old, Old Story" (1866) that lies behind the hymn of that name, as well as "I Love to Tell the Story" (1866). I take "Modern Times" from the title of a Bob Dylan album, which in turn may originate in a 1936 Charlie Chaplin film. Dylan also uses the phrase in his liner notes to *World Gone Wrong* (1993): "All their songs are raw to the bone & are faultlessly made for these modern times (the New Dark Ages); nothing effete about the Mississippi Sheiks."

As music fans, we inevitably open our lives to a surprising intimacy with our favorite songs, genres, and artists. Music is so much a part of all we do that we tend to associate sounds and lyrics with significant moments in our lives and the emotional apogees that accompany them. The music of our youth might remind us of our first taste of independence and rebellion, or deep friendship and love, or the sense of our potential at that formative stage. Perhaps the music we enjoy as adults provides solace from anxieties and escape from the monotonous demands and responsibilities of daily life. It follows that no two people will hear their most cherished songs in quite the same way. We internalize those sounds and words, making them our own as they mingle with our deepest feelings. Discussions about music and art, whether formal or informal, are often highly tendentious for this reason. Throughout this book, I return to reflections on ways fans contribute to the meaning they find in music. We construct something out of songs we want or need.

No doubt, many of the connections we make between our own stories and Bob Dylan's music would strike others as odd. My "relationship" with Bob Dylan's 1980s masterpiece "Brownsville Girl"

(*Knocked Out Loaded*, August 1986)[4] illustrates the point, a song I will forever (and weirdly) link to my educational experiences. I first heard *Knocked Out Loaded* in the fall of 1986, just weeks after leaving home for the first time and during my first year of undergraduate studies. I fancied myself like the protagonist in "Brownsville Girl": on the road, traveling and meeting new people, full of anxiety (though fortunately not at risk of getting my head shot off), and haunted by memories of all that I left behind. As a young adult on my own for the first time, I had major decisions to make (do I duck or run?) and yet acted with wild optimism and confidence, certain against all odds that somehow the roof would stay on.

The fall of 1986 was also my first foray into higher education, an opening of my mind to new ideas and ways of thinking that would forever change the way I see the world. With "Brownsville Girl" playing in the background of the school year, I found my travels from class to class, book to book, assignment to assignment, and subject to subject as an adventure every bit as mysterious and unpredictable as the one described in the lyrics. There, the narrator darts all over the map—San Antonio, the Alamo, Mexico, the Rockies, Brownsville (or New Danville, in another version of the song), Amarillo, and the French Quarter of New Orleans—a journey that I associated then, in my sophomoric attempts at poetic expression, to the liberation that education brings, the opening up of new worlds to explore. To this day, "Brownsville Girl" encapsulates the 1986–1987 school year for me. My memory for details—like the narrator of the song who struggles with his—is weak and yet somehow everything that matters from that year is contained in Dylan's lyrics and his performance of them. This is a strange way to hear the song, I realize, and no one else would or could ever replicate these associations in quite the same way.

"Brownsville Girl" also dominates my thoughts about the final years of my formal educational journey, which wrapped up in the fall of 2000. It reminds me of the happy but challenging years spent in "the French Quarter," which in my idiosyncratic, biographical commentary means Montréal, Québec, not the Vieux Carré of New Orleans, Louisiana. My wife Kyla and I look back at those sometimes-challenging years as poor starving students with affection, because even when things did not turn out the way we planned, we learned that those who suffer together have "stronger connections" than those who do not. (We remember hearing this "Brownsville Girl" lesson one evening in our favorite Irish pub— Ye Olde Orchard—as *Bob Dylan's Greatest Hits Volume 3* [1994] played over the sound system.) Just as the song's wild geography came to symbolize my undergraduate academic awakening, so too did its language encapsulate the setting and the challenges of postgraduate studies. Facing the task of preparing a doctoral dissertation—in theory, an original contribution to knowledge— the narrator's quasi-prayer took on new meaning: I could use "an original thought . . . right now." I played it/prayed it often in the days leading up to and during my oral defense of that dissertation. (The other image I carried to that examination, anticipating the questioning to come, was J. Alfred Prufrock, "sprawling on a pin, / . . . pinned and wriggling on the wall."[5])

Of course, all of this has absolutely nothing to do with any other Bob Dylan fan, and certainly nothing to do with Bob Dylan himself and his understanding of the story told in the song, whatever that is. This is one of the great pleasures of art. We experience it with this wonderful mix of unique individual memories and connections as well as the discourses of the broader listening community, which might include fans, reviewers, critics, and scholars. There are many formal and informal commentaries on "Brownsville Girl," some disciplined in terms of methodology and careful to avoid unrestrained subjectivism and others more casual, like the one I construct in my head each time I hear the song, and like those in forums permitting fan interaction (blogs, Web sites, and the like). This book combines a mix of both, drawing at times on academic resources, fan-based reflections, and my own personal interactions with Dylan's music.

My particular interest is Bob Dylan and religious discourse, and here too we face similar ambiguities as those presented by music generally. Matters of faith and opinions about organized religion are as private, idiosyncratic, and deeply felt as our experiences with music. Even those who have deep attachments to a religious tradition find it difficult to articulate the emotional content of this part of their lives exhaustively. Just as our reasons for liking this or that song remain vague the minute we try to express them, so too the limits of our "vocabulary" for expressing encounters with transcendence hamper our discourse. Because we bring unique personal perspectives to sacred subjects, the exploration of *religion in music*, *religion and music*, and even *religion as music* is doubly subjective and, again, highly individualistic.

"Brownsville Girl" illustrates the kind of blending of art and experience I describe. The song opens with the narrator musing about an unnamed Gregory Peck film he saw (clearly *The Gunfighter*, 1950), and soon after expresses confusion about why *he* was in it and what part *he* was supposed to play. Dylan did not just see the film; he was in some way a participant in the story told, just as we are somehow active participants in the formulation of meaning in the songs we love (compare remarks on Benjamin in the preface). The singer moves in and out of the story told in the film, at one moment chased by gunfighters (like Jimmy Ringo, Peck's character in *The Gunfighter*), at another standing in line at a theater to see his favorite actor on the silver screen. All music fans experience this blurring of the lines between music and autobiography. In some strange way I lived "Brownsville Girl" during my school years. To interpret a song is a confessional act.

Religious content is ubiquitous in popular music, so it is not surprising that songs become dialogue partners for our informal reflections on spiritual themes. This too is deeply subjective and often at quite a remove from both a songwriter's intentions and the "relationships" of other audience members to the same music. For instance, when I hear the narrator of "Brownsville Girl" refer to a memory that calls out like a "rollin' train," I tend to link this train with the "slow train comin'" of Dylan's gospel period (1979–1981).[6] I have no reason to do so, other than the repetition of the term.[7] Perhaps it is significant that Woody Guthrie, whose influence on Bob Dylan cannot be overestimated, combines the romance of the rails with a gospel sensibility in his singing and writing: "This train don't carry no rustlers, / Whores, pimps, or side-street hustlers; / This train is bound for glory, / This train. . . . 'Cause them guys is a singin' that this train is bound for glory, an' I'm gonna hug her breast till I find out where she's bound."[8] Presumably, Guthrie's words influenced Dylan's use of train imagery in his songs.

Here, too, I cannot escape my own story, and it tends to shape how I hear this songwriter. Like Dylan's experience a few years earlier (I fancy), I went through a religious awakening in 1980. One of the first artistic expressions of faith I encountered afterward was the album *Slow Train Coming*. Admittedly, my worldview at the time was quite naïve, and I saw the world as black and white— either you got faith or you got unbelief. I still associate Dylan's gospel albums with my early, simplistic encounter with religion, so when I hear about a memory calling out like a rolling train in "Brownsville Girl," it makes me think of someone looking back to a time of newfound faith. It was long ago and far away, but despite the distance, those memories remain persistent and noisy, even thunderous like that slow-moving train. Again, I do not suspect this was the intent of "Brownsville Girl," but every time I hear that song, it takes me back to 1980, just as it takes me back to the equally powerful memories of 1986 and 2000.

First Thoughts on Lyrics and Poems

As these opening remarks likely intimate, this book provides an unusual examination of the music and art of Bob Dylan, but since he is a highly unusual musician and artist, I hope this scrutiny is appropriate. I find that the most interesting works treating Bob Dylan are those breaking from traditional patterns of biographical and interpretive writing. For instance, Sam Shepard's collection *Rolling Thunder Logbook*, which I discuss later, includes poetry, photography, and even (references to) a stage play that explores aspects of Dylan's life and work. The book considers the mysteries surrounding the singer and the questions regularly raised by fans during a mid-1970s tour: "You see them staring hard into his white mask,[9] his gray-green eyes, trying to pick at the mystery. Who is he anyway? What's the source of his power? An apparition?"[10] We find another unconventional study of Dylan in Stephen Scobie's poetry. Those who read Dylan scholarship know this author best through his literary critical analysis *Alias Bob Dylan Revisited*, but his collection of poems inspired by the artist, *And Forget My Name: A Speculative Biography of Bob Dylan*, invites readers to leave the confines of mere prose and think about the singer in new ways. Consider also the fascinating 2007 Todd Haynes film *I'm Not There*, with its diverse presentations of Bob Dylan's story, or Paul Williams's writings, with their unabashed subjectivism and emphasis on the experience of albums and performances. Williams reminds us constantly that the question *How does it feel?* is as important as, if not more important than, *What does it mean?*[11] Some photographers capture insights with their cameras (e.g., Barry Feinstein, Ken Regan), but perhaps the most important interpreters of Dylan's art are his peers, those musicians who cover his songs. There is something profoundly correct about the Jimi Hendrix Experience's take on "All Along the Watchtower" (*Electric Ladyland*, 1968), or Lou Reed's version of "Foot of Pride" (in *Bob Dylan: The 30th Anniversary Collection*, 1993).

Determining *what* music means to audiences and *how* those songs have meaning is an extremely difficult matter that complicates music interpretation. The relationship of words to sounds is a particularly contentious issue. In chapter 2, I comment further on lyric analysis, but I include a few notes on the subject here because it is so fundamental to all that follows. Many analysts reject any approach to songs that divorces the words from the sound or places emphasis on lyrics over musicality. The sounds and live performances are what matter most.[12] Others complain about readings that overintellectualize Dylan's songs, particularly when interpreters pluck the Dylan canon out of its proper context, treating the songs as artifacts quite apart from their relevant biographical, social, and musical environments. One review of several 2007 publications on Bob Dylan notes this tendency to treat lyrical content separately, raising the perennial question of whether songs are truly poems or not, something text-based analysis usually assumes. "A preoccupation with the lyrics—and the lyrics only—is common to much Dylan scholarship," Louis P. Masur writes, "but a song is not a poem."[13] Instead, he stresses the physicality of our participation in music. When music is loud, when we sing along and move to the beat, it is in those moments "we are transformed, or at least transported. The music provides release and offers escape." In addition, even though fans know it may be illusory (since commercialism drives the pop-music industry), "music restores a sense of immediacy and authenticity." Masur highlights the place of physicality in Dylan appreciation in his brief remarks: " 'Like a Rolling Stone' plays, we close our eyes, point our fingers, and shout 'How does it feel!' The answer, more than forty years later, is that it still feels great."[14]

Sociologist of rock music Simon Frith touches on another concern when he refers to critics who treat all song lyrics the same, taking their meaning "to be transparent" with little or no account of musical setting and performance of those words. These analysts "tend to equate a song's popularity to public agreement with the message."[15] Others looking specifically at religious dimensions in music also question the emphasis on words. Religion-and-the-arts scholar Robin Sylvan chooses to examine music over lyrics because analysis of the latter "is superficial and has been overdone" and because "the major religious impact of the music takes place primarily at a nondiscursive level."[16] Jeremy S. Begbie's theological treatment of music includes the observation that "Christian assessments of popular music . . . have too often focused on scrutinizing lyrics alone—'content analysis' (a term that gives the game away)—as if the musical sounds were no more than a transparent varnish on the words, which alone carry content."[17]

It is not in dispute that musical *sound* carries meaning and that audience *participation* with performances—singing along, dancing—is often transformative. I listen to enough music and attend enough concerts to know this firsthand. Still, I maintain it is also true that *reading* the work of songwriters can be a meaningful experience, analogous to reading a fine play. It does not replace performances of that work, but no one denies that reading Shakespeare or Oscar Wilde is pleasurable and consequential in itself. I listen to recordings of Dylan constantly and attend live performances at every opportunity, and these are irreplaceable experiences. I also read Dylan, which affords a form of encounter very unlike that gained from a CD or concert. Critics who insist that words and sound must always remain together dismiss the value of a solitary reading of Bob Dylan's *Lyrics: 1962–2001*.

A further issue is whether the term *poetry* applies to song lyrics intended for musical accompaniment. Gordon Ball's fascinating account of his reasons for nominating Dylan to the Nobel Committee of the Swedish Academy helps put this discussion into some perspective. He reminds us of longstanding connections between verse and song, noting, "Poetry and music have shared common ground, from the [ancient] Greeks to Pound to Ginsberg."[18] By performing his verses, Dylan participates in an ancient union of words and sounds. Ball also observes that New Criticism—an emphasis on poetry as text that dominated literary criticism for much of the twentieth century—weakened the natural association of poetry and music. Dylan restores this balance, thus heeding an observation put forward by Ezra Pound:

> Both in Greece and in Provence the poetry attained its highest rhythmic and metrical brilliance at times when the arts of verse and music were most closely knit together, when each thing done by the poet had some definite musical urge or necessity bound up within it.[19]

Terms like *poetry* and *literature* are not easily compartmentalized. To suggest that rock songs cannot be poetry and that poetry must be confined to the page and reduced to a particular kind of performance (such as spoken word, without musical accompaniment) seems unnecessarily restrictive.

Ball's reflections on whether Dylan merits a Nobel Prize in Literature raise a further question about the evaluation of his art. If we acknowledge the vital link between poetry and music, the question remains whether Dylan's work, on the page, "can rest companionably with enshrined works of literature. The answer is decidedly positive," Ball concludes.[20] He compares Dylan favorably to Anton Chekhov in his ability to evoke complex settings in a few short words, to Arthur Rimbaud in his prophetic and visionary perspectives, to William Butler Yeats in his eclecticism and inventiveness, and to William Faulkner in his examination of the human condition.[21] To maintain that Dylan's lyrics are powerful apart from performance is not farfetched, and, again, there is pleasure and meaning in reading his words as well as hearing them in performance. I do not deny that I would rather attend a concert than spend an evening with *Lyrics* in hand, just as I would rather go to the theater than read *King Lear*. Unfortunately, Dylan is not always in town.

Though we will not resolve the Dylan-is-poet, lyrics-are-poetry debates here, I will make one simple observation on the matter. To my mind, it is significant that Dylan publishes in book format not only poetry[22] but also songs alongside poetry. His collection *Lyrics* first appeared in 1973, with a number of expansions and revisions appearing in the years following. If lyrics cannot signify apart from musical accompaniment, there would be little reason to publish a book like this. The implication is that the author intends these songs to be read, just as he does the nonlyrical texts that accompany them in this context, like "Last Thoughts on Woody Guthrie," "Joan Baez in Concert, Part 2," and "11 Outlined Epitaphs."[23] Publishing poetry with lyrics is not unique, but it does suggest that distinguishing the two writing forms is not always easy.[24]

Dylan's *Lyrics* raises other interesting questions about the matter of songs and poetry. The content of this book follows an album-by-album structure and regularly includes material not found on the official release in question, usually indicating songs written and/or recorded during the making of the album. These "additional lyrics" present us with copyrighted songs whose existence is completely or largely textual in nature, not musical. For instance, *Lyrics* includes the words to "Legionnaire's Disease," but according to Clinton Heylin, there is no known studio recording of the song or concert performance by Dylan.[25] In other cases, we know of songs included in *Lyrics* that Dylan recorded but did not release or perform in public, which is the case with "Long Ago, Far Away" and "Long Time Gone."[26] And there are still other songs found in *Lyrics* that Dylan performed in concert at least once but did not record in studio or release on an official album (e.g., "City of Gold").[27] In these examples, we have texts, words on a page, published by Bob Dylan. There is no musical accompaniment for them (except for some songs that circulate in unofficial, bootlegged albums). What do we call them if not poetry?

Chapter One

The *Flâneur* Plays Guitar

Who is this character anyway?
> Sam Shepard (referring to Bob Dylan)

Who is this man?
> Matthew 8:27; Mark 4:41; Luke 8:25
> (referring to Jesus of Nazareth)

Who do people say that I am? . . . Who do you say that I am?
> Jesus (Mark 8:27, 29)

A Picture on the Wall Near the Cage Where I Work

I taped a photocopied picture of Bob Dylan to my office door during the time I spent thinking about and writing this book. It is my favorite picture of the singer, taken likely in the fall of 1975. He is standing in a cemetery by a large crucifix, in the Catholic grotto in Lowell, Massachusetts.[1] Jack Kerouac's grave is in this cemetery, so the motley crew touring with Dylan at the time stopped by the Beat writer's hometown to pay their respects. There are other photographs of this visit to the Lowell cemetery showing Dylan and poet Allen Ginsberg sitting cross-legged at Kerouac's grave.[2]

The picture on my office door shows Dylan standing in front of the tall statue, his feathered hat just inches below Christ's nailed feet. He carries a large tree branch as a walking stick while the

1

camera looks up into his face, capturing both the singer's stoic expression and the Messiah's agony all at once. The picture has symbolic potential that illustrates challenges facing those interested in Bob Dylan's relationship to religion.

For one thing, though Christ is in the picture, Dylan is the focal point. Christ on the cross looks off into the distant heavens, remote and inaccessible. Dylan, on the other hand, stares penetratingly into the eyes of anyone looking at the photograph. It is actually difficult to focus on the crucified figure, which is off center. We view Christ at a slight angle. He appears high in the frame of the picture, and we cannot make eye contact with him. Bob Dylan's shadowed eyes, on the other hand, stare back at us from dead center of the picture. He has an authoritative, confident stance—one thumb coolly placed in a pocket, jacket thrown over his shoulder like a cape. The other hand grasps his walking stick firmly. He could be Moses leading his people, poised to strike against the rock (see Exod. 17:5–6).

Viewed this way, the picture brings to mind John Lennon's 1966 observation that the Beatles are "more popular than Jesus now."[3] Lennon's words always struck me as a reasonable observation rather than irreverence, despite the controversy that ensued. He calculated the shock value, no doubt, but it remains true that more kids flocked to Beatles concerts and record shops at the time than to churches. The picture on my door suggests something similar. It is hard to see religion—the figure on the cross in this case—with Dylan's imposing gaze commanding an audience. He is in the way, blocking a clear view of the icon behind him. The Dylan mystique is hard to ignore; moreover, many claim to find just as much wisdom in his canon of work as in the Sermon on the Mount.

This is not the end of it, however. The Ken Regan photograph on my office door suggests other things as well. For one thing, Dylan stands *at the feet* of the dying Jesus, just where his most devoted followers kept watch on the dark day the statue depicts. According to the evangelist John, "standing near the cross of Jesus" were various women, including his mother, his mother's sister, and Mary Magdalene. And there was another. Standing beside Jesus' mother was the mysterious, nameless, male figure known only as "the disciple whom [Jesus] loved" (19:25–26). This character shows up a few times in the Gospel of John and is the only male disciple[4] left standing by the side of the condemned Jesus, after all others had fled in fear (e.g., Mark 14:50). This close companion of Jesus sits at his teacher's side during a sacred meal (John 13:23; also see 21:20), hears the first reports of the resurrection, is second on the scene after Mary Magdalene to peer into the empty tomb (John 20:2–5), and recognizes the risen Lord ahead of St. Peter (John 21:7). The most touching reference concerns Jesus' mother, Mary. From the cross, the dying, eldest son entrusts her to the care of this close friend: "When Jesus saw his mother and the disciple whom he loved standing beside her, he said to his mother, 'Woman, here is your son.' Then he said to the disciple, 'Here is your mother.' And from that hour the disciple took her into his own home" (John 19:26–27).[5]

Bob Dylan stands in the very place of "the one whom Jesus loved," the only male disciple at the foot of the cross. Viewed this way, the photograph does not indicate a singer guilty of megalomania or showing any disrespect. Quite the opposite in fact—it suggests reverence for the one towering above him as he humbly takes his place at the master's feet.

There is a third possibility. Perhaps as we consider the Dylan presented in this photograph, standing menacingly or meekly at the foot of the cross, we should be thinking of the nameless Roman soldier also described in the New Testament Gospels. Apart from the beloved disciple, he is the only other man of note identified as standing in that place. Significantly, as we think of the joker that is Bob Dylan, this figure is of two minds. His presence at the scene implies, on the one hand, the actions of a sinister figure participating in the grisly execution. Perhaps it was this very soldier who pounded the nails or placed the spear in Jesus' side (John 19:34). On the other hand, the soldier at the foot of the cross experiences a profound transformation. Something happens to him as events surrounding the crucifixion unfold, because as Jesus takes his last breath this soldier declares, " 'Truly this man was God's Son!' " (Matt. 27:54; Mark 15:39) and " 'Certainly this man was innocent' " (Luke 23:47). Unlike the disciple whom Jesus loved and the women standing at the foot of the cross who were loyal friends from beginning to end, and unlike other villains in the Gospel narratives who do not change their opinions, this soldier evolves from killer to believer. Which is it in the photograph? Are we looking at the swagger of a murdering soldier or the humility of a new convert?

People will draw their own conclusions about this photograph: Does it depict the singer in the foreground, distracting the gaze away from Jesus? Is Dylan the musician at the foot of the cross, subservient to this religion, and standing in the place of the beloved disciple? Or is he the newly insightful Roman, transformed by an unexpected encounter? Some gladly embrace the idea of Dylan as a secular prophet, a term permitting a semblance of religiosity that does not actually connect the singer to a faith tradition in any way. He might pose with a crucifix, for instance, but this does not indicate any connection to Christianity. It makes sense, therefore, that Dylan draws the eye away from the crucifix, this symbol of what some consider vacuous organized religion, with its conformity, hypocrisy, irrelevance, and anachronism. Others, however, look to Dylan's songs as windows opening on something far bigger than the artist and his art. The songs allow us to catch glimpses of a never-defined but nonetheless genuine transcendence. It is all in the eye of the beholder. Ultimately, we see in Dylan what we want to see. We find in his songs what we want to find. Occasionally, one of my young students will look at the picture on my office door and ask, "Who's this?" Aware of his penchant for wearing literal and figurative masks, I am inclined to respond with the only honest answer I can think of: "I don't know. Who do you think he is?"

The great musician, humanitarian, and academic Albert Schweitzer once commented on the resemblance of biographers to their subjects. Remarkably, it is as if the writers look into a deep well and see their own reflections staring back at them, for in telling another's story, they reveal much about themselves. Schweitzer specifically had in mind nineteenth-century historians writing about Jesus of Nazareth, but if I may be so impertinent as to suggest a parallel situation, the same holds true for those writing about Bob Dylan. Schweitzer observes that biographers/historians approach their subjects with more than simple intellectual curiosity. "The historical investigation of the life of Jesus did not take its rise from a purely historical interest," he notes. "It turned to the Jesus of history as an ally in the struggle against the tyranny of dogma."[6] Schweitzer's comments raise an important question about those choosing to investigate Bob Dylan's life and work. What motivates them? Is there more than purely academic, historical, or biographical interest at play? If so, do we seek to claim Dylan as an ally in some kind of struggle in the same way nineteenth-century historians found their own "thoughts in Jesus"?[7] To return to the potential meanings of the picture on my door, do we find in Dylan a symbol of our preference for a secular prophetic voice apart from religion or for one subservient to the cross? Our point of departure determines where we end up.

Schweitzer presses his claim further by suggesting that the historian/biographer does not merely *find* his/her reflection in Jesus but instead "*create[s]* Jesus in accordance with his own character."[8] The Jesus that historians find is to some degree a fiction, Schweitzer suggests, and the same is true of analyses of the life and work of Bob Dylan. We find the Dylan we want to find. The endless ambiguities Dylan puts before audiences (like the photograph) contribute to our diverse conclusions, but, more to the point, the exercise of studying Dylan is self-revelatory.

The possible reactions to the picture on my door mentioned above might suggest polar opposite positions—either Dylan replaces religion in some sense (drawing one's gaze away from the crucifix), or he submits to it (standing at the foot of the cross as a longtime disciple or newly converted soldier). There is still another possibility, one presenting us with a middle ground most listeners of his music will likely accept. The crucifix stands behind Bob Dylan. If we consider this with attention to Dylan's art, putting to the side for the moment notions of religious meaning and his personal connections to it, we can allow this picture to symbolize an important background for Dylan's aesthetics. The singer's deep connection with American roots music indicates knowledge of a cultural inheritance soaked in the Bible and Christian tradition, in addition to the religious formation stemming from his Jewish heritage and his study of the New Testament later in life. Dylan enhances his knowledge of religious material by drawing from wells other than music. Literature he knows also conveys biblical and gospel content. For instance, Woody Guthrie's *Bound for Glory* mentions religious characters on occasion, like the preacher announcing, " 'The day of th' comin' of th' Lord is near! Jesus Christ of Nazareth will come down out of the clouds in all of His purity, all of His glory, and all of His power! Are you ready, brother and sister? Are you saved and sanctified and baptized in the spirit of the Holy Ghost? Are your garments spotless? Is your soul as white as the drifted snow?' "[9] Dylan employs some of these familiar phrases in the songs, stage remarks, and interviews during his gospel period (1979–1981). The account of the crucifixion in the Gospels and the infinite number of artists telling that old, old story inform Bob Dylan's musical ancestry, and there are signs of this influence everywhere in his work, from *Bob Dylan* (1962) to *Together Through Life* and *Christmas in the Heart* (2009). Dylan's position in front of the crucifix symbolizes this cultural, literary, musical, and religious backdrop and all its influence on his work.

One final thought about this picture. As mentioned, viewers look up into Dylan's face and beyond it to the figure on the cross. According to Christian tradition, Jesus speaks to God in heaven when he is on the cross, as in the words " 'Father, into your hands I commend my spirit' " (Luke 23:46). Christ in the picture is looking up to the open sky, to the one in heaven, who is high above Dylan as well. God is present in the picture to the extent that the crucifixion scene includes dialogue with the Father in heaven. It is God as mediated through Christian discourse, and this God is, in the language of the photo, *above* Dylan and *behind* all he does.

Bob Dylan often mentions God in his songs, and though he rarely attempts to define what the term means, he still points us toward that vague Other. Particularly in the post–*John Wesley Harding* period, one commentator observes, "Whether speaking of, to, for, or about God, . . . Dylan is consistently God-concerned."[10] Frequently this God-concerned language is biblical as well. During a period of convalescence following a motorcycle accident in 1966, the time leading up to *John Wesley Harding*, "Dylan had begun to read the Bible with conviction, keeping an open copy on a stand in his Woodstock study. He studied pertinent passages like a student seeking an advanced degree in religion. Biblical references now swarmed around his songs, taking his music into previously unexplored territories."[11] Whether interested in religion or not, listeners will agree that Dylan's perspective as a poet-singer often involves a grasping after and striving toward an indefinable Something, and he turns to the language of the Jewish and Christian Scriptures to help articulate this search. He sees a shadow and chases it. If and how we interpret that Other, that Something, is our business. Bob Dylan merely forces the issue on us, leaving us to reach our own conclusions. In my view, this is the good news according to Bob Dylan.

Just as a photograph elicits interpretations as diverse as those who view it, so also Bob Dylan's songs invite an endless array of analyses. The popular and critical writing committed to interpreting his work is remarkable both for its quantity and range of perspective. When we introduce religion and spirituality to conversations about Bob Dylan's art and propose ways he borrows from, reflects on, and contributes to discourses on transcendent themes, the conversation becomes even more complex. The term *religion* itself means different things to different people. It might suggest to some the rigidity of creed and to others some more loosely defined spirituality. For some, it offers personal solace and the promise of collective well-being, whereas others find in it only systemic injustice and violence. Some find meaning in a particular faith tradition, but others find transcendence in nature or art, or even popular culture. Everyone has an opinion.

This last form of religious experience deserves further comment. Kelton Cobb investigates the "kinds of religious impulses" active below the surfaces of popular culture, a phenomenon that includes distinct spiritualities that he enumerates using subscripted numbers. These spiritualities are "responses to a genuine stirring of the divine (religion$_1$), or resuscitations of ideals or perceptions from organized religion that were entrusted to the culture and are now reasserting themselves (religion$_3$)."[12] By religion$_1$ Cobb indicates, drawing on theologian Paul Tillich,[13] forces in culture, a preconscious faith that finds meaning and consequence in one's existence. We find this faith in the depths of all spheres of culture, including art, science, politics, family, economy, religion, and the media, all of which can sustain our conviction "that it is a meaningful act to participate in them."[14] This instinctive understanding of ultimate meaning stands apart from religion$_2$, which refers to the explicit practices, symbols, mythologies, and texts of organized religion. By religion$_3$, Cobb (but not Tillich) refers to ways "that the ideas and values of a particular religion$_2$ come to be absorbed—but not lost—by the culture in which that religion is or has been dominant."[15] These terms are helpful as we approach Bob Dylan's art with an interest in its religious content.

We might argue that all three of these definitions of religion appear in Bob Dylan's work. There is an instinctive awareness of the value of human life in every note of his music calling for justice or love (religion$_1$), and though he occasionally gives voice to the teachings of organized religion (religion$_2$), the vast majority of his work involves the absorption and creative rewriting of its terms and symbols, particularly those of the Jewish and Christian traditions (religion$_3$). The point I want to make here is simply that Dylan's fans and interpreters think of religion in very different ways. Some find Dylan merely using religious terms and imagery artistically but with no particular theological intent, whereas others find in his songs meaningful engagements with ultimate questions. The gospel according to Bob Dylan means something quite different from fan to fan. Again, everyone has an opinion.

Jack Kerouac, Sam Shepard, and *Chronicles*: Dylan's *Flânerie* as Paradigm of His Religious Speculations

What is it about Bob Dylan that introduces so much fascination, confusion, and speculation about his religious beliefs and the religious significance of his work? There are likely several reasons, not least among them his clear associations with Judaism and Christianity. Though many singer-songwriters[16] participate in religious life in one form or another and address religious subject matter in their songs, Bob Dylan is distinctive in that he is endlessly curious, giving free rein to an inquisitive nature in a way few others do. His lyrics are mysterious and cryptic, and he steadfastly refuses to provide interpretations of his songs satisfactory to those requesting them. Furthermore, he is oxymoronic in that he is a reclusive public figure.[17] He simultaneously draws an audience and keeps them at a distance, which fuels speculation about the meaning of his art and any possible connections it may have with his private life.

Throughout *The Rolling Thunder Logbook,* playwright Sam Shepard tries to understand who Bob Dylan is. This proves a difficult task. On the one hand, "Dylan has invented himself. He's made himself up from scratch." On the other, he is not one to reveal secrets. This constructed Dylan fascinates but eludes definition. Audiences remain enthralled but never quite figure him out. Dylan "creates a mythic atmosphere out of the land around us," managing to take the very land we tread "but never see until someone shows it to us."[18] A mystery attaches itself to Bob Dylan, a personality that attracts and bewilders all at once. "If a mystery is solved, the case is dropped. In this case, in the case of Dylan, the mystery is never solved, so the case keeps on. It keeps coming up again. Over and over the years. Who is this character anyway?" For audiences speculating about him (much as I am doing now), "all they can do is imagine what he's like. You see them staring hard into his white mask [referring to the white makeup he wore during a mid-1970s tour], his gray-green eyes, trying to pick at the mystery. *Who is he anyway?* What's the source of his power? An apparition?"[19]

In the opening pages of Bob Dylan's autobiographical *Chronicles,* Vol. 1, the singer claims he made his way to New York City "from the Midwest in a four-door sedan, '57 Impala."[20] It might sound petty to mention, but this is factually incorrect because Chevrolet did not produce its Impala model until 1958.[21] A gaffe by the author on such an insignificant detail and an oversight by the fact-checkers at Simon & Schuster are not so remarkable given that the moment recalled reaches back forty or so years. Yet we should remember this is the same person with a penchant for being evasive and a reputation for hiding behind masks, both literal and metaphorical. This writer famously changed his name and fabricated stories about his origins and early life experiences. He has used numerous pseudonyms throughout his career[22] and continuously hides from and baffles interlocutors. Interviews with Bob Dylan often present the songwriter employing various strategies of evasion. Commenting on examples found in Jonathan Cott's *Bob Dylan: The Essential Interviews*, Masur finds Dylan "engaging in theater and wordplay made all the more uproarious—and painful—by how seriously he is taken."[23] The 2007 Todd Haynes film *I'm Not There* captures well this pattern of interaction; its series of unusual vignettes brings Dylan's "sense of playfulness—and that desperate desire to elude definition—to compelling dramatic life."[24] This reluctant celebrity simultaneously draws a crowd and then playfully pushes it away, denying he is the one we need and warning us not to trust him.[25]

This pattern of obfuscation creates an enormous challenge for those seeking to represent the "real" Bob Dylan in biographical writing or to "find" him in interviews, concerts, movies, song lyrics, or even *Chronicles*, his long-awaited autobiography and first substantial prose work. He plays with the expectation of self-disclosure we bring to autobiographical writing. Mikal Gilmore claims, "I've always felt that there are parts of himself that he doesn't give up easily, if at all in an interview. I don't think he gives it up even in *Chronicles*, which is an autobiography of the mind. There are parts of his experience and frame of mind that he doesn't go into readily—he may eventually, though I don't think he has yet."[26] Readers might reasonably expect that since he is now writing a memoir (we have only volume 1 of *Chronicles* as I type this), he will come clean about his "real" identity and the meaning of his art. Strangely enough, by disappointing us in this regard once again, he gives us a far more interesting book!

I suspect Dylan knows he was not riding in a 1957 Impala. He is warning his readers here, letting them know at the outset of *Chronicles* that the story he tells is no mere encyclopedia entry, a list of facts and rehearsal of the dates and events that others deem significant. Instead, Dylan selects the moments and scenes he considers important, and he simultaneously reveals and conceals as he goes.

This tendency toward evasion is only one of the oddities of Dylan's autobiography. Though *Chronicles* earned critical recognition as a finalist for the 2005 National Book Critics Prize in Biography and Memoir and winner of the 2005 Quill Book Award in biography/memoir, as celebrity autobiographical writing goes, it remains distinctive in many respects and does not fit easily in this genre category. For the author, the poetry and imagination of his language appear to be at least as important as the incidents to which he refers. This collection of anecdotes and reminiscences is also rather episodic, focusing largely on the 1960s, early 1970s, and late 1980s. The resulting silences regarding major events in his career and personal life are striking, as is the lack of attention to strict chronology. Stories featuring Columbia talent scout John Hammond open and close the book,[27] for instance, flanking thirty years or so of other tales. To my mind, this return to the start resembles the structure of Jack Kerouac's *On the Road*, which also opens and closes in New York City after the principal characters wander around America.

Bob Dylan's *Chronicles* invites comparison with playwright Sam Shepard's *The Rolling Thunder Logbook* as well, another enigmatic presentation of the singer-songwriter. On October 30, 1975, Dylan's Rolling Thunder Revue tour officially opened in Plymouth, Massachusetts. The choice of Plymouth as a starting location is suggestive. The site of earliest settlement, a place of beginnings, is particularly suitable to commence what is a kind of American odyssey. Shepard's *Logbook* is an intriguing blend of reportage and poetic reflections on this unusual rock-and-roll road show that brought together a diverse collection of artists from Allen Ginsberg to T-Bone Burnett. The Rolling Thunder Revue mixed rock, folk, and country music with poetry readings and social-justice concern. While all of this was going on, Dylan and his traveling band of artists were making a movie, which would eventually see the light of day as *Renaldo and Clara*, released in 1978.

Shepard's *Logbook* reads like a diary, capturing impressions of life on the road with a diverse assortment of highly creative individuals. However, this is no typical tour, one centered on arenas and stadiums in large cities. Instead, Dylan and his friends perform mostly in small venues,[28] traveling town to town by road (like Sal Paradise and Dean Moriarty in Kerouac's novel), not plane. One consequence of this format—evident in Shepard's *Logbook* and Dylan's film *Renaldo and Clara*—is a string of semiscripted and largely random encounters with an assortment of people that provides an interesting cross section of American life.

The randomness of these encounters and the absurdities of the situations the actors experience during the Rolling Thunder Revue deserve notice. I say absurd because Dylan began filming *Renaldo and Clara* with minimal preparation. Indeed, as Shepard describes it, Dylan initially hired him to write dialogue for the film "on the spot." Dylan did not even want to discuss the film after the two first met, preferring, significantly, to wait until the touring group was on the road:

> [Shepard says] I tell him we're thinking of shooting some footage . . . . [Dylan answers] "I gotta wait til we get outa this city. Right now I just feel like gettin' outa here. Once we're up there *on the road* we'll be able to get into the film more. I'm just waitin' to get outa here now."[29]

Dylan shows no interest in planning his movie, of entering into the filming with a prepared script in hand. He trusts instead to serendipity, preferring improvisation and spontaneity. This in itself becomes a metaphor for freedom and openness to chance encounters and inspirations and, I propose, a modus operandi for his approach to religious meaning. The film offers some loosely scripted and choreographed scenes, but much of it involves ad-libbing and moments of creative, quick responses to situations as they present themselves.

The Rolling Thunder Revue as a whole, as represented in Shepard's *Logbook* and Dylan's *Renaldo and Clara*, attempts to experience the kind of idealized American freedom modeled in Jack Kerouac's *On the Road* (note the correspondence of Dylan's/

Shepard's language in the last citation and Kerouac's title). Wayne Robins describes *On the Road* as a "nonstop, amphetamine-fueled semi-fictional [*sic*] account of a trip across America in search of kicks, chicks, and jazz, with fictionalized portrayals of [Allen] Ginsberg and beat hero Neal Cassady. Reading it became a rite of passage for restless young people, and it became one of the essential parts of the literary canon of the 1960s."[30] A similar restlessness and longing for unencumbered artistic expression characterizes the activities of the Rolling Thunder Revue as depicted in Shepard's account. Freedom is an important theme in his *Logbook*, particularly in its longest section, which focuses on the incarceration and release of Rubin "Hurricane" Carter. This is not only an important concern for Dylan, who organized a benefit concert to raise awareness of the boxer's plight; the story becomes a metaphor that symbolizes something much larger. The climax of the book may be Dylan's words to Shepard, "Rubin's been acquitted! He'll be out by Christmas!"[31] The literal release of Hurricane Carter parallels the (artistic) freedom achieved by the unnatural experiences of the Rolling Thunder Revue. Shepard emphasizes the unnaturalness of the tour by regularly contrasting the experiences of life on the road with the normalcy of home and family life (e.g., "It's unreal to think of any place as permanent once movement has taken root as a way of life"[32]).

We find another intriguing vision of freedom in Woody Guthrie's *Bound for Glory*, a book Dylan acknowledges as formative and influential for his own writing.[33] For much of the second half of this *Bildungsroman*, Guthrie describes his travels from Pampa, Texas, to Sonora, California, after receiving an invitation from his wealthy Aunt Laura.[34] The journey he describes involves a series of iconic Guthrie scenes as he hitchhikes; travels on boxcars; endures hunger, heat, and cold; and makes friends with the poor and unemployed ramblers he meets along the way. After finally arriving at his destination, hungry and dirty and beaten down by privations and dangers, Guthrie stands at the impressive double doors of the gated mansion of his kinfolk. The doors have crosses on them and locks that remind him of both a funeral parlor and a jail.[35] After Guthrie takes in the beautiful yards and large windows before him, the butler answers his knock on the door, and at that moment, Guthrie has a sudden flash of insight and inspiration:

> The air from the house sifted past [the butler] on its way out the door, and there was a smell that made me know that the air had been hemmed up inside that house for a long time. Hemmed up. Walled in. Covered away from the moon and out of the reach of the sun. Cut away from the drift of the leaves and the wash of the waters. Hid out from the going and the coming of the people, cut loose from the thoughts of the crowds on the streets.[36] . . . I know, I know, I'm on the right hill, but I'm at the wrong house. This wasn't what I hung that boxcar for, nor hugged that iron ladder for, nor bellied down on top of that high rolling freight train for. The train was laughing and cussing and alive with human people.[37]

Even though the butler assures Guthrie he is standing at the right address, the grubby visitor keeps repeating he is at the wrong house, certain he made a mistake in coming. Interestingly, after he leaves the gated, isolated compound—after listening "to that iron gate snap locked behind [him]"—Guthrie leaves the home he described as a jail and funeral parlor only moments earlier, and says, "I was alive again."[38]

The Woody Guthrie we read about in *Bound for Glory* resembles in spirit the musicians in Shepard's *Logbook* and the restless travelers in Kerouac's *On the Road*, as well as Walter Benjamin's *flâneur* and the narrator of Edgar Allan Poe's "Man of the Crowd," which I discuss below and in chapter 6. They cannot sit still for long. The very idea of confinement—hemmed and walled in like the air in Aunt Laura's mansion—is untenable. Their curiosity to see and experience more of life is insatiable. This seems true of many ever-moving characters in Dylan's songs as well (e.g., the narrator in "Tangled Up in Blue," *Blood on the Tracks*, 1975), and even the singer himself, whose never-ending touring and recording suggests an aversion to inactivity and confinement.

Several clues suggest a link between Dylan, Shepard, and Kerouac's influential precursor *On the Road*. Shepard mentions Kerouac at various times throughout his book, including acknowledgment of the "dead Kerouac" in the preface to the 2004 edition.[39]

He also devotes a significant amount of space in his *Logbook*—including the pictures mentioned earlier—to the Rolling Thunder Revue's visit to Kerouac's hometown, Lowell, Massachusetts. As noted, Dylan and Allen Ginsberg spend time at Kerouac's grave, singing and reading a selection from his 1959 poem *Mexico City Blues*. Part of the scene appears in *Renaldo and Clara*.[40] Kerouac is, in effect, a character in Shepard's book. Dylan also refers to Kerouac's *On the Road* throughout *Chronicles*.[41]

The experience of random encounters Dylan was seeking for the film could not occur until they were, as he says, "on the road." Numerous scenes in both Shepard's *Logbook* and Dylan's *Renaldo and Clara* document chance conversations with strangers; some of these are in unusual and out-of-the-way venues, like trains, back roads, "middle of the sticks," "Massachusetts woods," and the like. Also suggestive is the interesting emphasis on mode of travel throughout *Logbook*. The Rolling Thunder Revue, unlike most major touring musical acts, deliberately avoids air travel. Shepard opens his book by refusing to travel by plane, announcing to Dylan's staff, "I don't fly either. I only take trains." By doing so, he enjoys one of the chance encounters his *Logbook* celebrates. Dylan drives himself from place to place in his camper.[42] Cheyette notes, "Dylan's personae . . . either write or dream on a train and, in doing so, reflect on the ever-moving grounds of their creativity."[43] This is a fitting description of the ever-moving Rolling Thunder Revue, though that specific creative burst occurred on the road, not the rails. Does this decision to drive involve deliberate mimicry of the adventures of Dean Moriarty and Sal Paradise, the protagonists in Kerouac's *On the Road*?

As I read Bob Dylan's autobiography and Sam Shepard's poetic biography, the image of the *flâneur* comes to mind, that figure best known to us from the writings of Charles Baudelaire (1821–1867) and Walter Benjamin (1892–1940) who wanders the urban streets and arcades of nineteenth-century Paris. "There was the pedestrian who would let himself be jostled by the crowd," writes Benjamin,

> . . . but there was also the *flâneur* who demanded elbow room and was unwilling to forgo the life of a gentleman of leisure.

Let the many attend to their daily affairs; the man of leisure can indulge in the perambulations of the *flâneur* only if as such he is already out of place. He is as much out of place in an atmosphere of complete leisure as in the feverish turmoil of the city.[44]

The *flâneur* is in a position to lead an idle life; however, as Benjamin's description indicates, his curiosity will not allow it. He chooses instead to wander and observe, finding meaning in the everyday and marginal. Similarly, Bob Dylan is no mere pedestrian. Like the *flâneur*, he too is wealthy, in a position to be a man of complete leisure, and he has been for most of his adult life. Yet also like Benjamin's *flâneur*, he would be out of place as a sybarite. As I write this, Dylan continues to be extremely active, even at an age when most of his peers enjoy a more settled, retired life. At the same time, strange as it sounds for a giant of the entertainment world, he also resembles the *flâneur* in his preference for solitude, something suggested by his ambivalent relationship to fame and his Herculean efforts to protect his privacy.[45] He is out of place in what Benjamin calls "the feverish turmoil of the city"—or at least this is the impression given by his Rolling Thunder Revue persona, who generally keeps off the beaten path, visiting out-of-the-way places. In a song released soon after the Revue, he complains to a lover who fails to recognize his need for solitude.[46]

Perhaps the most intriguing resemblance between the "Bob Dylan" character in *Chronicles* and *Logbook* and the *flâneur* described by Benjamin is their passionate quest for meaning and insight. Hannah Arendt describes the *flâneur* as "aimlessly strolling through the crowds in the big cities in studied contrast to their hurried, purposeful activity," and it is to him "that things reveal themselves in *their secret meaning.*"[47] S. Brent Plate imagines Benjamin's *flâneur* "wander[ing] the streets, ambling through its passages, and *revealing undisclosed secrets.*"[48] For Benjamin's *flâneur* and Dylan, the search for meaning is not limited to any predetermined trails, can include overlooked people and places, and is intuitive and original. Like the *flâneur*, Dylan moves away from the mainstream and takes time to consider the people and miscellany in out-of-the-way places. It is in such encounters that revelation can occur. We see this in his account of a visit to "an obscure roadside place, a gaunt shack called King Tut's Museum," after which he returns home with "a clear head."[49] Dylan also resembles Benjamin's *flâneur* in his emphasis on flashes of insight over larger, all-encompassing narratives: "Things were too big to see all at once." This phrase appears in a description of a party that not only provides the writer with chance encounters (like those described in Shepard's *Logbook*) but also moments of lucidity, clarity, and insight. As this section of the book opens, Dylan is frustrated and confused ("I wanted to understand things"), but after the experience of this social event, his "brain became wide awake."[50]

Categorizing Bob Dylan's *Chronicles* as autobiography and Sam Shepard's *Logbook* as biography stretches conventional definitions of these genres precisely because *flânerie* is a modus operandi in Bob Dylan's career. Dylan strays from conventional paths in a variety of ways. He finds meaning in out-of-the-way places, drawing on resources as diverse as American roots music, Amerindian mythology,[51] and the Bible. He is one of the most famous people in the world, yet he is unusually reclusive. He is a singer-songwriter but also writes books, makes films and acts, sketches pictures, and hosts a radio show.

Little about Dylan's career is typical, and it follows that some attempts to narrate that story are a little unconventional as well. For example, Jack Kerouac's novel *On the Road* inspired many of Dylan's generation, and I suggest Sam Shepard models his writings about the Rolling Thunder Revue on that influential story. This not only explains the attention Shepard gives to the "dead Kerouac"[52] in *The Rolling Thunder Logbook*, but it also helps us understand his presentation of Bob Dylan, the enigmatic figure at the center of his book. Sam Shepard's first-person account of the Rolling Thunder Revue recalls Sal Paradise's perspective as narrator of *On the Road*, but rather than beginning on the East Coast in New York and heading to the West Coast and California, Shepard makes the reverse journey. Shepard's attempt to echo the Kerouac novel implies that Bob Dylan is, for Shepard's purposes, Dean Moriarty, Sal Paradise's friend and traveling companion. According to Kerouac scholar Ann Charters, the narrator Sal Paradise goes in search of the American dream, pushing the limits of freedom "by following the example of Dean Moriarty. Dean is the dream's reality. . . . For Sal Paradise, his friend Moriarty is 'Beat—the road, the soul Beatific,' in possession of the key to unlock the door to the mysterious possibilities and richness of experience itself."[53] Many Dylan fans do the same. The paralleling of Shepard with Sal Paradise, Dylan with Dean Moriarty, and the *Logbook* with Kerouac's *On the Road* explains Shepard's highly mystical presentation of Dylan. Dylan is a visionary in *Logbook*, a unique individual with insights to which most are not privy. Throughout his story, Shepard works hard to figure out "Who is this character anyway?"[54] using the searching language of those mystified by Jesus of Nazareth (Matt. 8:27; Mark 4:41; Luke 8:25).

There is one further detail in Walter Benjamin's presentation of the *flâneur* I will mention at this point. Benjamin's work frequently introduces the idea of intoxication, both literal and metaphorical. The *flâneur* succumbs to an "anamnestic intoxication" while wandering through the city streets, feeding on "the sensory data taking shape before his eyes."[55] Similarly, Benjamin tells us, a gambler is lost within the game but simultaneously renewed, and a collector experiences a deep "enchantment" and "loses himself" in this activity of "practical memory."[56] In each case—the *flâneur*, the gambler, the collector—is an overwhelming sense of distraction within which are found illumination and a form of memory. As Howard Eiland puts it, "Being carried away—which is what distraction and intoxication have in common . . . does not necessarily exclude a certain profane illumination."[57] For these three figures, distraction does not dull recollection but heightens their sense of perception. As the *flâneur* wanders through the crowds in the city streets, he makes "unconscious and unwitting connections . . . thus putting into practice a 'reception in distraction'."[58] The collector, for instance, holds items from his showcase and is inspired by them, able "to look through them into their distance, like an augur." The items in a collection hold, for the collector, histories in themselves, "an encyclopedia of all knowledge."[59]

Forms of intoxication also figure in the cluster of American writings I refer to in these pages. Kerouac, Shepard, and Dylan all speak of intoxication—literal and metaphorical—as a precondition to moments of insight and clarity. While in Mexico, Sal Paradise and Dean Moriarty seek out some tea, "ma-ree-wa-na," from a young man named Victor. The comical consequence involves a miraculous ability to understand the Spanish language—"I thought Dean was understanding everything he said by sheer wild insight and sudden revelatory genius inconceivably inspired by his glowing happiness."[60]

Dylan also introduces language that speaks of absorption with some person, event, or subject matter that suggests a kind of intoxication. When speaking about Mike Seeger, he uses language reminiscent of Benjamin's references to unexpected flashes of insight:

> Sometimes you know things have to change. . . . Little things foreshadow what's coming. . . . Something immediate happens and you're in another world, you jump into the unknown, have an instinctive understanding of it—you're set free. . . . It happens fast, like magic. . . . Somebody holds the mirror up, unlocks the door. . . . Mike Seeger had that effect on me.

Later, when describing Seeger's arrival at a party, Dylan uses language that combines revelation and insight with a kind of disorientation. When Seeger unexpectedly enters the room, Dylan says his brain becomes "wide awake," adding, "Something hit me." Dylan finds himself in an intoxicated state, "so absorbed in listening to [Seeger] that I wasn't even aware of myself." It is during this moment that he has an epiphany of sorts. Dylan realizes he "would have to start believing in possibilities that [he] would not have allowed before" and that the way forward artistically must involve a change because he "had been closing [his] creativity down to a very narrow, controllable scale." In order to make such a change, Dylan concludes, "I might have to disorientate myself."[61]

A further example from *Chronicles* of this beneficial intoxication appears as Dylan describes a visit with U2's front man, Bono. Here the intoxication is literal. Bono "brought a case of Guinness with him" and before long, "the case of Guinness was almost gone." Here too Dylan couples the language of intoxication with freedom and artistic vision. Bono asks Dylan about unrecorded songs and before long calls producer Daniel Lanois, thus setting in motion events leading to the recording of *Oh Mercy* (1989). Liberation results from this intoxication, Dylan tells us: "I had a clear road ahead and didn't want to blow the chance to regain my musical freedom. I needed to let things straighten out and not get mixed up anymore."[62] Here, a story that involves a form of disorientation/intoxication leads to clarity of vision, "a clear road" and creativity. Elsewhere, Dylan speaks scornfully of a person he clearly does not respect: "He looked like he'd never been stoned a day in his life."[63]

Dylan's many interpreters recognize the difficulties involved in attempting to extrapolate biography from his songs. The same is true of his prose autobiography. This writer is witty and playful, hiding behind his ever-changing personae and masks. He is reluctant to offer commentaries on his work and is not beyond fabricating stories as a strategy for misleading those who pry. He did this in the 1960s (e.g., "I rode freight trains for kicks / An' got beat up for laughs" etc.[64]), and he does it in *Chronicles*, taking a ride in a nonexistent '57 Impala in order to avoid our attempts to get too close. Throughout *Chronicles* we find this blending of memory and creativity, this occasionally frustrating but always delightful habit of hiding from audiences . . . and his devoted fans expect nothing less.

At the same time, *Chronicles* does reveal something about Bob Dylan's way of seeing and exploring the world around him. As he does in his songs, he takes notice of characters and places easily missed by others. There is also a sense of randomness mingled in with his creative output. Walter Benjamin's *flâneur* provides us with an intriguing analogy to understand better this way of investigating the human condition.

Dylan's *Chronicles* and Shepard's *Logbook* also capture something of the Kerouac-ian version of *flânerie* we see in *On the Road*—that longing for newness, discovery, insight, and freedom. The *flâneur*, this restless seeker and wanderer described by Walter Benjamin and others, provides us with a way of imagining Dylan's dialogue with religious ideas and texts, an adventurous, unencumbered wandering after meaning.

Chapter Two

The Gospel according to Bob Dylan
Are You Serious?

An air of mystery surrounds Bob Dylan. He doesn't just sing songs . . . those songs must *mean* something. He doesn't just speak . . . those words must *involve a subtext* of some import. He commands an audience. Whether the songs actually carry depths of meaning or not, or whether there is an intended subtext, is quite beside the point. Audiences frequently *receive* Bob Dylan and his work this way, assuming it possesses gravitas. When they speak about him and his work, this magnification frequently includes religion-laden terms.

In the previous chapter, we examined the enigmatic Dylan persona, the artist wandering in search of meaning, drawing a crowd of spectators convinced he holds the answers they seek. This chapter brings into greater focus the religious qualities of that *flânerie*. Where does this perception of religious value originate? I approach the topic from different directions. First, as a convenient starting point, I anticipate responses to the title *The Gospel according to Bob Dylan*. What does this mean? Like the picture on my office door described earlier, showing Dylan standing before a crucifix, the use of religious symbols or words in relation to the singer can evoke different assessments. Audience members, whether religious or not, tend to use exaggerated language in relation to Bob Dylan, and I spend some time illustrating and reflecting on this curious phenomenon. Second, I consider reasons that some find particular meanings in the songs while others do not. As I do in other sections of the book, I turn to dialogue partners for ideas on how to engage the issue, and in this case, literary critic Stanley Fish's comments on the relationship of readers to texts prove particularly useful. With Fish's ideas in hand, the third section of this chapter examines connections between religion and popular culture generally, and Bob Dylan specifically, returning to and expanding on ideas presented in the first section. I close the chapter with a summary of findings and propose that intersections of religion and Bob Dylan fall broadly into four categories.

A Book That Nobody Should Write

'Αρχὴ τοῦ εὐαγγελίου Βοβοῦ Διλανοῦ: *"The gospel according to Bob Dylan."* When first invited to write a book focusing on Bob Dylan for the "Gospel according to" series I imagined two less-than-enthusiastic reactions, each objecting to what appears to be a frivolous treatment of something sacred. The first comes from those with religious sensibilities who might bristle at the notion of using a sacred term (*gospel*) to describe the work of a mere musician. To blur the distinction between language associated with the divine and celebrations of human achievement might seem disrespectful and unnecessarily provocative.

Despite this potential objection, the title remains appropriate because Bob Dylan's ardent fans often employ hyperbolic language soaked in religious concepts when discussing the man and his work (most commonly, "prophet"), and the songs include a great deal of content derived from religious discourse, particularly the Bible. Furthermore, Dylan occasionally introduces christological descriptors to lyrics using the first-person singular. This casts the songs' narrators (and for many, by extension, the singer himself) in an ethereal light. They wear thorny crowns just like Jesus, to give but one example.[1] As R. Clifton Spargo and Anne K. Ream put it, "Early Dylan is littered with references to saints, sinners, jokers, thieves, and faith healers, and sometimes he even casts himself, ironically, in the role of a Messiah."[2] This habit is not limited to Dylan's early work though, as a line about his body glowing with flame in a more recent song illustrates ("Tell Ol' Bill," *Tell Tale Signs*, 2008; see Rev. 1:14–16). Among various thematic overlaps between Dylan's stories and those told about Christ, references to betrayal and temptation are widespread.[3] In these examples, the songwriter is responsible for the Christ-singer/narrator parallels, but we might add that interpreters occasionally make connections of their own. For instance, Michael Gray comments on Dylan's physical resemblance to Jesus during the *Hard Rain* television special of 1976, suggesting Dylan looks "extraordinarily Christ-like," "uncannily like Jesus Christ."[4] Apparently, this is not an isolated opinion. Mark Allan Powell reports that marketers for Pat Robertson's Christian Broadcasting Network unwittingly incorporated a publicity photo of Dylan from this TV special as part of their design for a Bible cover. Why? Because they thought it looked like Jesus![5]

The second anticipated objection to the title of this book comes from Bob Dylan fans wary of something appearing to co-opt the artist for a cause. A book with such a title must surely attempt to present Dylan as endorsing a particular theology or ideological position. This is a reasonable concern, since many Christians did this very thing during the period bracketed by the albums *Street Legal* (1978) and *Infidels* (1983). Both of these concerns deserve a response.

Objection #1: Religious Labels Are Inappropriate

The phrase "gospel according to . . ." invokes not only the titles of the New Testament books Matthew, Mark, Luke, and John and a number of noncanonical writings from the ancient world claiming to document the life and/or teachings of Jesus, but also the core beliefs of Christianity itself, as in the phrase "the beginning of the gospel [or good news] of Jesus Christ" (Mark 1:1; words I paraphrase slightly in the opening Greek sentence of this chapter). A deliberate echo of the Scriptures and the central tenets of the Christian faith in a book about a rock star might sound a little brazen. Is he really equating the Bob Dylan canon with the sacred canon? one might ask. Worse still, is he equating Bob Dylan with Saints Matthew, Mark, Luke, and John? Worst of all, is he equating Bob Dylan's message with the gospel of Jesus Christ?

I raise this issue because of a relatively unique phenomenon associated with Bob Dylan. Many people *really do* speak of him in quasi-religious terms. We are accustomed to exaggerated claims about the artistic achievements of celebrities, and usually this tendency in itself is not particularly startling. Dylan certainly has his share of grandiose accolades that speak to his significance as a musician, writer, and thinker.

A. J. Weberman: "You know, a lot of people say Dylan is the Shakespeare of his time. Hey, Shakespeare was the Dylan of his time!"[6]

T-Bone Burnett: "There is no way to accurately or adequately laud Bob Dylan. He is the Homer of our time."[7]

Van Morrison: "Dylan is the greatest living poet."[8]

Colin Larkin: "Bob Dylan is unquestionably the greatest musical poet of the twentieth century and certainly one of the most important figures in the entire history of popular music."[9]

Louis P. Masur: "In short order [Dylan] issued *Bringing It All Back Home* (1965), *Highway 61 Revisited* (1965), and *Blonde on Blonde* (1966), perhaps the greatest burst of sustained creative genius since Faulkner published successively and annually *The Sound of Fury* (1929), *As I Lay Dying* (1930), *Sanctuary* (1931), and *Light in August* (1932)."[10]

Bruce Springsteen: "Dylan was a revolutionary. Bob freed your mind the way Elvis freed your body. He showed us that just because the music was innately physical did not mean that it was anti-intellectual. He had the vision and the talent to make a pop song that contained the whole world."[11]

Neil Young: "For *me,* Dylan is the greatest that ever lived in the singer/songwriter/poet vein. He's an original, like Woody Guthrie. From a literary sense? This guy's over the top. He's like Longfellow or one of those fuckin' guys, that's what Dylan is. He even named himself after a poet."[12]

Apparently, language is no barrier for recognizing his artistic power, as Régine Chassagne from the Canadian band Arcade Fire attests: "When I was 15, I would hear Bob Dylan songs. . . . I barely spoke English. I probably got 10 percent of it, just the basic words—'babe' and 'door.' But I could tell that there was something important there."[13] What Woody Guthrie says must be true: "Songs was [sic] a music and a language of all tongues."[14] Even characters in Dylan's stories play up the hype. An imagined world playfully echoes the real one in *Masked and Anonymous* as the reporter Tom Friend (Jeff Bridges) twice says to the singer Jack Fate (Bob Dylan), "You're supposed to have all the answers."

After identifying someone as having extraordinary artistic and visionary capacities, the jump to assigning quasi-divine attributes and inspirations—usually for hyperbolic flair—is a short one. Of course most of this comes with tongue firmly in cheek, an indulgence in grandiose language by devoted fans, much like the graffiti declarations that "Clapton is God."[15] Yet there remains something different about Dylan's stature within contemporary culture, a reception of the artist that goes beyond mere fandom. Consider a selection of comments about Dylan and his artistry that drift toward something bigger than his art, something approaching the sphere of religion:

> **Ken Kesey** (author of *One Flew Over the Cuckoo's Nest*): "I've just figured out who this weird little fuck [Dylan] is. . . . Same guy who wrote the Book of Revelations [sic]."[16]

> **Bob Johnston:** "I truly believe that in a couple of hundred years they'll find out he was a prophet. I think he is the only prophet we've had since Jesus."[17]

> **Sam Shepard:** "Two [Dylan] concerts sold out. . . . College types going to see the prophet."[18]

> **Barry Feinstein** (referring to audiences in the U.K. in 1966): "He was the god, he was their god of the times."[19]

Each remark introduces religious terminology in relation to Dylan and credits the singer with an ability to see and understand things that most do not. *You're supposed to have all the answers*, and legions of fans agree. We see this adoration expressed in the negative as well, in the rather extreme reactions to certain artistic decisions Dylan makes. For audiences and critics, his artistic successes may touch on the sublime, but his (perceived) failures evoke unusually harsh condemnations, and occasionally they include religious terminology to express the depth of feeling involved: "Judas!"[20]

Dylan alludes to the prophet label bestowed on him so often by fans in "I Feel a Change Comin' On" (*Together Through Life*, 2009), as he sings about some hearing the blood of the land in his voice. As is so often the case, there is an echo of biblical phrasing in his lyric: "The land is full of bloody crimes" (Ezek. 7:23 KJV); "The land was polluted with blood" (Ps. 106:38 KJV; see also Exod. 4:9; 12:13; Num. 35:33; Deut. 19:10; Ezek. 9:9). Though fans hear in the songs modern-day jeremiads every bit as forceful as the ancients, the singer himself usually resists such labels, insisting he is neither a prophet nor a prophet's son in "Long Time Gone."[21] Of course, the prophet Amos said the same thing ("'I am no prophet, nor a prophet's son'" [Amos 7:14]), and he could not shake the title any better than Dylan can.

Such over-the-top reverence puzzles Dylan, and it has puzzled him throughout his career. As Powell puts it, "As one who was accorded unsought mythic status before his time, he resents exaggerated estimates of his significance, repels idolatrous would-be disciples, and seems to enjoy being regarded as enigmatic."[22] In a 2004 interview for the CBS program *60 Minutes*, Ed Bradley asks about this phenomenon. Dylan's response suggests some discomfort with grandiose labels:

> You feel like an impostor when someone thinks you're something and you're not. . . . You're just not that person everybody thinks you are, though they call you that all the time. "You're the prophet. You're the savior." I never wanted to be a prophet or savior. Elvis maybe. I could easily see myself becoming him. But prophet? No.[23]

In the same interview Dylan denies his songs are "sermons" and that he is a spokesperson for anybody or anything, but Bradley presses him further about the laudatory claims put forward by fans and their tendency to celebrate him and his songs as prophetic.

Bradley: But they [i.e., Dylan's fans] saw it.

Dylan: They must not have heard the songs.

Bradley: It's ironic, you know, that the way that people viewed you was just the polar opposite of the way you viewed yourself.

Dylan: [understatedly] Isn't that something?

Dylan seems similarly bewildered by audience interest when interviewer Bill Flanagan mentions his career album sales to date—more than a hundred million: "Yeah I know. It's a mystery to me too."[24] "Music, my writing," he insisted in an interview more than forty years before his conversation with Ed Bradley, "is something special, not sacred."[25] Woody Guthrie faced a similar dissonance, with those around him attributing skills and assigning titles he knew to be unwarranted: "They thought I was a mind reader. I didn't claim to be, so some of them called me a fortune teller and a healer. But I never claimed to be different from you or anybody else."[26] Some of the honorific titles included religious labels, which he, along with at least one skeptic, rejected. Here's how Guthrie relates his responses to calls from one crowd:

> "This is th' final battle! Battle of Armageddon! . . ." "Now you tell us somethin', Mister Fortune Teller!" "Hell yes, that's what we come here for! Tell us a vision 'bout all of this stuff!". . . . "You ain't no prophet!" one big boy yelled. "Hell, any of us could say that same thing! You're a dam fake!" [Guthrie responds.] "An' you're a Goddam fool!" I hollered out at him. "I told ya I didn't claim ta be nothin' fancy! Yer own dam head's jist as good as mine! Hell, yes!"[27]

Dylan must read these words and smile. He has been arguing with a very similar crowd and making the same reply to their demands his whole career.

Dylan rejects such excesses for good reason. It is dangerous. Elvis is the most celebrated pop musician of all time and a clear example of the dangers facing one who is object of such devotion, as Bobbie Ann Mason makes clear:

> He had found the perfect drug in his youth, being the King, and to sustain that transcendent experience he needed more and more affirmation. He needed fortifying chemicals to help him stay on his emotional mountaintop, or alternately to shut down to find momentary release. But he couldn't give up that original fabulous apotheosis, when he became god on earth. He was addicted to being Elvis.[28]

Dylan's high regard for Elvis Presley is obvious, and so is the lesson of the Elvis tragedy. Mason's remarks suggest Elvis struggled to live up to his celebrity status. Stephen Scobie's reading of "Brownsville Girl" (*Knocked Out Loaded*, 1986) is instructive here. Dylan, with cowriter Sam Shepard, bases this song loosely on the 1950 movie *The Gunfighter*, a film in which a young fame seeker shoots the protagonist, the famous gunslinger Jimmy Ringo, in the back. The song closes with a haunting reference to the tearing down of stars,[29] which Scobie links to Dylan's concerns about his celebrity status; it haunts him and raises the possibility that it will destroy him.[30] Dylan's line recalls a story told by Shepard in his *Logbook* about Roger McGuinn, in which the Byrds' singer confesses his fear of audiences, specifically that someone might shoot him.[31] Perhaps it is noteworthy that Dylan wrote the song only a few years after John Lennon's assassination, making the appeal of a movie featuring the gunning down of a well-known hero understandable.

His uneasiness about audience expectations is also a recurring theme in *Chronicles*, where he complains about the absurdity of the press's attentions:

> It seems like the world has always needed . . . someone to lead the charge against the Roman Empire. . . . I really was never any more than what I was—a folk musician who gazed into the gray mist with tear-blinded eyes. . . . Now it had blown up in my face. . . . I wasn't a preacher performing miracles.[32]

While Dylan seems truly mystified about his audiences, he is not above nurturing this mystique and indulging occasionally, no doubt with a sense of irony, in exaggerated self-description. When looking back to his early days as a new arrival to New York City, he acknowledges his youthful idealism and admits a certain self-aggrandizement: "I could transcend . . . limitations. . . . [I] had a heightened sense of awareness, was set in my ways, impractical and a visionary to boot." He also speaks of his destiny at times in such a way that highlights his uniqueness: "Destiny was about to manifest itself. I felt like it was looking right at me and nobody else."[33] In 1975, he told *People* magazine, "I didn't consciously pursue the Bob Dylan myth. It was given to me by God. Inspiration is what we're looking for. You just have to be receptive to it."[34]

The tendency toward hyperbole in fan assessments of Dylan does draw criticism. Something of the kind appears in Pope Benedict XVI's *Pope John Paul II, My Beloved Predecessor,* in which then-Cardinal Ratzinger mentions his concerns about Bob Dylan's participation in the 1997 World Eucharistic Congress in Bologna, Italy, for Pope John Paul II.

> The stars, Bob Dylan and others whose names I don't remember, arrived for the young people. They had a message completely different from the one for which the pope labors. There was reason to be skeptical—I was then and, to some extent, still am—and to question whether it was right to bring in these kinds of "prophets." But all of a sudden their message seemed weak and outdated when the pope put aside the hand-written text in front of him and began to speak to the young people from his heart, saying things to them that, at first glance, one would not have the courage to say. He spoke to them of the meaning of failure, sacrifice, the acceptance of suffering, the cross.[35]

Ratzinger might think Bob Dylan is the wrong "prophet" for such an occasion, but it is interesting to note he still refers to him by that term. Ratzinger's remarks make it clear that religious labels placed on Dylan stick, following him even as far as the palace of the pope. Pope John Paul II did not share Cardinal Ratzinger's opinion and looked at Dylan's presence on that occasion quite differently.[36] During his sermon immediately after Dylan's performance, the pontiff quoted the songwriter's best-known song: "You say the answer is blowing in the wind, my friend, and so it is, but it is not the wind that blows things away; it is the wind that is the breath and the Life of the Holy Spirit." Furthermore, the pope answers one of the questions raised by the song: "How many roads must a man walk down? One, there is only one road for man and it is the road of Jesus Christ."[37]

While it is certainly true that fans nurture Bob Dylan's mystique through their endless attention to his life and work, it is also true that Dylan participates in this myth making to some extent. Marketing and strategies for winning and holding an audience are part of it. So is the necessity of creating a sense of space between one's private and public life. Bono points out that Dylan "kept his privacy by creating disinformation by a series of elaborate masks, by avoiding the mainstream and creating his own path through the thicket,"[38] an insight that goes a long way toward explaining subsequent fascination. Here we have a universally recognized celebrity who shies away from the spotlight, an artist who places himself in the public eye by continuously touring, yet one who limits media access to his private life. This simultaneous presence and absence, disclosure and closure, combined with provocative artistry create the sense of mystery that so intrigues Bobheads. We never have quite enough. Is the motive behind these limits on public access personal protection or the machinations of an astute businessperson who knows how to work a crowd? Perhaps a bit of both.

Objection #2: Claiming Dylan as a Religious Spokesperson is Inappropriate

While some (like Pope Benedict XVI) might complain about the high esteem bestowed on Bob Dylan, especially when fans employ religious language to celebrate his achievements, the reverse is also true. Others will read this book's title and groan, fearing it indicates yet another attempt to claim Bob Dylan for a cause to which he has no connection (say, the Christian right), or to reduce his work to a singularity that cannot possibly do justice to his genius (say, the Bible or religious thought). This too is an objection to the perceived trivializing of something sacred, but here we have a reverse of the situation just described. Dylan is now himself a revered object, and to connect him to some particular cause or theology is the equivalent of saying he belongs uniquely to some but not to others. He is ours, not yours!

These concerns are understandable. In the late 1970s and early 1980s, Christian conservatives latched on to Bob Dylan's fame as a way of raising their own profiles and furthering their agendas. Christian media sources reported on his activities following news of his conversion, and there were attempts to profit in one way or another from his celebrity. Pastor Bill Dwyer of the Vineyard Christian fellowship, with which Dylan had some connections, speculates that one problem facing Dylan "was that there were a lot of people that wanted to use him and push him up to the front, put him on TV, put him on the stage and have him say something."[39]

Not surprisingly, many Christian organizations hoped to take advantage of having one of the world's most famous people suddenly in their midst, now that he had joined their ranks as a believer. According to Dwyer, there was concern among the staff of the Vineyard that "Bob would be co-opted or drawn off by somebody who had their own agenda for [him], and they would try to use him. There is a lot of media in the Christian world, and a lot of churches in the Christian world who, if a celebrity comes to Christ, wants to put them up front right away in order to expand their own ministry, in order to attract more people to their church." The documentary *Bob Dylan 1975–1981: Rolling Thunder and the Gospel Years* also includes similar remarks by songwriter Al Kasha, who knew Dylan during the Vineyard days: "I'm going to be very candid. Where I think he [Dylan] got hurt, not by Jesus Christ but by other Christians, is [that] a lot of Christian evangelists, I felt, took advantage of him."[40]

There were even some unusual efforts made to protect Dylan from supposed dangerous influences. Dylan biographer Clinton Heylin refers to individuals "seeking to ensure that he remained an isolated, enthusiastic advocate of the Vineyard Fellowship's particular brand of evangelism," something that included extreme measures like banning his publicist Paul Wasserman from backstage "because he was an infidel."[41] The high expectations placed on Dylan by Christians resemble the demands of the folk community in the 1960s once they anointed him as their unofficial high priest. It is not surprising that the singer moved away from such stifling environments.

While many audiences—not just Christians, folkies, and social-justice advocates—would like to claim Dylan as their spokesperson, the truth is that his work defies easy compartmentalization. He does not sing about any one subject any more than he rests content within any one musical style. For my part, I emphasize here that Dylan's significance lies not in his conformity to or association with any particular worldview, but rather in the encounter between his art and the individuals who engage it. Music audiences are amorphous; they are not monolithic, a cohesive unit that adheres to a fixed creed or a political one committed to a rigid ideology. How can we speak of this individual experience of the music?

Listening to Dylan with Stanley Fish

As noted earlier, not everyone agrees that focusing on words apart from sound is the best way to approach popular music lyrics. If the title of the book presents an obstacle for some, my decision to focus on lyrics will do the same for others. To be sure, those who look closely at the lyrics of popular songs apart from musical accompaniment open themselves to valid criticisms. Deena Weinstein's comments on analyses of progressive rock highlight some of the concerns:

> Lyrics have never been much of a selling point for rock. . . . They're ignored, misinterpreted, or misheard. When words are grasped, it is fragmentarily through phrases or a chorus rather than as the full lyrical text. Fans and fan-pandering critics attempt interpretations, but they tend to be superficial and naive. They hear the singer's "I" as a literal reflection of the author,

indicating a failure to see that art may be something beyond giving vent to one's personal feelings and experiences.[42]

Weinstein goes on to appeal to Michel Foucault's observation that an author is not "a human being, but a subject position," something created *by* the text. Rock critics and fans have the tendency to approach lyrical interpretation the other way around, beginning with biographical considerations and moving toward the songs, the "VH1-profile romantic fantasy of a text [song] created by a 'life.' "[43]

Another issue is the tendency to approach lyrics with the assumption that there is an underlying second sense, as if mysterious or enigmatic words must be codes for the audience to decipher. This is analogous to a bad habit identified by Umberto Eco, who observes modern readers "finding" symbolic meaning in everything they read, so much so that "the symbolic diamond, which was meant to flash in the dark and dazzle us at sudden but ideally very rare moments, has become a neon strip that pervades the texture of every discourse. This is too much of a good thing."[44] Eco reminds us that texts can include "open unintentionality" as well. If we proceed in reading everything as though it has a "second sense," then everything becomes "flat and dull," and the "lust for a second sense ruins our ability to see second or even one thousand senses where they actually exist, or have been placed."[45] Over-interpretation is an enormous temptation for Bobheads (myself included), who often mistake playfulness for riddles, arbitrariness for intentionality, and spontaneity for premeditation. Consider the lyrics to *The Basement Tapes* songs, which show Dylan engaging in wordplay, not politicking or philosophizing: "Language, for one thing, is completely unfettered. A good number of the songs seem as cryptic, or as nonsensical, as a misnumbered crossword puzzle—that is, if you listen only for words, and not for what the singing and the music say—but the open spirit of the songs is as straightforward as their unmatched vitality and spunk."[46]

With these cautions in place, I proceed with the assumption that there is no singular way to read and interpret a song because meaning resides in the listener, not in the music or lyrics. To gain a few

insights about the dynamics involved in our reception of music and
to introduce some ideas about why audiences fall into the interpretive traps Weinstein and others describe, I turn to Stanley Fish
and his reflections on reading and the discovery of meaning in the
written word. His remarks provide us with a useful methodological
analogy that we can adapt for our consideration of religious meaning in Bob Dylan's song lyrics.

Stanley Fish answers his titular question rather playfully in the
preface to *Is There a Text in This Class?* and suggests, "There is
and there isn't."[47] There is not, he goes on to explain, if by text we
understand an unchanging entity, one that is stable from moment
to moment. However, there is a text if by the term we refer to the
perceived meaning that presents itself to an interpretive community guided by particular assumptions. Said differently, protocols
guide all readers, invariably shaping the expectations we place on
the texts we read. This understanding of text as something unsta-
ble and fluid, and the shift away from author- and text-centered
interpretation toward an audience-centered theory of reading, is
particularly helpful when considering the unique ways audiences
listen to popular music generally and Bob Dylan in particular.
People hear all kinds of things in Dylan's songs, and many focus
on one or more particular threads running through his collected
works as being the quintessential substance of his art as a whole:
social justice, politics, philosophy, romance and sexuality, religion, literary and poetic self-consciousness, homage to American
musical precursors, and so on. Regardless of our views about what
constitutes the core of Dylan's art, Fish would have us remember
that our experiences of art vary and that reading and hearing do not
occur in a vacuum. Our environments shape us, provide us with
guiding assumptions, and move us toward certain conclusions. We
tend to find that which we expect.

Fish concludes that the reader's experience, not the text itself,
is "the proper object of analysis."[48] The reader needs to ask what
it is that individual words, phrases, sentences, paragraphs, chapters, novels, plays, and poems do, not what authors intend. This
approach to text provides us with a way of thinking about religious
meaning in Bob Dylan's music. It is not so much the content of his

songs that carry meaning but our engagements with the lyrics and music that matter in this regard.

We should not confuse the information readers find in an utterance, what they identify as the text's message, as the equivalent to some absolute, fixed purpose for the text put there by the author. Instead, it "is the experience of an utterance—all of it and not anything that could be said about it, including anything I could say—that is its meaning."[49] He could just as easily be referring to a rock song here. Readers of books or poems, and those listening to music, generate meaning. He speaks of *"meaning as an event*, something that is happening between the words and in the reader's mind, something not visible to the naked eye but which can be made visible (or at least palpable) by the regular introduction of a 'searching' question (what does this do?)."[50]

Fish also refers to our environment as readers, which influences our perceptions about discovered meaning. When making his point that environment shapes interpretation, he provides a sample reading of a passage from *Paradise Lost* that produces a conclusion "not discovered by the analytical method but produced by it." He says elsewhere, "I 'saw' what my interpretive principles permitted or directed me to see, and then I turned around and attributed what I had 'seen' to a text and an intention."[51] Such a discovery is not the product of individual acumen in reading a difficult text, but rather the result of a particular reading strategy.

Notice that reading (and listening) strategies exist *prior to the act of reading*. It matters what expectations we bring to songs, if any. These expectations represent a precondition that determines what conclusions individual audience members will reach. There is a link between the truth/meaning we find in Dylan's songs and the presuppositions guiding us as we listen to them. A religiously inclined, spiritually open fan will likely discover a kind of richness in a song quite different from what is found by those looking for a voice to articulate their politics. Others who are pining over a broken relationship will have another kind of experience when listening to the same album. Complex lyrics like Dylan's address all kinds of subjects, so all three groups might hear the same songs but reach very different conclusions because of their "needs" at a particular moment. They will gravitate to particular ideas. So what is the album largely about? Religion, politics, or romance? It is any one of these, and all of these.

For Stanley Fish, reading is a generative act and a form of writing. The text is no longer a "privileged container of meaning"; instead the reader possesses "joint responsibility for the production of meaning." Fish questions the narrow reading strategies of critics who find meaning only in the text itself. Similarly problematic is any attempt to locate meaning in authorial intention, which is necessarily beyond the reach of critics. Again, Fish insists that the experience of the reader, not the text, is the proper object of analysis.[52] It follows that *what we want or need* from a Bob Dylan song is at least as important as *what is in* a Bob Dylan song.

Finding Religious Meaning in Bob Dylan, or It's Up to Me

There is a third less-than-enthusiastic response to the phrase "the gospel according to Bob Dylan" indicated by my chapter subtitle, "Are You Serious?" I have in mind those with only passing exposure to Bob Dylan's life and work who may be surprised to discover there is anything here of interest to religious studies. They may not bring objections like the other hypothetical readers described above—those concerned that either religion or Dylan are treated with inappropriate levity—but they might raise an eyebrow and ask what one has to do with the other. The remainder of this chapter explores reasons that the religious dimensions of Bob Dylan's work are so fascinating and deserving of close attention.

When people discover my interest in biblical and religious themes in Bob Dylan's writings, they often ask a familiar question: So, what does he believe? Interestingly, this does not happen with other artists I write about on occasion, whose work also includes conspicuous religious subject matter. Heavy metal music, for instance, typically draws on religion for its lyrics and symbols, yet most people do not confuse Ozzy Osbourne's stage persona with his personal beliefs. He might wear crosses, call himself the Prince of Darkness, and sell "unholy water" at concerts, but this does not usually lead to speculation about the presence or absence of religious orientation in his private life.[53] Here audiences readily appreciate that the fusion of music and religion is simply part of the genre in question, as is also the case with country music. In some other instances, a musician's personal beliefs are obvious enough that speculation is unnecessary. Most know that Yusuf Islam (Cat Stevens) is a Muslim; that George Harrison is a Hindu; that Alice Cooper and Sinéad O'Connor are Christians. All of these musicians share their religious views openly in interviews, various writings, and their music. George Harrison's Hinduism is transparent in his book *I, Me, Mine* and the albums *All Things Must Pass* (1970) and *Brainwashed* (2002), for example, which bookend his solo career. Alice Cooper announced his conversion to Christianity with the album *The Last Temptation* (1994) and speaks openly about his faith journey in the autobiographical *Alice Cooper, Golf Monster: A Rock 'N' Roller's 12 Steps to Becoming a Golf Addict*.[54] Sinéad O'Connor's faith (schismatic Catholic) is evident in her album *Theology* (2007), while Yusuf Islam's *An Other Cup* (2006) and *Roadsinger* (2009) are beautiful, clear statements of his Muslim faith. In each case, these artists sing and speak openly about their spirituality—no ambiguity, no need for relentless questions and speculation. In far more cases still, audiences realize religious terms, phrases, and images serve artistic ends and do not express any personal positions on matters of faith. The use of language connected to organized religion and sacred texts is ubiquitous in popular music, but most listeners know instinctively that a gap exists between singers and the songs they write.

Somehow, the situation is different with Bob Dylan, for fans and critics often connect this artist to his art. One reason they do so may be the cryptic nature of many of his lyrics that gives the impression something more is going on below the surface, which in turn invites a search for deeper meaning. He nurtures this sense of mystery: "All the great performers that I'd seen who I wanted to be like . . . all had one thing in common. It was in their eyes. There was something in their eyes that would say . . . 'I know something you don't know.' I wanted to be that kind of performer."[55] The presence of ambiguity in songs tends to make a biographically based strategy of interpretation attractive to many who hope clues useful for interpretation may present themselves.

When asked about Dylan's religious beliefs, my answer is always the same. I do not know.[56] Ultimately, it is none of my business. All I can say with any confidence is that religious language is everywhere in the songs, which accounts for my academic interest in the subject. The presence of religious content in song lyrics, however, does not necessarily reveal anything about the personal life of the one who wrote them, and we should be cautious about making the leap back and forth from songs to biography and from biography to songs. At the same time, when on the rare occasion Dylan speaks about his personal beliefs, he tends to be vague, often pointing toward music rather than organized religion as a source of spiritual sustenance:

> I find religiosity and philosophy in the music. I don't find it any-where else. . . . I don't adhere to rabbis, preachers, evangelists. . . . I've learned more from the songs than I've learned from any of this kind of entity. The songs are my lexicon. I believe the songs.[57]

Notice that he *finds* religiosity and philosophy in the music; he does not put it there. Whatever we think of Dylan's religious views, it is clear that he links spirituality with music. He makes comments to this effect quite often: "When Frank [Sinatra] sang that song ["Ebb Tide"], I could hear everything in his voice—death, God and the universe, everything."[58] Woody Guthrie thinks of songs in much the same way: "I sung out by myself. . . . All kinds of hats, caps, sweaters, and dresses stood around tapping shoes against the concrete, patting hands, like getting new hope out of old religion. . . ."[59]

For a songwriter who delights in evading questions and who guards his privacy so fiercely, it is almost certain that our curiosity about Dylan's personal beliefs will remain unsatisfied. Maybe someday he will speak openly about his spirituality in a way analogous to artists like George Harrison and Yusuf Islam. I would listen with interest to such an interview should it ever hit the wires, but I doubt it will.

Even Dylan's gospel songs and stage sermons of the late 1970s and early 1980s are ambiguous to a degree. His earnestness and sincerity are not in question, but we should remember that much of the material he relayed to audiences at that time was not fully his own. Instead, he passed along a received discourse, one echoing the church's dogma and the writings of particular teachers (like the bizarre eschatological ideas of Hal Lindsey). Consider these words from a concert sermon:

> I read the Bible a lot; it just happens I do. It tells you specific things in the book of Daniel and the book of Revelation which might apply to these times here. Because Russia is going to come down and attack the Middle East; it says this in the Bible. And I've been reading all kinds of books my whole life, and I really never found any truth in any of them. These things in the Bible, they seem to uplift me and tell me the truth.[60]

Here and elsewhere, Dylan modeled his speech and demeanor at this time according to certain conventions of gospel music performance. This is what gospel musicians do. They proclaim the old, old story in modern times. They pass along the Christian teachings they received, just like St. Paul himself: "I handed on to you as of first importance what I in turn had received" (1 Cor. 15:3). Christians and Christian musicians repeat and preserve the basic elements of the gospel tradition as they receive it, without innovation. Does it follow that Dylan believed or understood all aspects of this new teaching? He certainly did not tether himself to this one form of religious discourse (Christian fundamentalism). As he moved on from gospel music and its various conventions, his religious *flânerie* brought him into new conversations, including associations with Lubavitcher Hasidism, a sect of Orthodox Judaism.[61]

A Short Personal Note on the Study of Religion
in Popular Culture

I introduce again the term *flânerie* to make a few remarks on the study of religion in popular culture. At a conference, a theologian once chastised me for suggesting we can find religious meaning outside the walls of the church. Such a postmodern approach to spiritual inquiry leads nowhere, he warned. Years later this comment still rankles because it oversimplifies the matter to a blunt either/or and rejects the possibility of a both/and approach to meaning and God. The fact is, I remain inside the church walls, theologically speaking, and grounded in the historic creeds, and yet I enjoy looking beyond the stained-glass windows and strolling (*flânerie*) outside the church doors. My professional life illustrates what I mean. I have the best job imaginable, teaching both biblical and English literature to undergraduate students. I move from lectures on Paul and the Gospels in the mornings to Shakespeare and Jane Austen in the afternoons. And without losing sight of the theological distinction between biblical canon and literary canon, I remain convinced these diverse bodies of literature remain, in their own ways, true. The best art—literature, painting, dance, sculpture, and so on—is revelatory. Is this true of the popular arts as well?

Spirituality in Popular Culture

It will come as no surprise to most that Don Saliers, a theologian (not the one I refer to above), professor of sacred music, and musician, claims that folk and popular music "often express and explore deeply religious questions." However, Saliers does not end there. Though his book focuses on the church's music and classical compositions and hymns, he adds, "We may find stronger prophetic texts and musical lines outside the churches than inside."[62] He recommends, in fact, that we do away with the usual dichotomies of sacred and secular music and "attend to what can be called the 'sacrality' or even the 'sacramentality' of music wherever and whenever we are moved out of ourselves and our habitual, common-sense world." The theological significance of music, he insists, is not unique to the traditions of high art.[63]

Bob Dylan's music moves many listeners out of themselves, out of their "habitual, common-sense world." Falling under his dancing spell, we end up chasing the shadow he sees. This escape from the common-sense world leads a few listeners to something approaching religious meaning. Their thoughts might turn, no matter how far removed from organized religion, to the *idea* of justice, to the *idea* of a divine being, to the *idea* of reliable, meaningful, enduring love. The music creates space for such concepts, pressing at the walls of our habitual patterns of thought, allowing us room to contemplate new possibilities. One writer goes so far as to call Dylan a "musical theologian."[64] Spargo and Ream argue that "even without the rebirth of 1979, Jewish and Christian idioms persist in his work to such a degree that Dylan would have to be reckoned one of the most powerful interpreters of religious language and sensibility in all of American pop culture."[65] It is no wonder that Dylan opens up our minds about spiritual matters and forces us to think about them. What we do with this newly opened "space" is our own business.

The study of connections between religion and the arts is a burgeoning academic field, and the diversity of recent books exploring this subject area is remarkable. As a field of study, links between religion and culture go far beyond the kinds of curiosity exemplified by devotees of particular genres or entertainment icons. Scholars are increasingly cognizant that popular culture not only includes religious content but in some sense functions as a rough equivalent to religious experience, providing audiences with a venue to explore and a shared vocabulary to articulate their own spirituality. Links between the arts and personal religiosity exist despite declining adherence to organized religion.[66] As Robin Sylvan puts it, "Traditional institutional religion has become increasingly irrelevant to many people [and] the sector of popular culture has become the new arena for their religious expression."[67] Similarly, Kelton Cobb argues that popular culture "has become, for most, the primary instrument for forging personal identity and probing the cosmos for meaning." What is more, the various art forms falling under this rubric popular culture, its "plotlines, characters, look and feel, poetry, rhythms, colors, and preoccupations," provide audiences with "a fundamental resource . . . for making meaning." From these raw materials, "we contrive our symbols, myths, rituals, ethics, and any notions we might have about more transcendent goods like love, truth, beauty, happiness and the divine."[68]

If we consider Bob Dylan's art in light of these excerpts, we begin to see that the search for deep meaning in his music by so many is not so strange after all. Pop culture provides forms of spiritual encounter that the consumer helps construct. As noted above, the religious significance of Bob Dylan does not lie entirely in the man himself, or even in his music and lyrics. He is not a systematic theologian or self-conscious religious teacher, presenting a single, consistent, fully expressed and nuanced worldview or religious perspective. Rather, religious meaning and insight—the gospel according to Bob Dylan—spring from the engagement of the individual fan with his art. If we find answers in Dylan, it is because we are already asking particular questions. If we find comfort or meaning in the songs, it is because we are looking for ways to articulate preexisting conditions. We integrate his words and sounds with the ideas, knowledge, needs, and assumptions we bring to the music.[69] This, in my view, is why the religious material in Bob Dylan's songs and writings matter, why it warrants close examination, along with the songs of other musicians who deal with religious questions. Bob Dylan's imaginative work provides an artistic world in which to explore our own ideas and questions about religion.

Engaging Religious Content in Dylan's Work: Four Approaches

Bruce David Forbes introduces a collection of studies on religion and popular culture by identifying four ways these worlds intersect: 1) religion in popular culture; 2) popular culture in religion; 3) popular culture as religion; and 4) religion and popular culture in dialogue.[70] By *religion in culture*, Forbes indicates "the appearance, explicitly or implicitly, of religious themes, language, imagery, and subject matter in elements of popular culture."[71] This is a straightforward idea for music fans who know well how often songwriters introduce religious content to their work. The second category may be less familiar. For Forbes, *popular culture in religion* indicates "the appropriation of aspects of popular culture by religious groups and institutions."[72] Many churches, for instance, reflect contemporary music styles in their worship services, and occasionally "secular" songs find their way into the worship life of religious communities.

The most intriguing category in Forbes's list is *popular culture as religion*, meaning that popular culture "serves as religion or functions like religion for many people."[73] We find excellent examples of this phenomenon in Robin Sylvan's fascinating *Traces of the Spirit*, noted earlier, in which he examines the subcultures associated with the Grateful Dead, house/rave/electronic dance music, heavy metal, and rap/hip-hop. He finds that many participants enjoy a vibrant spirituality in these contexts, complete with ritual, community, and experiences of transcendence. "I have come to understand," he concludes, "just how profound and significant a religious phenomenon is taking place in these musical subcultures."[74] We read of another intriguing example of culture cum religion in Gregory L. Reece's study of Elvis worship. Reece investigates, among other things, whether Graceland is "a center of a new religious movement," a "sacred shrine at the center of a religious pilgrimage."[75] Other artists touch their audiences deeply in ways resembling an encounter with the sacred. When speaking about the lyrics of Led Zeppelin, Susan Fast speaks of an "undefined (or at least underdefined and therefore more interpretively open) spirituality,"[76] a description that is equally fitting for much of Dylan's work.

By *religion and popular culture in dialogue*, Forbes refers to the various conversations possible between these disparate worlds.[77] Hostility often divides the faithful and the creative forces behind such media as film and television, largely over ethical concerns (like the presence of violence or sexuality). However, constructive conversations between the two are also possible: "Often, religion critiques the values and assumptions of popular culture, offering appreciation, criticism, or both. Yet commentators also can use themes and insights from popular culture to critique religion, raising questions about its relevance or adequacy. In either case, the discussions provoke clarification of implicit values and assumptions in both religion and popular culture."[78]

Forbes's four categories provide a useful way to think about Bob Dylan's art because we can see religion in his songs; his songs embraced by religion; Dylan as religion; and religion and Dylan in dialogue. First, the presence of *religion in Dylan's songs* is obvious and, I hope, illustrated sufficiently in other parts of this book. This material is usually Judeo-Christian in origin, and the Bible specifically is present everywhere in his work.[79] There is a wide cast of named characters who migrate from the Scriptures to the songs—Cain and Abel, Abraham, Judas, the Good Samaritan, and so on. Allusions to others abound as well, as in the reference to one living a long time ago who brought the dead back to life ("Girl from the Red River Shore," *Tell Tale Signs*, 2008). There is a seemingly endless string of terms and phrases that one can trace back to Dylan's reading of the Bible, often specifically the King James Version.

Second, we find examples of *Dylan in religion* when organized religion and its representatives find in the artist or his creations some kind of resource to promote a particular cause. During his gospel music period (if measured by the albums, 1979–1981), many found in Dylan a powerful endorsement for Christianity. Dylan contributed a harmonica solo to Christian musician Keith Green's song "Pledge My Head to Heaven" (*So You Wanna Go Back to Egypt*, 1980), thus allowing Green to broaden his platform. Some presentations of Dylan's religious journey use his story as a way of teaching aspects of the Christian faith (e.g., Marshall's *Restless Pilgrim*; and Steve Stockman's chapter on Dylan in *The Rock Cries Out*), and gospel musicians often cover his songs.[80]

Third, as discussed earlier, Dylan's fans regularly celebrate their hero using hyperbolic, quasi-religious terms and categories, in effect treating *Dylan as religion*. When they do so, their language resembles Dylan's "worship" of his own musical heroes. He describes watching saxophone player John Hart and noticing his striking resemblance to Blind Gary Davis, adding that he suddenly felt he "was seeing the sight of a god's face."[81] Reflecting in Martin Scorsese's documentary *No Direction Home* (2005) on his first meetings with Johnny Cash, Dylan describes the country star as "more like a religious figure to me." I discuss this deep respect for fellow artists further in the next chapter, but for now we might observe that this exaggerated language follows naturally on Dylan's insistence that music provides a connection to the sacred and that music *is* sacred. ("I find religiosity and philosophy in the music. I don't find it anywhere else. . . . The songs are my lexicon. I believe the songs."[82])

The nature of *Dylan's dialogue with religion* is an interesting issue. He does not claim any formal adherence to organized religion (see citation of his interview with Pareles below). However, from his childhood days in a Jewish family, through his discovery of the religious content of American roots music in the 1960s and later, the exploration of Christianity in the late 1970s and early 1980s, and his continuing artistic exploration of religious themes and texts, it is at least informally part of his life and art. Dylan respects religion. Performing for the pope would suggest this (there is no reason to suggest cynically that money or publicity would motivate such a thing—he does not lack either), as does his dutiful attention to his children's bar mitzvahs.[83] Comments Dylan made during an episode of his *Theme Time Radio Hour* focused on the Bible (which first aired September 6, 2006) also strike me as a respectful and appreciative reflection on that collection of stories and ancient wisdom.

To return for a moment to Forbes's third category of popular culture as religion, Dylan's elevation of music to a kind of sacredness is worth repeating. "There's only two kinds of music: death music and healing music," he said on one occasion.[84] Folk music in particular feeds his mind and spirit. "My songs come out of folk music," he says. "I love that whole pantheon."[85] He uses folk songs to explore the universe and claims the folk genre "was all [he] needed to exist."[86] This deep affection for early American musical traditions is a well-known part of his story, and many writers examine Dylan's love and theft of this great body of early, recorded work.[87] One need only listen to his rhapsodies on *Theme Time Radio Hour* about those singers and songwriters that went before him, whether folk, blues, gospel, or early rock and roll, to find evidence of a profound respect for this musical heritage.

On some occasions, Dylan's choice of terms for celebrating musical influences is striking, for it moves far beyond mere admiration for the talent and ingenuity of individual players, singers, and writers and appreciation for the musical lineage of which they are a part. His laudatory language approaches reverence, complete with the use of religious expression. The use of hyperbole in celebrating musical genius is familiar enough ("Clapton is God," for instance), but it is not to the musicians themselves that Dylan bends the knee, so to speak. Speaking of himself on one occasion, he admits that performers come and go and that "songs are the star of the show, not me."[88] Music, the spirit of the songs, moves him toward something resembling a sacred space.

> "Those old songs are my lexicon and my prayer book," he adds [in an interview for *The New York Times* in 1997]. "All my beliefs come out of those old songs, literally, anything from 'Let Me Rest on That Peaceful Mountain' to 'Keep on the Sunny Side.' You can find all my philosophy in those old songs. I believe in a God of time and space, but if people ask me about that, my impulse is to point them back toward those songs. I believe in Hank Williams singing 'I Saw the Light.' I've seen the light, too." Dylan says he now subscribes to no organized religion.[89]

Other musicians make similar remarks about the sacredness and spirituality of music. Canadian producer and musician Daniel Lanois, producer of Dylan's *Oh Mercy* and *Time Out of Mind*, prefaces his song "Sacred and Secular" (*Here Is What Is*, 2008) by referring to the pedal steel guitar as his favorite instrument. "I've been playing it since I was a kid," he says. "It takes me to a sacred place. It's my little church in a suitcase. That's what I like to call it, my church in a suitcase."[90] Bono also links spirituality and music making:

> I stopped going to churches and got myself into a different kind of religion. Don't laugh, that's what being in a rock 'n' roll band is, not pseudo-religion either. . . . Show-business is Shamanism:

Music is Worship; whether it's worship of women or their designer, the world or its destroyer, whether it comes from that ancient place we call soul or simply the spinal cortex, whether the prayers are on fire with a dumb rage or dove-like desire . . . the smoke goes upwards . . . to God or something you replace God with . . . usually yourself.[91]

Audiences find meaning in the music they hear just as performers do.

For those of us who confess Dylan's music functions as lexicon and prayer book, we do well to remember that our experience of this Dylanesque mysticism is a construction. He refuses to interpret his own songs for us, so it follows that whatever we take from them is a product of our own making. "I'm not good at defining things," he told Robert Hilburn in a 2004 interview. "Even if I could tell you what the song was about I wouldn't. It's up to the listener to figure out what it means to him."[92] The song in question is "Just Like a Woman" (*Blonde on Blonde*, 1966), but the point remains for all his music. Meaning resides with the listener and her experience of the music, not in the song on its own but the song as mingled with her own emotions and circumstances. Musicians function as mediums, priests, stained-glass windows, or icons, pointing beyond themselves to something far bigger, but they cannot define that vague something for the listener.

Chapter Three

Not a Prophet or Savior . . .
Elvis Maybe
Bob Dylan's Devoted Disciples

*W*e continue teasing out the quasi-religious relationships between music and listener, celebrity and fan, in this chapter, though now we come at it from another direction, asking first, Where does the prophet find prophetic voices? Where does the inspirational Bob Dylan turn for inspiration? We thus pick up and expand on ideas introduced at the end of the last chapter. Just as his fans go into raptures over his music, Dylan celebrates music and its master practitioners in the most exalted terms. We fans speak of Bob Dylan just as he speaks of his musical heroes.

The second part of this chapter considers ways Bob Dylan plays with his audiences' overuse of hyperbole. Knowing fans and critics employ grandiose terms to describe him and his music, he *writes back* to that discourse, playfully dialoguing with audiences, occasionally with self-deprecating, mock parody of his own celebrity. The bulk of this section explores his 2003 film *Masked and Anonymous*, in which he casts himself as a failed messiah.

All His Beliefs Come Out of Those Old Songs

Bob Dylan finds deep meaning, even spirituality, in music, and his esteem for other musicians takes several forms. Consider an interesting news item coming out of Winnipeg, Manitoba, Canada, soon after a Dylan concert there on November 2, 2008. News outlets began reporting that the singer had stopped by Neil Young's childhood home in the hours before the show. As the story goes, the current owner of the house saw two men standing in the front yard speaking to his wife, and after figuring out it was Bob Dylan with his tour manager, he invited them in for a look around. According to the homeowner, Dylan was particularly interested to know which bedroom belonged to Neil when he lived there.[1]

Why would visiting this house matter to Dylan? One suspects he finds in this home a musical equivalent to sacred space. Dylan wants to be in the very room where Young (presumably) learned guitar, maybe discovered great music by radio, and first dreamed of being a performer. This sense of admiration and affection for artistic genius is familiar in music circles. Neil Young himself seeks out forms of connection with musical greatness. While performing at the Ryman Auditorium in Nashville, Young acknowledges that Hank Williams stood on that very stage years earlier. "His spirit's still here," he notes, "and that's a beautiful thing." Later in the same concert, before singing "This Old Guitar" (from the album *Prairie Wind*, 2005), Young makes a further connection to the iconic singer: "This guitar here . . . this is Hank's old guitar. It was here [at the Ryman Auditorium] in 1951, I think. . . . I'm glad to see it back here."[2] There is a picture of this guitar on the *Prairie Wind* liner notes.

Young's appreciation for vintage musical equipment is well known. William Echard, building on Paul Théberge, refers to this use of old equipment as a way of "sonically encoding nostalgia." Use of vintage equipment "gives a connection to, or allows appropriation of, the past, both symbolically and literally."[3] Dylan's visit to Young's childhood home resembles this interest in finding symbolic and literal connections with the past. He also reveres (imaginatively) an old musical instrument in a scene from *Masked and Anonymous*, when Bobby Cupid (Luke Wilson) presents Jack Fate (Dylan) with Blind Lemon's guitar. These physical and spatial connections permit tangible links to admired musical traditions.[4]

A second example of Dylan's quasi-spiritual connection to music involves his first encounter with Robert Johnson's work. Columbia Records's John Hammond is largely responsible for getting Dylan's career underway, recognizing in the young folk musician something special: "Hammond had only heard two of my original compositions," writes Dylan, "but he had a premonition that there would be more."[5] What did he see in this youngster? Conventional wisdom might suggest talent scouts would look forward, trying to anticipate new trends, but Hammond also looked backwards. "He saw me as someone in the long line of a tradition, the tradition of blues, jazz and folk and not as some newfangled wunderkind on the cutting edge," Dylan said.[6]

Hammond passed along some Robert Johnson recordings to the young singer, including Johnson's compilation *King of the Delta Blues* (1961). "From the first note," Dylan relates, "the vibrations from the loudspeaker made my hair stand up." It clearly left an impression on the young performer:

> When Johnson started singing, he seemed like a guy who could have sprung from the head of Zeus in full armor. I immediately differentiated between him and anyone else I had ever heard. The songs weren't customary blues songs. They were perfected pieces—each song contained four or five verses, every couplet intertwined with the next but in no obvious way. They were so utterly fluid. . . . They jumped all over the place in range and subject matter, short punchy verses that resulted in some panoramic story—fires of mankind blasting off the surface of this spinning piece of plastic.[7]

Presumably, John Hammond recognized affinities between Johnson and Dylan that he hoped to nurture by introducing the blues legend's work to the new performer. Dylan credits Johnson with various contributions to his own development as a songwriter. He studied the blues musician's songs, copying the words so he could "more closely examine the lyrics and patterns, the construction of his old-style lines and the free association that he used."[8] "I wanted to be like that, too," Dylan adds. Allusions to Johnson's music appear in Dylan's songwriting, as in "Tweedle Dee & Tweedle Dum," and "High Water (For Charley Patton)," both on *"Love and Theft"* (2001),[9] but his influence on Dylan certainly goes much deeper.

What is interesting about Dylan's description of Johnson is how suitable it is as a description of Dylan himself. Put Dylan's name in place of Johnson's in the opening sentence of the citation above, and you have a paragraph out of any gushing reviewer's assessment of the latest album to hit the shelves. Dylan's fans indulge in hyperbolic flourishes all the time, easily conferring divine honors on the singer in much the same way Dylan elegizes Robert Johnson ("sprung from . . . Zeus," etc.). Furthermore, when Dylan describes Johnson's songs as characterized by "free association . . . [with] sparkling allegories, big-ass truths wrapped in the hard shell of nonsensical abstraction—themes that flew through the air with the greatest of ease,"[10] he uses words that would be appropriate in describing any one of his own songs.

Third, Dylan also finds meaning-laden musicality in the life and art of Woody Guthrie. As a young singer, he learned Guthrie's songs, mimicked his dress and style, and even visited the ailing folkie in the hospital.[11] Guthrie's music and his storytelling abilities are both important influences on Dylan's art, as he readily admits:

> One guy said, "Hey there, you're singing a Woody Guthrie song." He gave me a book that [Woody] wrote called *Bound for Glory* and I read it. I identified with the *Bound for Glory* book more than I even did with [Jack Kerouac's] *On the Road*.[12]

The poem "Last Thoughts on Woody Guthrie" is an early tribute to his musical hero. The poem explores a profound sense of existential disorientation, and because of constant shifts back and forth between the second and first person, readers/listeners inevitably participate in the poet's disillusionments and anxieties: "to yourself you sometimes say / 'I never knew it was gonna be this way . . .'"[13] The role models and options available to the poet are less than desirable, something complicating the search for an authentic sense of identity: "'Christ do I gotta be like that / . . . / Good God Almighty / THAT STUFF AIN'T REAL'." The poet resolves the dilemma by looking for answers in places not previously investigated. One needs to look elsewhere for hope, he concludes, and there are two possibilities. Either visit "the church of your choice" where you will find God, or the "Brooklyn State

Hospital" where you will find Woody Guthrie. The paralleling of church and hospital, God and Guthrie, makes several statements simultaneously. Obviously, it expresses the writer's high esteem for the legendary folk icon. But beyond this, the paralleling of music with religion suggests one can find authenticity, meaning, and "hope" in both. The poet is not prescriptive and remains modest about his assertions: "It's only my opinion / I may be right or wrong." The poem ends by claiming seekers will find both God and Guthrie "In the Grand Canyon / At sundown." This phrase brings to mind the romanticism of the American West, the wandering minstrel tradition of which Guthrie is a part, and the grandeur of the Creator's handiwork.

Dylan's fascination with Neil Young, Robert Johnson, and Woody Guthrie illustrates two qualities of the "religion" audiences find in music more generally. First, it is spirituality independent of the usual venues of religious expression. The music Dylan identifies with provides him with a different canon and an alternative kind of authentic religious encounter. He finds truth, beauty, and significance in voices outside the discourses of traditional religious expression (i.e., not the church). Second, we find Dylan using hyperbolic claims about other musicians (e.g., "sprung from . . . Zeus") in much the same way that his own fans speak of him, indulging in this blurring of religiosity and the experience of great music.[14]

What Dylan finds in Guthrie, Johnson, and Young, I find in Dylan. As is the case with all fans, "my Bob Dylan" is a construct, an idealized fabrication of the man and his art that is inevitably quite unlike the way others see him. There are some songs and albums I play constantly, others I rarely turn on. I prefer some periods of his career to others. It is likely significant that I enjoy reading Dylan—*Lyrics*, *Chronicles*, *Tarantula*—whereas others are less inclined to appreciate the texts alongside the music. Of course, the concerts always leave an impression on audiences though no two shows are alike. For me, an outdoor concert in Montreal on August 5, 1997, stands out as a moment of crazy synergy with the artist and the songs that I could never fully explain. The highlight of the night for me was Dylan's performance of "Blind Willie McTell," apparently the first time he played the song in concert. I had hit something of a rough patch in the summer of 1997; it was a moment when I thought no one could sing the blues like me. On that cool evening, "Blind Willie McTell" had a particular resonance that no one else could have shared. Of course, the fact that Dylan chose to perform that song for the first time that particular night, while I watched (somewhat oxymoronically) in low spirits, is pure coincidence. I know that. However, I am not able to shake my amazement at the perfect timing of that moment, nor do I want to.

I am not alone in experiencing such transcendence through the popular arts. In one of his studies of celebrity culture, Ellis Cashmore observes that the phenomenon of "bestowing divine status on mere mortals" is not unique to Western society or the modern era. "History is full of characters," says Cashmore, "[that] actually encouraged their followers to do so."[15] What is fascinating is the way that celebrities enter a place in the popular imagination typically and perhaps most logically reserved for those in positions of power, whether deriving from royal lineage, the state, or the spiritual realm. "Even musicians who have scorned such attributions, like Bob Marley or Bob Dylan, have been endowed with deistic eminence by fans," Cashmore observes. "Marley had an oracular presence and his songs were infused with Rastafarian prophecy. Dylan perplexed one generation, while inspiring another with his sour condemnations of war and prejudice. Their influence makes their veneration comprehensible."[16] Cashmore colorfully explains his remark about the comprehensible veneration of highly influential musicians like Marley and Dylan by contrasting the excessive adoration of minor celebrities, which is much harder to understand because it is less deserving.[17]

By far, the most striking example of the near deification of a celebrity is the ongoing fascination with Elvis Presley among his devoted fans more than thirty years after his death. For some, this phenomenon resembles the birth of a new cult or religion. Writers point to parallels between the celebration of Elvis and the activities associated with established religions. Consider, for example, the use of the phrase "the King" with reference to the singer, the collection of souvenirs that resembles the role of sacred relics and fetishes, the evolution of Graceland into a sacred space in the post-1977 era, the priestly role of Elvis impersonators, and ritualized activities marking the dates of the King's birth and death. Many, of course, claim he is still alive.[18] As Gregory L. Reece puts it, "People see fit to respond to the life and death of Elvis Presley in ways that rely on the resources of their religious beliefs."[19]

The very fact that Reece and others pursue this line of questioning—is Elvis fan culture a kind of cult or emerging religion?—is telling. Adoration of Michael Jackson also borders on religious devotion. Since pallbearers carried his casket into the public memorial as a gospel choir sang Andraé Crouch's "Soon and Very Soon," one suspects many blurred the sense of the words "We are going to see the king," mingling notions of the King of Kings with the King of Pop. Dylan indulged in a similarly honorific gesture in comments about Elvis in 1997. When discussing a serious illness, he quipped, "I really thought I'd be seeing Elvis soon." There is a playful double entendre here. For many, death means being ushered into the presence of Jesus, the King of Kings (as in Luke 23:43). For a musician, speaking of meeting Elvis in death involves meeting the King of Rock and Roll.

There are probably many reasons for such hyperbolic flourishes in honor of celebrities. Perhaps we long to see a normal, real person accomplish amazing things. Religious traditions elevate in status both gods and prophets, but most of them—at least in the traditional, established religions—represent times and places modern devotees cannot identify with very easily. We might revere Moses or Mohammed but ultimately find it easier to understand and identify with kings born in Tupelo, Mississippi, and Gary, Indiana, or a prophet born in Duluth, Minnesota. We may remain Jewish, Muslim, Hindu, or Christian, but celebrity culture provides more immediate connections to greatness.

The Bible in the First-Person Singular

According to one definition, parody "imitates the serious manner and characteristic features of a particular literary work, or the distinctive style of a particular author, or the typical stylistic and other features of a serious literary genre, and deflates the original by applying the imitation to a lowly or comically inappropriate subject."[20] According to another definition, parody operates "as a method of inscribing continuity while permitting critical distance. It can, indeed, function as a conservative force in both retaining and mocking other aesthetic forms; but it is also capable of transformative power in creating new syntheses."[21] Allowing these definitions, we might suggest that Dylan's deliberate use of biblical and sacred terms can be both playful and subversive; it is a self-conscious critical engagement with religion, and entertainment at the same time. There may be mockery, but parody need not be negative. Hutcheon finds it is also potentially transformative: "What has traditionally been called parody privileges the normative impulse, but today's art abounds as well in examples of parody's power to revitalize."[22] Parody involves dialogue and the identification of perceived weaknesses and flaws with varying degrees of mockery. We find this in Dylan's interactions with religion, particularly on those occasions when he ridicules those who abuse it. He knows well that not every person claiming to be a Christian (for example) is a worthy representative of the faith. Bob Dylan parodies biblical subjects on other occasions, such as those moments when he represents himself as a character in one of its stories. This self-referential, first-person description of Dylan's narrators/characters in biblical (often, christological) terms tends to be humorous, as in the exaggerated depiction of one's troubles as a form of crucifixion.

We hear this in song lyrics and see it played out in film. For instance, early in *Renaldo and Clara* there is a scene with two street preachers proclaiming their hellfire gospel to passersby from the top of a Volkswagen van.[23] They are intolerant and aggressive, and one of them even roughs up a heckler. We see them again later in the film, this time with the camera cutting back and forth between them and Dylan riding in a vehicle with his song "What Will You Do When Jesus Comes?"[24] playing in the background. As he answers his titular question with another interrogative— "Will you tear out your hair?"—the camera turns appropriately to the angry preachers who are doing just that, figuratively speaking. The song also asks if you will kick Jesus out into the street when he comes. As we hear these words, the music fades, and we see Dylan getting out of the vehicle onto the city sidewalk, perhaps playfully suggesting *he* is the awaited messiah.

Dylan's commentaries on religion occasionally have a critical edge, usually when referring to people who cloak themselves in a disingenuous or intolerant spirituality, as in his condemnation of those who speak in religion's name ("Slow Train," *Slow Train Coming*, 1979).[25] Maybe the Bible-quoting figure in the long black coat is the sort of religion-talkin' character he has in mind here ("Man in the Long Black Coat," *Oh Mercy*, 1989). "The lyrics try to tell you about someone whose body doesn't belong to him," Dylan writes of this song. "Someone who loved life but cannot live, and it rankles his soul that others should be able to live."[26] Such superficiality is a familiar target for Dylan, who deftly deflates those with only a veneer of spirituality rather than a genuine depth of faith, character, and kindness. We could read the street-preacher scenes in *Renaldo and Clara* this way, as a censure of the kind of religiosity represented by those angry moralizers who clearly look at most walking by with disdain, condemning them as degenerates deserving the hellfire they proclaim. When Dylan suggests *he himself* is the awaited messiah by singing, "What will you do when Jesus comes?" as the preachers condemn their onlookers in the background, the scene drips with irony and ridicule. Rather than the vengeful messiah anticipated by the preachers, *this* messiah is tolerant. He does not condemn but rather sides with the weak and vulnerable, as in his advocacy of the wrongly convicted Rubin "Hurricane" Carter, which features so prominently in the film (and in Shepard's *Logbook*). *This* messiah is also loved by the crowds who flock to see him during concerts; he is not dreaded like the vengeful God proclaimed by these fear-mongering soapbox prophets.

Like *Renaldo and Clara*, several stories told in his songs make use of christological characters and narrators. Dylan frequently "casts himself as the larger-than-life and often martyred hero of his own songs, which ties his fans to the idiosyncratic development of his own mythicised life story—which is full of an American dream of self-fashioning and self-transformation."[27] What is more, he tends to dress his pain and sense of martyrdom and self-sacrifice in messianic terms, identifying with, or at least resembling, Christ himself. The language is often ironic and playful, with hints of self-mockery. We find this on the album *Modern Times* (2006). Here we read stories about slippery and morally ambiguous individuals. The narrator of "Spirit on the Water," for one, is at one moment praying to higher powers as he sweats blood and, at another, barred from returning to paradise after committing murder. Dylan moves from Christ in the garden (Luke 22:44) to Cain in the wilderness (Gen. 4:8) in the space of a few words.

The opening verse of "Spirit on the Water" echoes the Genesis creation narrative, thus locating the narrator's tale in the midst of chaos (compare the first two lines of the song with Gen. 1:1–2). Within this scene of primordial turmoil, his thoughts turn to the woman he loves. He flatters her not only with a string of pop-song clichés but also sacred terms that elevate the sense of tragedy resulting from their separation. He may sweat blood like the meek, innocent, sacrificial Son of God, but in reality he is the perpetrator of a crime; he is not a victim of violence but one who commits violent acts, brawling one moment, killing a man in another. Because of his actions, Cain becomes a fugitive and wanders the earth (Gen. 4:11–16), barred like his parents from returning to paradise (3:23–24), and forced to live in the land east of Eden (4:16). The narrator of the song suffers a similarly cruel fate, forced to wander alone because his lover remains in Eden. Though he admits he would be happy to live always with her, he is unable to do so. He wants to be with her "in paradise," but this is not possible. While it sounds rather dark, there is subtle play in this scene as well. The narrator's call to the woman in paradise is as much a seduction as a lament. Though he is barred entry to paradise himself, the gates of Eden seem more permeable for her. He hears her sweet voice calling and remains confident she cannot forget him. The song closes with an invitation. Though his best days are behind him, he can still offer her a good time.

This penchant for biblical and specifically christological imagery in *Modern Times* and elsewhere appears somewhat melodramatic, if not megalomaniacal. His enemies refuse him as they refused Jesus ("Bob Dylan's 115th Dream," *Bringing It All Back Home*, 1965; e.g., John 1:11),[28] he wears a crown of thorns while some gamble for his clothes ("Shelter from the Storm," *Blood on the Tracks*, 1975; see e.g., Luke 23:34);[29] and he extends a love greater than all others ("Maybe Someday," *Knocked Out Loaded*, 1986; see John 15:13).[30] However, rather than an unhealthy ego, the language shows Dylan indulging in poetic hyperbole, irony, and good humor. As "Spirit on the Water" illustrates, he is equally comfortable playing the villain in his songs and on occasion is explicit about the potential threat he poses to others. While some characters and narrators in his songs are heroes and saviors, others are cowards (e.g., the one in "Brownsville Girl" [*Knocked Out Loaded*, 1986] who runs from a dangerous situation) and deceivers (potentially like the narrator in "Trust Yourself," *Empire Burlesque*, 1985). Sometimes, we are uncertain about where characters' loyalties lie (e.g., "Jokerman," *Infidels*, 1983). For a more sustained example of parody in Bob Dylan's art, I turn now to his film *Masked and Anonymous* (2003).

It Ain't Easy Being Human: *Masked and Anonymous*

Bob Dylan's on-screen performances are quite varied, including a hilarious cameo in the television sitcom *Dharma and Greg* (1999) and an appearance in a 2004 Victoria's Secret commercial, featuring his song "Love Sick" from 1997's *Time Out of Mind*. (This commercial reveals the singer's brilliant if subtle sense of humor. In 1965, an interviewer asked Dylan, *"If you were going to sell out to a commercial interest, which one would you choose?"* His response: "Ladies garments."[31] Apparently he wasn't kidding.) The highlight of his on-screen career is arguably D. A. Pennebaker's documentary *Dont* [*sic*] *Look Back* (1967), which followed Dylan for three weeks during a tour of England in 1965. One of the first music videos appears in this production, in which Dylan flips through large cards with the words to "Subterranean Homesick Blues" (*Bringing It All Back Home*, 1965). Dylan's many other projects include film roles, television concerts, and appearances in various documentaries, including Martin Scorsese's 2005 offering *No Direction Home*. But one of the most compelling performances comes in the 2003 film *Masked and Anonymous*.

This film is in a league of its own as far as Dylan's on-screen projects go. Though not a huge critical success, *Masked and Anonymous* is witty and thought-provoking, and the fact that Dylan cowrote the screenplay (under the pseudonym Sergei Petrov, with director Larry Charles, who uses the pseudonym Rene Fontaine) only adds to the enjoyment. Dylan plays Jack Fate, a singer released from prison to perform a benefit concert in a fictional America reeling from civil strife and subject to a paranoid government. Thanks to some strong performances by Jeff Bridges, Penélope Cruz, John Goodman, Val Kilmer, Jessica Lange, Cheech Morin, Mickey Rourke, and Luke Wilson; cameo appearances by Angela Bassett, Bruce Dern, Ed Harris, Giovanni Ribisi, and Christian Slater; and brilliant musical performances by Dylan and his touring band, *Masked and Anonymous* quickly emerged as a cult favorite among Bobheads. Dylan's own songs make up most of the soundtrack, often as covered by other musicians representing a wide array of styles.

Quite apart from marvelous musical performances and some great acting by the supporting cast, this movie is intriguing for viewers with an interest in religion, specifically the Christian Bible. It contains numerous echoes of biblical stories, but I focus here on four closely related characters. The story centers on the vaguely Christlike musician Jack Fate, who finds himself surrounded by Judas/Satan counterparts (Edmund, Tom Friend, and Uncle Sweetheart). Each one threatens and tempts the protagonist in his own way.

The movie begins with a montage featuring various scenes of violence (war, heavy-handed arrests) and natural disasters (a volcano, flooding waters) while a radio evangelist announces, "God has turned his back on this nation." These disasters come as no surprise to the preacher, who asks rhetorically, "Does the Bible lie?" The preacher might have questions put to Jesus in Matthew 24:3–8 in mind:

> "Tell us . . . what will be the sign[32] of your coming and of the end of the age?" Jesus answered them, "Beware that no one leads you astray. For many will come in my name, saying, 'I am the Messiah!' and they will lead many astray. And you will hear of wars and rumors of wars; see that you are not alarmed; for this must take place, but the end is not yet. For nation will rise against nation, and kingdom against kingdom, and there will be famines and earthquakes in various places: all this is but the beginning of the birth pangs."

The opening montage of violence and destruction in *Masked and Anonymous*, combined with the radio preacher's announcement of impending judgment, appear to represent visually these and similar words found in the Bible. Though we know little of the setting of the story, it takes place in a chaotic, perhaps revolutionary, somewhat Orwellian America (there are posters in some scenes featuring the visage of the dictator/president, Fate's father). The explicit reference to the Bible in the opening seconds of the film prepares the viewer for the numerous other allusions that follow and provides warrant for an analysis of the film concerned with biblical imagery.

The first of the four characters I discuss here is Jack Fate, the central protagonist played by Bob Dylan. There are several christological overtones attached to this singer, some obvious—for instance, his dead mother's name is Mary, which we learn from a gravestone—and others subtle, as in various parallels between Jack Fate's experiences and Christ's incarnation, resurrection, ascension, and second coming. We first meet Fate emerging from a tomblike jail and ascending the stairs (a resurrection/ascension of sorts). As he is leaving this cave/cell the guard says, "Some angels must have intervened on your behalf. " This calls to mind Matthew 28:2–7, which describes an angel's activities in connection with the resurrection story, including rolling back the stone covering the entrance to the tomb, a cave/cell. In his very next appearance he is descending stairs with guitar case in hand, a descent that suggests that Jack is about to begin his musical second coming/comeback. Various passing comments also indicate that Fate's release is an incarnation/second coming. As Fate descends the stairs following his "resurrection," a man named Prospero (Cheech Morin) asks him if he is "coming back," to which Fate replies, "I did come back." As he is leaving the prison in the previous scene, one of the prisoners asks Fate where he is going, to which Fate answers, "Roswell." This playful reference to the famous alien landing near Roswell, New Mexico, may be another way of illustrating the incarnation idea. Prospero and Fate dialogue about which direction Fate will go—the lack of precision hints at John 3:8: " 'The wind blows where it chooses, and you hear the sound of it, but you do not know where it comes from or where it goes. So it is with everyone who is born of the Spirit.' " Later, when checking into the hotel, Fate observes, "I've been here before," and later still his mistress says, "I wondered when you would return."

The christological overtones continue following the resurrection/ascension/"descension" sequence when we shift to a conversation between Uncle Sweetheart (John Goodman) and Nina Veronica (Jessica Lange). Uncle Sweetheart is the second of the four key characters of interest here. Nina questions the currency of Fate's celebrity, after which Sweetheart retorts, "Did Jesus have to walk on water twice to make his point?" When she tells him that "the Network" responded with silence to the announcement that Jack Fate would headline the benefit concert, he interprets this silence as "reverence, like prayer." Uncle Sweetheart is close to Jack Fate ("We go way back") and despite his dubious, financially driven motives for hiring the musician, he did arrange for his release from prison and appears to be a friend. At the very least, he is an appreciative fan, as his astute analysis of "Drifter's Escape" during a performance suggests. Like Judas (his office is actually in the "Judas Building"), he is both friend and foe, and he manipulates for financial gain, just like Jesus' erstwhile disciple who was himself a thief (see John 12:6).

Sweetheart often serves as a foil to bring the Fate-Christ parallels to the surface. At one point, he observes that the concert featuring the (artistically) resurrected Fate has the potential to "save the world" (see below). This is a difficult task, Fate observes—"It ain't easy being human." This comment alludes to the Roswell reference and the New Testament teaching that the divine becomes flesh (John 1:14). Nevertheless, this incarnation story is not straightforward. Jack Fate's name is from Dylan's 1975 album *Blood on the Tracks* and the song "Simple Twist of Fate" (which serves also as the name of the cover band that will back him for performances in the movie). Yes, Fate is some kind of Christ figure but one with a "twist." The twist may lie in his close connection with sinister individuals like Sweetheart and also in the fact that he ultimately fails in his musical comeback/second coming.[33]

The third character of interest is Tom Friend (Jeff Bridges), who also reinforces the christological associations attached to Jack Fate and, like Sweetheart, introduces sinister designs against the singer, which recall the machinations of Satan tempting Christ in the wilderness. According to the director's commentary on the DVD release of the film, Tom Friend wears clothes similar to those worn by Bob Dylan during various stages of his career, which suggests he represents a dimension of Dylan's/Fate's persona. The fourth character, Edmund (Mickey Rourke), also has close ties to Fate. The two are brothers, either literally (since we are told that Fate had a twin brother who disappeared—though the connection is never made explicit) or figuratively (Edmund says to Fate, "I was the son your father [the president] never had"). After Jack's fall from his father's good favor, Edmund (son of the family's servant) steps in to take Fate's position within the family and government, ultimately becoming the president's heir and successor. Of course, the parallels with Edmund's villainous, usurping namesake in *King Lear* are hard to miss, perhaps indicating he is the president's illegitimate son (just as the Shakespearean Edmund is the illegitimate child of the Earl of Gloucester).[34] The closeness of these four characters calls attention to a significant ambiguity, a blurring of the lines between good and evil, Christ and antichrist.

If we allow that the predominant—though not always consistent—Christ figure in the film is Jack Fate, we find corresponding Judas/Satan figures in Edmund, Tom Friend, and Uncle Sweetheart. The reporter Tom Friend offers fame to Jack Fate ("I can put your face on every magazine"). Sweetheart also offers Fate an opportunity at fortune, just as the devil promises Jesus:

> The devil took him to a very high mountain and showed him all the kingdoms of the world and their splendor; and he said to him, "All these I will give you, if you will fall down and worship me." (Matt. 4:8–9; Luke 4:5–7)

Uncle Sweetheart, who at one point boasts of "eating from the tree of good and evil" (compare the serpent in the garden of Eden), puts it this way:

> You do this show, this benefit, it will be seen all over the world. You put your career back on track, maybe a tour, maybe a record, maybe both, make a little money and save the world all at the same time.

This implied denigration of material success (i.e., it is coming from the mouth of Satan/Judas/Sweetheart) and career advancement is further explored in the frequent references to the Network's expectations about the songs Jack Fate will perform for the benefit concert. They keep making requests for famous songs by rock royalty like the Beatles, the Rolling Stones, and the Who but while rehearsing, Fate and his band usually play old folk and gospel standards (e.g., "Look Away, Dixie Land") or some of Fate's/Dylan's more recent (and therefore generally less-known) work. The only song actually performed at the benefit concert is Dylan's "Cold Irons Bound" (*Time Out of Mind*, 1997). We see further the contrast between mere commercial success and respect for the integrity of quality, time-honored roots music when Bobby Cupid (Luke Wilson) gives blues-legend Blind Lemon's guitar to Jack Fate as a gift. Cupid and Fate treat it with reverence. The money-driven Sweetheart just sneers.

Every Christ figure needs a Judas, and though Nina Veronica is responsible for the final act of (coerced) betrayal against Fate at the end of the film, an ensemble cast, not a single individual, plays the Judas figure in this story. If Edmund, Sweetheart, and Friend contrast with and reflect characteristics of Jack Fate, it would be consistent with recurring themes in Dylan's songs where we regularly find such alternatives as friend and foe, Christ and antichrist, and love and hate in close proximity. Ambiguity often causes the unwary to mistake error for truth, violence for kindness, and so on.

Tom Friend's religiously inclined girlfriend Pagan Lace (Pené-lope Cruz) plays a supporting role in the film's Jesus-meets-Judas/Satan theme. She loves Jack Fate's songs because they are not precise but "completely open to interpretation." When we first meet her she is praying before lit candles and wearing a Metal-lica t-shirt (with crosses and the name of their album *Master of Puppets* on it). She is repeating the phrase "Christ, O Lord, save me." At one point we notice "333" tattooed on her hand. While the allusion to the infamous "666" of Revelation 13:18 is obvious, the use of the divine number "3" may suggest the Trinity and perhaps more specifically the Holy Spirit as its third member. This conclu-sion is supported by Tom Friend's dying words; he whispers into her ear that he once passed a cathedral and saw a white dove (a symbol of the Holy Spirit in the New Testament). Like the dove in the Gospels, it appears she is a manifestation of the Holy Spirit. It is striking that a character named "Pagan" aligns with the Holy Spirit. The image is transgressive, suggesting perhaps that we find divine illumination and grace in unexpected places. There are links between Pagan Lace and music—her Metallica t-shirt, her appreciation of Jack Fate's songs—so music might be one of those unexpected, "pagan" sources of spiritual insight.

Pagan Lace's relationship with Tom Friend is important. Friend is the character most resembling Bob Dylan in terms of attitude and beliefs. The young Dylan portrayed in *Dont* [*sic*] *Look Back* was angry, suspicious, and at war with reporters, constantly respond-ing harshly to their questions. The roles are reversed in *Masked and Anonymous*. Friend is an early-Dylan-like *reporter* who chal-lenges and questions the later-Dylan-like *musician* (namely, Jack Fate). Penélope Cruz (Tom's girlfriend, as we've seen) even bears a striking resemblance to Joan Baez, who appears in *Dont Look Back* and was at the time romantically involved with Dylan. This fact, coupled with the circa '65 Dylan clothes worn by Friend, takes us back to that earlier film. The dialogue between Friend and Fate therefore suggests a conversation between a younger and an older Dylan. Pagan Lace insists on staying close to Tom Friend, even when he suggests she leave him. She also speaks well of Jack Fate ("I love his music"). She remains a virtuous, religious, and faithful friend to both characters, to the Fate/Friend persona, perhaps intimating they are the same person, two sides of the same coin.

Masked and Anonymous treats themes we find elsewhere in Dylan's story and art. He is a prophet to many of his fans, something also true of Jack Fate. As Tom Friend says to him two times, "You're supposed to have all the answers." Despite the reverence shown by fans, the artist Bob Dylan/Jack Fate also faces harsh criticism and knows that following his artistic vision results in conflict with those same audiences. One issue the film explores is the fickle nature of fans. While some celebrate and understand Jack Fate, many more misunderstand and ridicule. He could avoid this by making what others consider better choices, by compromising his artistic instincts. The Judases in the movie conspire against the artist, urging him to betray his artistic vision, his muse, and to play the music acceptable to the unscrupulous Network. Of course, Jack Fate, like Bob Dylan, does not allow the preferences of others to determine his artistic choices.

This theme comes to a head in what I believe is the most important scene in the movie. Toward the end of *Masked and Anonymous*, a character in Al Jolson–like black makeup appears to Jack Fate shortly before the concert begins. Oscar Vogel (Ed Harris) was, he explains to Fate, one of "your father's [the president's] favorite performers." Vogel spoke out against some of the president's actions, however, "because [he] had a forum to speak" as an entertainer. His short speech includes the words "It's not what goes into your mouth, but what comes out," echoing Jesus in Mark 7:15. This points to the importance of words, indicating that an artist must speak the truth even when doing so is dangerous. Vogel indicates that one's decisions about what to say or sing, or not say or sing, can defile. You can compromise to protect yourself and your career, or you can speak and sing according to your convictions. Vogel explains that the president killed him when he chose to speak out against wrongdoing—obviously, he appears to Fate as a ghost. This important scene closes when Fate excuses himself in order to perform at his own show—the benefit concert—where he will sing out of his own convictions.

The benefit concert begins immediately after this visitation, a concert in which Fate sings only his own material, not the songs preselected by the government-controlled Network, thus following through with Vogel's advice. Fate does not compromise. The concert begins and ends with Fate performing—appropriately— "Cold Irons Bound" from Dylan's album *Time Out of Mind* (1997), and while the band plays, the scene cuts from the stage to the dying president's bedroom. After the president dies, with "Cold Irons Bound" still playing in the background, Edmund steps from the bedroom to a podium where he announces his claim to the now-vacant president's office. This regime will be a violent one, and the new president will rule with an iron fist. Indeed, his inaugural speech, given as "Cold Irons Bound" continues, contains the promise that the media will be under his control. As the song and the speech end, we see the police moving in, ending the benefit concert. Fate will be one of the first victims of this powerful, abusive new regime. Police arrest him (wrongly) for the murder of Tom Friend; the authorities force Nina Veronica to accuse him of the crime.

At one point in the film, Jack Fate asks the question "Whose side are you on?" This question is never easy to answer. In his songs, Bob Dylan regularly explores the idea that wolves disguise themselves in sheep's clothing (e.g., "Jokerman," *Infidels*, 1983; "Trust Yourself," *Empire Burlesque*, 1985). In *Masked and Anonymous*, he covers similar ground. By imitating story lines and characters from the Bible, the movie makes a statement about artistic integrity.[35]

Chapter Four

"He's the Property of Jesus"
The Gospel Period

Well, I can understand why they [are] rebellious about it [i.e., audience reception of the *Slow Train Coming* material], because . . . up until the time . . . the Lord came into my life, I'd known nothing about him, and was just as rebellious, and . . . didn't think much about it either way. I never did care much for preachers who just ask for donations all the time, and . . . talk about the world to come. I was always growing up with what's right here and now, and . . . until Jesus became real to me in that way I couldn't understand.

Bob Dylan[1]

Things Have Changed: Dylan Meets Jesus

Any artist who takes his life and art in radically new directions will generate disappointment among fans who prefer the old life and art. Cat Stevens became a Muslim and transformed himself into Yusuf Islam at around the same time Dylan was exploring the Christian faith. Many of Stevens's fans were both puzzled and disappointed—I say disappointed because his conversion signaled his (at least temporary) retirement from the mainstream music industry.[2] Another very public turn to religion in the pop music world occurred in George Harrison's post-Beatles solo recordings. There were Eastern influences on the Beatles' work, but Harrison's 1970 album *All Things Must Pass* showcased his zealous

Hindu faith in its full artistic expression. The singer's embrace of Hinduism perplexed and occasionally frustrated fans wanting to understand his songs. Although some critics thought him sancti-monious, there is another way of looking at it: "George should be admired for having something distinctive to say, and for saying it knowing that many would not be sympathetic. He had the courage of his convictions to sing to the public what he sang to himself in his heart."[3] Dylan did the same.

In 1979 with the release of *Slow Train Coming*, Bob Dylan announced to the world that he—like George Harrison and Cat Stevens—would take his life and art in a radically new direction.[4] What distinguishes Dylan's experience from Stevens's and Har-rison's, however, is the disdain generated by his turn to religion. The others had their critics, to be sure, but the reactions of those naysayers paled in intensity next to Dylan's detractors. He pro-vides some sense of the sharpness of their criticisms in songs like "Property of Jesus," where he sings about those who laugh at him, resent him, and call him a loser because of his beliefs (*Shot of Love*, 1981).[5] His peers also voiced their opinions. John Lennon's "Serve Yourself" (*John Lennon Anthology*, 1998) is apparently a "polemical response to Bob Dylan's Christian 'You Gotta Serve Somebody,' [one that] belittles faith in Jesus Christ, Buddha, Mohammed, and Krishna, and . . . contemptuously associates reli-gion with wars."[6] George Harrison's fans did not react this way. Why was Dylan the object of such a backlash?

It is interesting to speculate about the vitriol directed at Dylan. Certainly, audiences do not attend rock concerts to hear sermons, nor do they buy tickets to learn they are degenerates facing impending judgment. Dylan would offer both. Strangely enough though, Harrison's religious lyrics are every bit as evangelistic in tone, but somehow they did not offend in quite the same way:

> You don't need no church house,
> You don't need no Temple
> . . . . . .
> To know that you have fallen[7]

Similarly, Yusuf Islam's "In the End" warns that individuals cannot bargain with truth "'Cause one day you're gonna die /

And good's going high, / And evil's going down—in the end" (*An Other Cup*, 2006 [liner notes]). If the intensity of reaction to Dylan's spiritual journey differs compared to Harrison and Stevens and others—and they faced their own hostile responses, to be sure[8]—an explanation may lie in the perceived exoticism of the faith traditions they adopted. For the most part, their audiences knew relatively little of Hinduism and Islam. Furthermore, the particular expression of Christianity Dylan embraced—fundamentalism—carries a lot of baggage. Outsiders often perceive it to be a naïve way of looking at the world; it is anti-intellectual, rigidly intolerant, quick to condemn and impose morality, and lacking in aesthetic appeal, compassion, and beauty. Whereas George Harrison and Cat Stevens were exploring truths off the beaten path for most in the English-speaking world, Bob Dylan was retreating into a worldview that many listeners found passé, narrow-minded, bigoted, and just plain boring.

The release of *Slow Train Coming* in August 1979 and his performance of songs from that album on NBC's *Saturday Night Live* on October 20 that same year ("Gotta Serve Somebody," "I Believe in You," and "When You Gonna Wake Up") declared his infatuation with Jesus. A number of theories attempt to explain this sudden turn to the Son of God. One traces Dylan's decision to heed the example of a highly influential woman, presumably the "Precious Angel" referred to in *Slow Train Coming*. Ron Rosenbaum mentions this idea in a 1979 *New York Magazine* article, noting witnesses saw Dylan with a woman "said to be the person most responsible for encouraging him to undergo the conversion."[9] This was a difficult period for him, now newly divorced and facing fallout from certain artistic missteps. As the theory goes, such vicissitudes made Dylan ripe for the comforting message of the Christian gospel. Rosenbaum adds that lines in "Precious Angel" contrast his wife with this other woman, this religious guide. The former may have told him about Buddha and Mohammed, but she never mentioned the one who died as a criminal. The precious angel, on the other hand, guided him toward the gospel, showing the songwriter he was previously blind to the truth (John 9:39) and standing on a weak foundation (Matt. 7:24–27).[10] There might be something to this theory, but it remains a little thin. Dylan is a very thoughtful individual and not likely to be easily swayed on such a major issue by the promptings of just one person.

Another theory Rosenbaum discusses is Dylan's interest in escaping the intense scrutiny of Jewish interpreters.[11] "Dylan had complained about how he was constantly besieged by queries from Jewish quarterlies and freelance cabbalists doing elaborate analyses of the Old Testament imagery in his songs," writes Rosenbaum, who surmises that Dylan found a way to escape this beleaguering attention through conversion to Christianity.[12] This theory is not convincing either. Dylan is certainly wise enough to know that a change of religious allegiance would not solve the matter of endless overinterpretation of his songs. Those who read his songs from a Christian perspective bombard the songwriter with just as many queries as their Jewish counterparts. This theory also suggests Dylan is rather casual and erratic in his religious life, and there is no reason to suppose this is the case.

While it is not possible to isolate all the factors behind the religious awakening evident in these gospel albums, Paul Williams may be on to something when he writes about the surprising number of peers, acquaintances, and friends who died in the years leading up to and included in the so-called gospel period. Mortality and eternal questions were on the singer's mind. Williams's investigations of Dylan's newly displayed Christian beliefs began with a marvelous booklet released in 1979, a quickly written, intuitive response to the conversion in which he tries to explain the singer's metamorphosis. In "Dylan—What Happened?" he credits the usual suspects as causal agents leading the singer to the Christianity of *Slow Train Coming*, among them the breakup of Dylan's marriage and negative responses to some of his recent work, like *Renaldo and Clara*. Presumably Williams touched a nerve here, because Dylan himself reportedly bought one hundred copies of his booklet "because he wanted some people he knew to read it."[13] As an account of Dylan's transformation, however, Williams admits missing a crucial issue suggested to him by Dylan's friend Howard Alk.

In his later article "Bob Dylan and Death," which first appeared in *The Telegraph* in 1988, Williams reports Alk's suggestion that "a major possible factor in Dylan's conversion to Christianity [was] awareness of and fear of death."[14] Williams then speculates that Elvis Presley's death in August of 1977 "must have had a subtle but very powerful effect on Dylan, particularly in light of Elvis's age and the fact that Dylan in 1977 was 36 and closing fast on the big 40. Forty is mid-life for a lot of us, but for one who identifies himself with other rock stars and culture heroes it can look like the end of the line."[15] Williams goes on to trace the fascination with death as a subject in some of Dylan's work, an interest reaching as far back as his eponymous debut album of 1962 and his cover of the Blind Lemon Jefferson song "See That My Grave Is Kept Clean": "Did you ever hear that coffin sound / Means another poor boy is underground. / Did you ever hear them church bells toll / . . . Means another poor boy is dead and gone."[16]

Approaching Bob Dylan's Gospel Period through *Street Legal* (1978)

Whatever the reasons behind his dramatic turn toward Christian faith, the 1978 album *Street Legal* anticipates the gospel material of *Slow Train Coming* (1979), *Saved* (1980), and *Shot of Love* (1981). The songs on this album include lyrical gestures that find the singer on a hunt for stability, contentment, and peace. Though it is not a Christian album, it remains, as Spargo and Ream suggest, "a harbinger of things to come."[17] Again, one must be careful to distinguish the songwriter Dylan from the persona adopted in his songs, because the two are not necessarily the same. My interest here is the narrative arc suggested by the transition from *Street Legal* to the more religiously focused lyrics of 1979–1981.

To return to Alk's (and Williams's) insight, one notices immediately the presence of violence (swords, shooting, pistol, Armageddon, overturned tables, Russian roulette, hanging by rope) and death throughout this album. We hear that death is cruel ("Changing of the Guards") and that one faces life in death ("No Time to Think"). He sings of plague ("No Time to Think") and death's ability to disarm ("No Time to Think"). The singer also admits,

"Horseplay and disease is killing me" ("Where Are You Tonight? [Journey Through Dark Heat]").[18] The *Street Legal* section of *Lyrics* also includes "Legionnaire's Disease," a song with the line "I wish I had a dollar for everyone that died within that year."[19] This album seems to confirm Howard Alk's observation that questions about mortality and death concerned the singer at this period. Alk, a longtime friend and collaborator with Dylan whose credits include work on the film *Eat the Document* (1971), took his own life in late 1981.

Street Legal segues into the overtly Christian lyrics of *Slow Train Coming*, generally charting a trajectory from despair to hope, crisis to solution, and ignorance to illumination. The album hints at what culminates in the faith perspective of the music to follow—namely, a restless search for meaning and comfort—but it lacks specificity. Anthony Varesi finds Dylan's turn toward evangelical Christianity more comprehensible "in the context of these songs."[20] This reaching toward a spiritual resource is a little vague. Dylan biographer Sounes refers to the *Street Legal* lyrics as "mystical mumbo-jumbo," but still they are "perhaps indicative of Bob searching for something to give meaning to his life."[21] I suspect Dylan was well on his way to the Christianity of *Slow Train Coming* when writing and recording *Street Legal*. Certainly by the later stages of the 1978 tour "there were signs . . . that Bob had become caught up in this enthusiasm for Jesus Christ."[22] It appears Dylan began writing about this new religious interest with subtlety and caution (the songs of *Street Legal*) and only later made this faith explicit (the songs of *Slow Train Coming*). In *Street Legal*, Bob Dylan tells the story of his turn to faith. I highlight a few ideas emerging from four songs to illustrate this point.

"Changing of the Guards"

Biblical allusions abound in *Street Legal,* and suggestive turns of phrase present the singer looking for a way out of his despair. The "story" told on this album begins with "Changing of the Guards,"[23] in which the singer rides past ditches full of destruction. This situation clearly leaves few options for travelers because veering to the left or right toward those ditches is perilous. Either way he turns there is looming disaster. This image is in fact a recurring biblical trope:

> Ye shall not turn aside to the right hand or to the left. (Deut. 5:32 KJV)

> Let me pass through thy land: I will go along by the high way, I will neither turn unto the right hand nor to the left. (Deut. 2:27 KJV)

> That his heart be not lifted up above his brethren, and that he turn not aside from the commandment, *to* the right hand, or *to* the left: to the end that he may prolong *his* days in his kingdom, he, and his children, in the midst of Israel. (Deut. 17:20 KJV)

> And thou shalt not go aside from any of the words which I command thee this day, *to* the right hand, or *to* the left, to go after other gods to serve them. (Deut. 28:14 KJV)

However, as he moves forward, avoiding those ditches on the left and right, there is illumination and rest. The song opens with a reference to the good shepherd's grief but closes with the more hopeful announcement of an expected time of peace.

"Is Your Love in Vain?"

The song "Is Your Love in Vain?" presents the narrator interrogating a would-be lover, asking among other things, "Do you understand my pain?"[24] This lover is guilty of intruding on the singer's solitude and darkness, and it is tempting to read such lines as a circumlocution for a newly encountered spirituality. The singer has been hurt before and is understandably wary of putting his trust in a new offer of solace. He needs to know if he can count on the one holding out this gift of comfort or if this offer of love is in vain. If this song indicates a guarded, critical evaluation of the promises of religious faith, the offer of wings extended to the singer could indicate Dylan was already thinking about the particular escape offered by Christianity at the time of writing. If so, he is already aware of and concerned about the price required of him. The closing question about his willingness to risk everything may turn the interrogation back on himself. No longer is the genuineness of Christ's love under scrutiny. Rather, by the song's end he begins to question his own openness to love a religious Other. As it turns out, this closing question is appropriate because indeed, the cost of his Christian faith in terms of sales and audience and general critical reaction proved to be quite high for Dylan in the years to come.

"Señor (Tales of Yankee Power)"

The sequence of "Is Your Love In Vain?" and "Señor (Tales of Yankee Power)"[25] is significant, fitting the general line of spiritual inquiry I am proposing here. The former presents the singer directing a series of questions at a newly encountered, potential (spiritual) lover. There is no sense of clear resolution in the earlier song because it ends with the unanswered titular question. In "Señor (Tales of Yankee Power)," however, there is a striking shift. The singer still asks a long list of questions (nine of them in total), but now there is movement with the spiritualized (but not feminized) Other. The masculine señor (a term of respect but also one with religious overtones, meaning "lord") now leads the way on a journey. The singer accompanies him but does not have a clear sense of the destination, for he asks where they are going. Perhaps significantly, one possible destination is Armageddon, a biblically rooted place name (Rev. 16:16) and a loaded term carrying significant meaning in the theological world Dylan would soon inhabit. In those Christian circles, premillennial eschatology and theories about the end times are prominent in preaching and teaching, and the apocalyptic emphases of Dylan's early gospel songs reflect these concerns:

> Behold, I come as a thief. Blessed *is* he that watcheth, and keepeth his garments, lest he walk naked, and they see his shame.
> And he gathered them together into a place called in the Hebrew tongue Armageddon. (Rev. 16:15–16 KJV)

The singer is not yet out of danger as he travels along with this señor, facing wicked winds, a dragon, and suspense, but there is an emerging resignation and acceptance of his fate. The singer strips and kneels, an image of submission, and then picks himself up from the floor and announces to the señor that he is ready. These words suggest a willingness to follow and participate in that person's work. The final verse provides a specific link to the biblical Christ. Using the first-person plural to indicate his participation in the señor's activities, the singer wants to turn over "these tables" in an unambiguous echo of the biblical story in which Jesus does the same thing.

> And Jesus went into the temple of God, and cast out all them that sold and bought in the temple, and overthrew the tables of the moneychangers, and the seats of them that sold doves,
>   And said unto them, It is written, My house shall be called the house of prayer; but ye have made it a den of thieves. (Matt. 21:12–13 KJV; pars. Mark 11:15–17; Luke 19:45–46; John 2:13–21)

Dylan's allusion to this story not only clarifies the identity of the señor (Jesus) but also anticipates the aggressive, judgmental tone of Dylan's earliest gospel songs. The transition from the despair and limited options of "Changing of the Guards" (ditches to the left and right), through to the singer's first tentative responses to the offer of (religious) love and assistance in "Is Your Love in Vain?" and onto the submission of "Señor (Tales of Yankee Power)," provides a trajectory paralleling his more explicit summaries of religious conversion in later songs. We might compare the loosely structured, somewhat cryptic narrative suggested by *Street Legal* with, for instance, the more direct confessions of Christian faith in "When He Returns" on *Slow Train Coming* and "Saving Grace" on *Saved*.[26]

The singer's perspective in the music of 1979–1981 is quite different from that represented in *Street Legal*. For the most part, those later albums presuppose faith and reflect a degree of certainty regarding the distinction of truth from error. The singer of the *Street Legal* songs is much less certain. There is a tentative acceptance of the spiritual alternative offered to him ("I stripped and kneeled") though very little understanding of what this might entail (e.g., he needs to ask the señor where they are heading).

"Where Are You Tonight? (Journey Through Dark Heat)"

Street Legal closes with the enigmatic but lovely "Where Are You Tonight? (Journey Through Dark Heat)"[27] which again suits the kind of religious orientation I am proposing for the songs on this album. Of course, the "long-distance train" of the opening line anticipates the slow train coming of the next album, and various biblical and religious terms and phrases in the song (*sacrifice, demon, forbidden fruit, paradise*) contribute to its mysterious and mystical atmosphere. The search that began with "Changing of the Guards" continues, but he is approaching resolution by the album's end. There is a new day, and the singer announces he has "finally arrived." There is also an answer to one of the questions asked earlier in the album, in "Is Your Love in Vain?" There the narrator wonders if he is willing to risk everything. Now, in "Where Are You Tonight? (Journey Through Dark Heat)," he claims he is. He knows firsthand that sacrifice is "the code of the road" and that paradise will not come cheap. The singer makes the costly, frightening leap into the unknown, choosing to follow the señor and take the pathway to the stars.

The unresolved question of the song—"Where are you tonight?"—is particularly poignant. Dylan is an artist, and if we imagine *Street Legal* as a movement toward a religious worldview previously unknown to him experientially, a certain amount of trepidation is understandable. What will an embrace of Christianity mean? He is open about his fears in this album, and in this song in particular. The vague "truth" of *Street Legal* (which at the time of writing might be the Christian truth explored explicitly in *Slow Train Coming*, that is, the Christian gospel) was both obscure and too profound.[28] In many of his earlier songs, Dylan is reluctant to reduce "truth" to simple formulas. In "My Back Pages," for instance, he backs off from his early idealism, admitting that truth is something far more complex than he once thought (*Another Side of Bob Dylan*, 1964). Indeed, for most of his career he insists that answers are elusive, always blowing in the wind. In "Where Are You Tonight? (Journey Through Dark Heat)," however, there is a hint that this new foray into something new, something rigidly defined as "truth" now staring him in the face, presents a particularly frightening possibility.

In the sixth verse, the narrator describes a female character with the capacity to discover his innermost thoughts. She is both invisible and disappearing slowly. As she strips, her beauty fades, and at precisely the moment he sees this, in the next line, we hear the singer hesitate. Uncharacteristically, the most brilliant songwriter of the day is apparently at a loss for words: "*I won't but then again, maybe I might*" (italics added).[29]

The equivocation here is not a misstep, even though it sounds awkward. To live the newly discovered truth he is speaking about—living it amounts to an explosion—requires disruption of the relationship he has with this mysterious woman. This beautiful, invisible stripper fades from his sight as the song closes, as he takes that step toward the "long-distance train"/"slow train" of the Christian gospel.[30] This woman is, I suspect, his artistic muse. He is moving toward a difficult truth that is profound and obscure, but it is truth, indeed *the* Truth. If the world lacked ambiguity, if there were clear answers for all life's questions (as opposed to answers blowing in the wind), there would be no need for artists. Dylan is singing here about the ultimate sacrifice he, as a songwriter and artist, must make. Sacrifice is a requirement in this new world he is about to enter, the world of faith. Here, there is no need for an inspirational muse because the answers are plain for all to see, read, and hear. He hesitates in the italicized line above for good reason, and even in the closing lines of the song he admits that without her (his muse, his art), things do not seem right.

If this reading of *Street Legal* were anywhere close to the mark, it would allow us to group *Street Legal* alongside the gospel trilogy. Similarly, just as *Street Legal* anticipates many of the more explicit religious interests of *Slow Train Coming*, *Saved*, and *Shot of Love*, 1983's *Infidels* continues to explore various religious concerns treated in those earlier albums. Rigid divisions of Dylan's writing into such categories as gospel and nongospel are not particularly helpful, but I will continue grouping them as such for the sake of convenience.

Reactions to Bob Dylan's Gospel Sound

> The greater the decrease in the social significance of an art form, the sharper the distinction between criticism and enjoyment by the public. The conventional is uncritically enjoyed, and the truly new is criticized with aversion.
>
> Walter Benjamin, "The Work of Art in the Age of Mechanical Reproduction"[31]

Reactions to this remarkable transformation of Dylan's art—as shocking a metamorphosis as his turn from acoustic to electric guitars a few years earlier—were swift in coming and intense in expression, coming from both outside the church and inside. It may be that the force of reaction to Bob Dylan's conversion was unparalleled, but other musicians faced similar criticisms when they turned to Christianity. I mentioned Alice Cooper earlier. When he released his equivalent to *Slow Train Coming* in 1994, *The Last Temptation*, this series of songs narrating his conversion to Christianity created a stir among his fans.[32]

> When I finally wrote *Last Temptation*, I saw a way of doing something clever, making a rock record that was as good as any rock record I'd ever made . . . but with Alice talking about morality.[33] For people who aren't paying attention to the lyrics, they'll give the album a thumbs-up when normally they might not be into religious music. It's one of the best records I've ever made. Sure, I was walking on thin ice using Alice as the medium, but I felt like I was being guided through the process.

Through this album, Alice Cooper announced his conversion, and as one might expect, reactions from fans were not positive. "My commitment to Christianity hit the newswires. I was now officially off the fence, intellectually, spiritually, and publicly. I immediately lost sales and bookings," wrote Cooper.[34] Similarly, cynical reactions to Dylan's religious beliefs are widespread and something of a fixture in the popular imagination. The very fact that *The Simpsons* can spoof Dylan's faith journey makes it clear that the mass-market American audience is at least generally familiar with the broad strokes of his associations with religion (raised Jewish, embraced Christianity later in life, at least for a short time); otherwise, the satire would not work. In the scene in question, the family watches television as an interview program hosted by Marge's high school friend (played by Kim Cattrall) begins. Her guest for this particular episode is Bob Dylan (though not played by him):

Announcer: *"The Talbot Report*, with Chloe Talbot. Tonight, Chloe interviews Bob Dylan."

Chloe: "So Bob, what religion are you converting to now?"

Bob Dylan: "Well I'll tell ya one thing [incomprehensible mumbling] no more. Shalom."[35]

Not only does this rehearse the hackneyed and absurd complaint that Bob Dylan cannot sing or speak clearly, this scene reflects a common perception about Dylan's religious attachments, namely, that they change frequently over time. The assumption behind the joke, presumably shared by many since *The Simpsons* targets a large audience, is that stasis is the true indicator of sincere, genuine religiosity. If Dylan were serious about his religious convictions in the 1970s and 1980s, so this line of thinking goes, he would have continued expressing himself in much the same way long after *Shot of Love*. However, *moving on* to something new does not necessarily mean *moving away*. Genuine spirituality need not be overt, nor does meaningful Christian faith find expression in evangelical fundamentalism alone. Furthermore, such views negate the possibility that Dylan may be exploring his Judaism in parallel with Christianity.

I think Bryan Cheyette is on the right track when he locates Dylan with the American-Jewish efforts to deal with a profound sense of difference and otherness, describing him as "devotedly impure . . .

now [riding] equally on the carnival and slow trains as Judas and Jesus, Jew and Christian." Cheyette interprets Dylan's adoption of a Christian worldview, at least temporarily, as a form of response to the dominant culture and a sense of dislocation. His Christian songs "radically rewrite his previous work as they introduce an alternative set of values which are specifically designed to resolve a lack of a fixed identity and an abiding sense of homelessness." Cheyette pictures the post–*Shot of Love* period as a return to "the foundational ambivalences of his Jewishness by bringing together his converted and unconverted selves in the imagined homeland of the Bible." The Jewish and Christian identities are not easily separated, however, as the former provides the precondition of the latter. Furthermore, in the first album following the overtly gospel albums, Dylan significantly includes the song "I and I" that not only recalls the biblical encounter between God and Moses (Exod. 3:14) but also speaks of his double identity, his "divided persona [which] is both Jewish and Christian, converted and unconverted . . . no longer waiting for the slow train to come."[36] Others also hold Dylan's Jewish and Christian selves in close proximity, though they explain it in more theological terms.[37]

Howard Sounes mentions peer reactions to Dylan's turn toward Christianity, including doubts about his sincerity and speculations about underlying motives. Some suspected finances had something to do with it. Keith Richards of the Rolling Stones called Dylan the "prophet of profit." Similarly, Ronnie Hawkins told Dylan, "After this [record] sells a few, you are gonna be an atheist and sell to all them cats who don't believe nothing." This, Hawkins told Sounes, did not go over well with Dylan: "He didn't laugh. He just looked at me. But I knew what he was doing. And he knew I knew what he was doing—he was selling records. That's his business."[38] Sounes is far more generous to Dylan as he answers such charges, finding Hawkins's cynicism about Dylan's religiosity "to be unfair." By all indications, "he genuinely believed in what he was singing and, ultimately, he suffered for making his faith so public. . . . Bob's Christian conversion had a detrimental effect on his long-term career."[39]

Questions about Dylan's motives and sincerity also came from

Christians with a public platform to voice their opinion. We find one simple example in a song by Christian musician and parodist Steve Taylor, who likens judgment day to a meltdown at Madame Tussaud's wax museum: "Elvis and the Beatles have seen a better day / better off to burn out than to melt away / Dylan may be fillin' the puddle they designed / is it gonna take a miracle to make up his mind?" ("Meltdown [At Madame Tussaud's]").[40] This reference to Dylan's indecision, appearing on Taylor's 1984 album *Meltdown*, echoes an overly simplistic response shared by many in the post-*Infidels* period (and as late as the episode of *The Simpsons* mentioned above).[41] Taylor assumes Dylan casually jumped into religion in 1979 and then jumped out just as quickly in 1983 with the appearance of *Infidels*, the album title alone suggesting as much.

Another interesting response to Bob Dylan's music from within the borders of fundamentalist Christianity appears in the widely distributed book by Dan and Steve Peters, *Why Knock Rock?* (1984). Peters and Peters view the folk music scene of the 1960s with a great deal of suspicion because the "answers" folk singers presented to impressionable youth of the day were "unfortunately, increasingly devoid of hope. In fact, there were far more questions raised than answers given. The answers, they were told, were blowin' in the wind. Folk music took on a quality of desperation and an element of hypocrisy."[42] They obviously allude to Dylan's famous song in this statement, but it is interesting to note they do not mention him by name in this section. The reason for this is clear later in the book when they promote Contemporary Christian Music as an alternative to the dangerous and devilish secular music industry, listing Dylan as a recommended artist under the category "Rock."[43] Presumably, they refer here to the rock albums *Slow Train Coming*, *Saved*, and *Shot of Love*. I suspect they did not know about Dylan's 1983 release *Infidels*, which is more ambiguous in its religious content. Dylan's reflections on the Middle East and sympathies for Israel's situation in "Neighborhood Bully," the abundance of allusions to the Hebrew Scriptures (e.g., "I and I" and "Jokerman"), and the inclusion of a photograph of the singer in Jerusalem suggested to many a turn away from Christianity and a return to his Jewish roots.[44] Details from his family life also contributed to speculations about Dylan's religiosity around this time.

> This song ["Neighborhood Bully"], and the photograph of Bob in Jerusalem on the inside sleeve of *Infidels*, appeared to confirm press reports that he had taken up with a fundamentalist Hasidic group. In the fall of 1983, Bob's seventeen-year-old son Jesse had a belated bar mitzvah in Jerusalem—Jakob and Samuel had already been bar mitzvahed in California—and Bob was photographed wearing a yarmulke at the Wailing Wall, adding to speculation that he had returned to Judaism. "As far as we're concerned, he was a confused Jew," Rabbi Kasriel Kastel told *Christianity Today*. "We feel he's coming back."[45]

One summary of the reactions to these activities puts it this way:

> Rumours persisted about his having abandoned Christianity and re-embraced the Jewish faith [around the time of *Infidels*]. His name began to be linked with the ultra-orthodox Lubavitcher sect: the inner sleeve of *Infidels* pictured him touching the soil of a hill above Jerusalem, while 'Neighbourhood [*sic*] Bully' was a fairly transparent defence of Israel's policies toward its neighbours. Dylan, as ever, refused to confirm or deny his state of spiritual health.[46]

One suspects the Christian conservatives Peters and Peters, who published *Why Knock Rock?* in 1984, would not have recommended Bob Dylan for their impressionable Christian readers had they known all this. Since Dylan's 1983 album signaled a departure from the more overtly Christian material of 1979–1981, it seems likely they would have dismissed the new material as unsuitable for their lists of recommended artists. I say this because they are so quick to condemn musicians and unwilling to appreciate the complexities and profundities found in some "secular" popular songs dealing with religious themes.

Personally, I find these church-based responses to Dylan's foray into gospel music more troubling than criticisms coming from peers who would understandably find the turn toward religion perplexing. When those outside the church, with little or no interest in religious matters to begin with, voice concern about Dylan's sudden infatuation with Jesus, it is not particularly surprising. When friends (or the artists we love) change dramatically, it is natural to feel a sense of loss and betrayal. C. S. Lewis observes, "Change is a threat to Affection." He speaks of the close ties of people who share much in common and "a dreadful thing" that often happens that creates intense disappointment, anger, and sadness:

> One of them flashes ahead—discovers poetry or science or serious music or perhaps undergoes a religious conversion. His life is flooded with the new interest. The other cannot share it; he is left behind. I doubt whether even the infidelity of a wife or husband raises a more miserable sense of desertion or a fiercer jealousy than this can sometimes do.[47]

This sense of desertion, I suspect, is what Dylan's critics experienced in the fall of 1979. The artist with whom many identified so fiercely, the one often called a prophet, flashed ahead. Nothing new about that for Dylan, except this time he moved in a direction few could follow. Previously they had hung on to his every word, but now he embraced a lifestyle and a discourse (fundamentalist Christianity) they found wholly inappropriate, even distasteful. "He was accused of being 'apocalyptic' and 'judgmental,'" according to Powell, "which of course he had always been. Still, it is one thing for a prophet to speak against his disciples' enemies and quite another to begin pronouncing oracles of woe and doom on those disciples themselves."[48]

Lewis's observations about the nature of love and friendship and about this idea of conversion (of whatever sort) as a threat to affection are perceptive. He continues by noting, "It is not yet jealousy of the new friends whom the deserter will soon be making. This will come; at first it is jealousy of the thing itself—of this science, this music, of God. . . . The jealousy will probably be expressed by ridicule."[49] What an insightful remark as we consider responses to Dylan's gospel period (e.g., Keith Richards, Ronnie Hawkins). For some, it was not the fact that he found religion but rather an objection to the particular kind of religion he claimed.

> Listening to the new Bob Dylan album [*Slow Train Coming*] is something like being accosted in an airport. "Hello," a voice

seems to say as Dylan twists his voice around the gospel chords of "When He returns [*sic*]." "Can I talk with you for a moment? Are you new in town? You know, a few months ago I accepted Jesus into my life—" "Uh, sorry, got a plane to catch!" "—and if *you don't* you'll rot in hell!"[50]

> I'm sorry for you Bobby / And I know that it's been hard / But my eyes can't see the glory / Of your bloody-minded God.[51]

Compare these reviews to further remarks by Lewis:

> The jealousy will probably be expressed by ridicule. The new interest is "all silly nonsense," contemptibly childish (or contemptibly grown-up), or else the deserter is not really interested in it at all—he's showing off, swanking; it's all affectation.[52]

If we bring Lewis's observations to Dylan's Christian phase, we find a useful commentary on that remarkable metamorphosis. Many fans saw the conversion as a traitorous act, and their anger regularly took the form of ridicule. Some mocked him for being so gullible.

Lewis also refers to making new friends when one adopts a new interest, something that occurred for Dylan during the late 1970s. Some who knew Dylan prior to his conversion had themselves embraced the Christian faith around this time (e.g., T-Bone Burnett), but his circle of friends and professional acquaintances sharing the faith expanded in these years, including among them the well-known Christian musician Keith Green. According to Green's wife, Melody, Dylan consulted the couple concerning the lyrics to *Slow Train Coming*,[53] and he even contributed a harmonica solo to Green's song "Pledge My Head to Heaven" (*So You Wanna Go Back to Egypt*, 1980). The friendship between Dylan and the Greens appears to have been a short-lived but close one:

> We had invited him over for dinner and I cooked him hamburgers at our house. . . . Bob Dylan was one of the most famous people in the world, and here we were just having a casual meal together on the second-hand fold-out table in our living room! . . . Keith really loved Bob, and they talked a lot . . . there seemed to be something very special taking place between them.[54]

And all those earlier fans who claimed Dylan as their own winced when they read such a thing. He's ours! Why are these Christians enjoying a barbeque with the man? They just met him, but I've been following his career for nearly twenty years! "It is not yet jealousy of the new friends whom the deserter will soon be making. This will come. . . ."[55]

Perhaps one of the most troublesome things about Dylan's conversion was his sudden modesty and dependence on others. Then, as now, fans credited Dylan constantly with unique insights. They also saw him as antiestablishment, not needing anyone to point the way—not the government, not the university, and certainly not the church. He followed his muse, and his clarity of thought and judgment were impeccable. In the gospel period, however, which included participation in a church-run Bible school, Dylan was the student. (Compare the language of *Street Legal*, discussed earlier, with its language of humble submission.) The free spirit who brushed off lectures at the University of Minnesota now dutifully attended Bible classes. Dylan refers to this explicitly in the liner notes to *Biograph* (1985), mentioning his attendance at "Bible school" (about which, see below). Even the comment about the Christian musicians Keith and Melody Green advising Dylan on song lyrics—Bob Dylan, the greatest songwriter of all time—is a little surprising. To their credit, the strangeness of that moment was not lost on them:

> He wanted to know what we thought [about the lyrics to *Slow Train Coming*] and we told him—the lyrics were great. Then Keith and I exchanged glances, both thinking, *Can you believe one of the world's greatest songwriters is asking our opinion?* Maybe it was his vulnerability that bonded our hearts to his in a special way.[56]

Bob Dylan the vulnerable songwriter—what an oxymoron.

Those observing and complaining about Dylan's entrance to the Christian community *from the outside* is one thing; those criticizing Dylan *from the inside* is quite another. As said, I personally find many of the responses directed at him from Christians to be quite distasteful. Christian responses to Dylan often lack charity and sensitivity and show very little appreciation for the unique challenges he faces as a celebrity, as a Jew, and as a profoundly nuanced thinker. No thoughtful Christian can sustain a simplistic, black-and-white view of the world like the one implied by the phrase "Ya either got faith or ya got unbelief and there ain't no neutral ground" ("Precious Angel," *Slow Train Coming*, 1979).[57] The gospel albums present Dylan wandering into a new religious and musical culture, zealously soaking up all he could. There is intensity and immediacy in the songs that capture vividly a moment in time, but forward movement is necessary and inevitable. All romances begin with the absurdities of flirtation and courting behavior, but those strange rituals die out as relationships mature. The various charges directed at Dylan by Christians in response to his activities during and following the gospel period are frequently misguided, even mean-spirited. I offer here a few reasons for making such a claim.

To begin with, those lodging criticisms appear to operate with a narrow definition of what makes a person Christian. Dylan's lyrics may not be overtly religious in the post–*Shot of Love* (1981) period, but this does not imply that his interests in Christian subjects diminished or disappeared, as though he experimented with religion one minute and then decided to move on to something else the next. Dylan did not discover religion for the first time in the late 1970s, nor did he abandon it in the early 1980s. All of his music—from *Bob Dylan* (1962) to *Together Through Life* (2009)—involves creative, original, and profound dialogue with biblical religion. Those wanting to make sense of Dylan's brief, public burst of enthusiasm for the gospel between 1979 and 1981 need to contextualize that work within the Dylan canon as a whole and his life story as a whole. That context needs to include the experiences and formation of his Jewish upbringing, especially as part of a minority group within a predominantly Christian society. That context should also include the ubiquity of religious themes in literature and the American music tradition Dylan knows, mimics, and adapts so well, not to mention personal circumstances and the influences of friends and acquaintances. The sudden enthusiasm for Jesus, the New Testament, and certain Christian teachings quite popular at that time (e.g., premillennialism) did not occur out of nowhere.

A second problem with the kind of criticism represented by Taylor's charge of indecision is the assumption that spirituality and religious devotion are somehow static. It is absurd to imagine religious experience as merely an *arrival* to some new insight and not a *process* of discovery. The biblical writings themselves present faith as a journey, using metaphors indicating progress and maturation (see 1 Cor. 13:12–13; Gal. 5:16–26; Heb. 6:1–3), so it ridiculous to accuse Dylan of some kind of betrayal because he moved on from the gospel music genre and continued developing in his thinking and writing. What Dylan recognized many years earlier with respect to political issues holds true for religious convictions as well: "I was so much older then / I'm younger than that now" ("My Back Pages," *Another Side of Bob Dylan*, 1964).[58] This song's acknowledgment of change does not imply abandonment of concern for "equality," but there is recognition that he might not know everything about the subject. Similarly, Dylan's religious views evolve and mature over time and across the lyrics of his songs, indicating a growing awareness of the complexities of faith.

Dylan's grasp of Christianity may appear simplistic at times on *Slow Train Coming*, *Saved*, and *Shot of Love*, but certainly not uniformly. Even some songs that appear rather unsophisticated prove to be remarkably clever under close examination. For instance, Ruvik Danieli and Anat Biletzki conclude that "Man Gave Names to All the Animals" (*Slow Train Coming*) is easily mistaken as a children's tune. However, "to ascribe merely a juvenile intent to [this song] is to miss this metaphysical poet at his most profound."[59] There are flashes of insight throughout these albums. No one complains that "Grain of Sand" (*Shot of Love*) is juvenile song writing. True, Dylan does not fit comfortably in any single interpretation of the Christian faith (i.e., a particular denomination or theological perspective), but this is no reason to question his sincerity or profundity. I return for a moment to biblical scholar and theologian Dale Allison Jr.'s comments about George Harrison, noted earlier. He maintains, "George should be admired for having something distinctive to say, and for saying it knowing that many would not be sympathetic. He had the courage of his convictions to sing to the public what he sang to himself in his heart."[60] This strikes me as a very appropriate way to think about Dylan's experiences.

Pastor Bill Dwyer of Valley Vineyard Church Christian Fellowship in Reseda, California, kindly answered some of my questions concerning Bob Dylan's associations with the church in the late seventies and early eighties. Dylan attended one of Dwyer's classes: "My class focused on the Sermon on the Mount, but it was really called 'The Sermons of the King,' and we covered five major sermons in Matthew including the Olivet Discourse, but most of our time was on [Matthew] 5–7." Dwyer's responses to my queries demonstrate how seriously and sincerely Dylan tackled his studies during this period, as the following excerpts from our correspondence make clear.

> **Gilmour:** Can you provide some sense of the kind of assignments students were doing?
>
> **Pastor Dwyer:** It varied. Most of the students were involved in active ministry projects surrounding evangelism, ministry to the poor. I don't think Bob did anything like this. I assume that this was due to his notoriety (it was hard for him to go anywhere publicly) and his own reclusive nature. In my class people had to memorize and meditate on the Beatitudes, and I think I was the only class that administered a . . . final exam. The goal was not information, but spiritual formation. Bob made a huge sacrifice to attend the school by turning down an international tour at that time and very humbly attended our classes in a converted office on Reseda Blvd. in Reseda. Reseda is where my church is located and is a low income area in the Valley.

This reference to the cost of Dylan's study recalls lines from "Is Your Love in Vain?" discussed above: "Are you willing to risk it all[?]"[61] The financial ramifications are obvious enough, but one also wonders how high a price attaches to the sacrifice of privacy for this "reclusive" student.

I also wondered about other studies Dylan engaged in while at the Reseda school and asked Pastor Dwyer what other courses he took:

> **Dwyer:** Pastor Kenn Gulliksen taught a class on discipleship where he went over all the fundamentals of the Christian life, like prayer, study, forgiveness, fasting, evangelism, etc. Kenn was very much focused on character. I always think of him as a Colossians 3 kind of guy. Very sincere and very spiritual. There were two other classes, but I can't recall their themes. I'm pretty sure it wasn't eschatology.

The third chapter of Paul's letter to the Colossians includes several instructions to Christians about day-to-day living, listing behaviors to avoid (e.g., greed, anger, slander) and others to practice (e.g., compassion, kindness, patience). Elsewhere in this letter, and throughout his writings, Paul is often more theologically abstract. Pastor Gulliksen's course on "the fundamentals" of Christian living clearly had a very practical focus.

I asked also about theological instruction, particularly the emphasis on end-times teaching, which figures so prominently in some of Dylan's songs (e.g., "When He Returns," *Slow Train Coming*; "Are You Ready?" *Saved*).

> **Gilmour:** Was eschatology an emphasis at the school? Judging from some of Dylan's on-stage remarks in the early '80s, I suspect he was reading Hal Lindsey and studying dispensationalism. Would this have been part of the school's program?

To explain my question somewhat, Hal Lindsey[62] wrote pop-level theology with an emphasis on events preceding the return of Christ and the judgment of the world. The term *dispensationalism* indicates a school of thought in biblical interpretation popular among American evangelicals in the 1970s. It emphasizes, among other things, God's plans for Israel, the rapture (the removal of Christians from the world before judgment), and the literal return of Christ. Lindsey's writings identify supposed "signs of the times" that indicate the imminence of these events. His interpretive strategies include observing significant political events involving major powers like Russia, China, the United States, and the (then-anticipated) European Union, and looking for ways their activities correspond with cryptic language in the Bible. As Pastor Dwyer mentions in his response, Lindsey had connections to the Reseda fellowship.

> **Dwyer:** Our church was definitely focused on the end times. Kenn brought it up frequently from the pulpit, and it gave a lot of momentum to our evangelism. Most of our leaders were pretrib[ulation] and/or premill[ennial], but it wasn't the theory of eschatology but [the fact that] the Lord might return any moment that was the real issue. Hal Lindsey hung around the church as well, and I guess Bob was very interested in this topic and talked to various people. He did not take a course on the end times. Quite honestly, I was a little surprised by *Slow Train* and how much Bob had adopted an end-times message. I'm sure that was not just from our school. Bob had a variety of contacts and influences. He loves to digest information and thinks deeply about these things.

The term *pretribulation* refers to the timing of the rapture (i.e., it will occur before a period of intense suffering on earth, therefore sparing Christians from this judgment). The cheesy Donald W. Thompson film *A Thief in the Night* (1972), so popular in conservative Christian circles throughout the decade, acts out this strange theological scenario (people disappearing, leaving those left behind to wonder where they went, etc.). Inevitably, many connected with the Reseda church would have known this film. The term *premillennialism* indicates a theological perspective maintaining that Christ will return to inaugurate a literal thousand-year kingdom before the final judgment. It is interesting to note Dylan did not study eschatology formally at the school, so presumably his investigations into this subject involved private study and/or conversations with others. Lindsey's teachings appear to influence Dylan's remarks from the stage during a Toronto concert on April 17, 1980, an unofficial recording of which circulates widely.

Keith Green's music also includes an emphasis on end times, and he was, as mentioned earlier, one of Dylan's friends during this period. I asked Pastor Dwyer if he knew anything about their relationship.

> **Gilmour:** Did Keith Green have any connection to the school? Melody Green mentions they first met Bob through the Vineyard,[63] and I was wondering if this involved a teaching role for Keith, perhaps like his later lectures at Last Days Ministries [the Greens' mission organization, based in Texas].
>
> **Dwyer:** Keith did not teach. Keith had been in the one-year program the year before but left it to pursue doing concerts/ministry. Keith was a very hyper young Christian, an artistic type, and did not do well in three–four hours of classroom [time]. He did get together with Bob a few times, and I believe Bob was touched by Keith's passion. Keith also understood the record industry and the pressures. Keith's dad was Jewish, and so he and Bob shared a few things in common, but Keith moved to Texas and I do not believe maintained any significant relationship with Bob.

These glimpses into Dylan's brief relationship with this church community at the very least suggest we can rule out some proposed motives for his decisions. He was not after a new audience and the money it would bring. There would be no financial benefit in passing up a touring opportunity and investing so much time in study if this were the case.

Any attempt to explain Bob Dylan's turn to Christianity must remain incomplete. Even if he spoke at length about his experiences, the story would remain partial because efforts to capture moods and emotions or influences and ideas must always remain so. The narrator of "Thunder on the Mountain" (*Modern Times*, 2006) tells us his soul is expanding. Notice, however, that one looking into his heart will only "*sort of* understand."[64] This is the best we can hope for in asking questions about Bob Dylan, his faith, and his art. There are limits to what we can know. Whenever we intrude on another's private world and attempt to explain what is ultimately out of reach, the results are bound to be deficient in one way or another, and inescapably tendentious.

Accounting for his eventual departure from a musical form that is overtly religious in perspective and from associations with organized Christianity is easier. Just like the folk music community of the 1960s, the Christian world of the late 1970s and early 1980s assumed they had Bob Dylan pinned down, pigeonholed, and defined. "We got him cornered in the churchyard," as it were.[65] Simplistic categorization is not something Dylan accepts, so his decision to move on is not very surprising. "Greed and lust I can understand," Bob Dylan once said, "but I can't understand the values of definition and confinement. Definition destroys." Commenting on this statement, Jonathan Cott describes Dylan as "elusive, oblique, mercurial, and always in motion," adding, "he has resisted in both his life and his work being categorized, encapsulated, finalized, conventionalized, canonized, and deified."[66] His unwillingness to allow others to restrain and define him and his art is a well-known feature of Bob Dylan's mystique.

We can reach a few conclusions about Bob Dylan's exploration of Christianity. For one thing, as anyone who listens to his music knows, *Bob Dylan is not a fool.* I find it puzzling that many of his most ardent, loyal fans so quickly dismissed then and still disregard now his work during this stage of his career, declaring it little more than a folly. Was he brainwashed? Was he less intelligent during his late thirties than he was in his late twenties? Of course not. Commentary on his life and music that descends into ridicule is pompous and inconsistent. Naturally, some artistic choices he makes are better than others, but if we remember that he is a songwriter constantly in process, exploring and experimenting, trying to tap into whatever inspirational wellsprings he stumbles on, then we should allow him the freedom of movement.

Personally, I do not think the gospel albums were a mistake, and I certainly do not question his sincerity. Since my academic field is biblical studies, I admit to cringing at some of his interpretations and theological positions, but this does not mean I want to jettison the whole gospel project. We should remember that the gospel lyrics, interviews, and stage speeches[67] are the work of someone coming into the evangelical Christian subculture only recently. Most biographers seem to place Dylan's first encounters with the church and his conversion to Christianity in 1978 and wrap up this period with the release of *Shot of Love* in 1981. That is not a lot of time. Of course, Dylan's grasp of this particular theology occasionally lacks sophistication and nuance, but there is also evidence of his growing insight. It is also a significant achievement that many within that gospel subculture appreciated Dylan (e.g., the Gospel Music Association gave Dylan a Dove Award for *Slow Train Coming* in 1980). Bob Dylan does not sit still as an artist or a thinker. *Saved* is not a mistake, nor is *Infidels*. If he merely repeated the content of the earlier album, choosing to remain in one intellectual, spiritual, and artistic space, *that* would have been a mistake. He fed off this period and then moved on to something artistically new.

I think we can also safely surmise that *Bob Dylan genuinely enjoys gospel music*. Quite apart from theories of personal crisis and conversion or theological questions both Jewish and Christian, we should remember that gospel music has deep roots in American culture. Dylan's longstanding appreciation for and knowledge of the American music tradition is well documented. Between 1979 and 1981, he indulged himself in gospel as yet another musical form.[68] The artist known for exploring and enriching American folk, rock, and country music now happily introduced the background vocals of gospel singers and explored a completely new (to him) way of writing. Those uncomfortable with the religious dimensions of *Slow Train Coming*, *Saved*, and *Shot of Love* might do well to think of Dylan's so-called conversion as a transformation analogous to his earlier musical twists and turns.

So how should we "read" the gospel albums? If we cannot reconstruct an artist's life story from the art produced, and if Dylan is serious when he says, "What I do in the studio doesn't define me as a person," we need to be very careful to avoid overemphasis on biographical reading of songs. We might catch glimpses of his personal beliefs and experiences, but these are immaterial; we must recognize the distance between his public personas (deliberate plural), characters in his songs, even the "I" of his lyrics, and the songwriter himself. In the end, he tells us, "all of these songs added together doesn't even come close to my whole vision of life."[69]

We should also be wary of isolating these albums from the rest of Dylan's music. It is easy to forget that the Bible and religious reflection are ubiquitous throughout all of his works, both before and after his gospel recordings. "Dylan's so-called Christian phase is nowhere near as out-of-sync with his overall career as most of his fans seem wont to believe," Mark Allan Powell reminds us. The Christian songs "were of a piece" with his earlier and later work to a degree that many fail to appreciate. There are continuities between *Infidels* (1983) and the earlier gospel albums and "nothing on the album that conflicted with Christian teachings or morality." *CCM* magazine (formerly *Contemporary Christian Music*) even "chose *Infidels* as one of their Ten Best Christian Albums of 1983."[70] Surprisingly, some critics feel the religious perspectives in albums before and after 1979–1981 carry more moral/ethical force than the gospel music. Steve Stockman suggests that in some ways the gospel albums are "not as prophetic in a biblical sense" as his other work: "The Old Testament prophets were those who would say it straight and sharp, cutting to the heart of society's injustice and individual selfishness. They were the weird eccentrics on the fringes who sent shockwaves right to the center."[71] This description matches Dylan nicely.

In the end, Dylan's gospel period resembles other musical transformations occurring throughout his career, such as his transitions from folk to rock, and rock to country. Every exploration of a new musical style involves a shift in vocabulary and idiom, and this was another instance of the same. Approaching the gospel songs as part of that ongoing evolution also helps us avoid the pitfalls of an overly fixed periodization of his work. As suggested earlier, certain themes appearing in the pre-gospel *Street Legal*

(1978) appear to anticipate ideas found in the gospel album *Slow Train Coming* (1979). Similarly, the postgospel *Infidels* (1983) is as rich in biblical allusions as the preceding gospel album *Shot of Love* (1981). The boundaries between his pregospel, gospel, and postgospel writing are porous and fluid, not rigid.[72] We can explore this, highlighting some of the continuities and discontinuities between the gospel albums and the others, by examining Dylan's use of the Jewish and Christian Scriptures.

Chapter Five

That Most Serious of Subjects
The Good Book, the Testaments
Both Old and New

The Dylan canon—consider, for instance, his selective, six-hundred-page book *Lyrics: 1962–2001*—presents us with a persistent engagement with the Bible over a forty-year period.[1] If we add to this canon other projects, such as his films *Renaldo and Clara* (1978) and *Masked and Anonymous* (2003), published poetry (*Tarantula: Poems*, 1971), album liner notes, and his prose autobiographical writing *Chronicles* (Vol. 1, 2004), each of which dialogues with the Bible in one way or another, we clearly have an extended engagement with the Scriptures.

There is nothing systematic about this use of the Bible, however. It is far more like a montage, a prophetic pastiche. "A folk song," Bob Dylan writes, "has over a thousand faces and you must meet them all if you want to play this stuff. A folk song might vary in meaning and it might not appear the same from one moment to the next. It depends on who's playing and who's listening."[2] This freedom to adapt and rewrite, while remaining tethered to a "textual" tradition, also characterizes his use of the Bible. He returns to it constantly yet never uses it the same way twice. As texts, images, and ideas pass from one setting and medium to another, their meanings evolve in the process. It follows, then, that as Dylan brings biblical content into the world of his songs, something original emerges. Adaptation always involves change.[3]

As a preamble to Bob Dylan's use of the Bible, this eclecticism deserves further attention. Once again, Dylan resembles other writers noted earlier on, including Woody Guthrie, a key source influencing his work, and Walter Benjamin, whose writings illuminate the songwriter's creations in various ways. One habit of writing all three share is the use of lists. How do they function? What does this device reveal about Dylan's use of the Bible and approach to religious reflection?

Walter Benjamin and Unstructured Collections, Bob Dylan and Lists

Movie people, hoss wranglers, dead enders, stew bums; stealers, dealers, sidewalk spielers; con men, sly flies, flat foots, reefer riders; dopers, smokers, boiler stokers; sailors, whalers, bar flies, brass railers; spittoon tuners, fruit-tree pruners; cobbers, spiders, three-way riders; honest people, fakes, vamps and bleeders; saviors, saved, and side-street singers; whore-house hunters, door-bell ringers; footloosers, rod riders, caboosers, outsiders; honky tonk and whiskey setters, tight-wads, spendthrifts, race-horse betters; black-mailers, gin soaks, comers, goers; good girls, bad girls, teasers, whores; buskers, corn huskers, dust bowlers, dust panners; waddlers, toddlers, dose packers, syph carriers; money men, honey men, sad men, funny men; ramblers, gamblers, highway anklers; cowards, brave guys, stools and snitches; nice people, bastards, sonsabitches; fair, square, and honest folks; low, sneaking greedy people; and somewhere, in amongst all of these Skid Row skidders—Cisco and me sung for our chips.[4]

Woody Guthrie

Near the beginning of *The Arcades Project*, Walter Benjamin describes his work as involving the art of citing without quotation, an idea related to a montage.[5] A montage is a collage, a collection of smaller bits and pieces, even pictures, put together to form a larger image. In a montage, no single fragment in itself can represent the whole, which only reveals itself when combined with the other fragments. Small pieces contribute (they are cited; they are included), but this does not constitute a quotation where a single source is set apart as uniquely revealing and authoritative—the important revelations only emerge when the cluster of citations are pulled together, permitting something larger to appear. When Benjamin brings the idea of the montage to the study of history, he describes the historian's task as one of assembling "large-scale constructions out of the smallest and most precisely cut components. Indeed, to discover in the analysis of the small individual moment the crystal of the total event." Such an approach allows for the construction of a narrative out of concrete, historical moments. His stated method for the *Arcades Project* is literary montage. "I needn't say anything," Benjamin tells us, "Merely show."[6]

The seemingly endless allusions and references to the Bible in Bob Dylan's work resembles *The Arcades Project* in form, a series of loosely related quotations that somehow reveals something beyond the sum of its parts. Consider also a brief section in Benjamin's *One-Way Street* called "Construction Site":

> Children are particularly fond of haunting any site where things are being visibly worked upon. They are irresistibly drawn by the detritus generated by building, gardening, housework, tailoring, or carpentry. In waste products they recognize the face that the world of things turns directly and solely to them. In using these things they do not so much imitate the works of adults as bring together, in the artifact produced in play, materials of widely differing kinds in a new, intuitive relationship. Children thus produce their own small world of things within the greater one.[7]

Benjamin builds *One-Way Street* itself out of the debris overlooked and ignored by others, and it requires a kind of reading that adapts to a new, montaged, and nonnarrative way of thinking. One can read the story of the children picking through the debris figuratively, as Benjamin himself, the historical materialist. He is a garbage collector, "seeking his material and inspiration not in the officially sanctioned sites of a cultural text but in the refuse and debris that has been overlooked, repressed, or marginalized."[8]

Our topic in this chapter is Bob Dylan's use of the Bible, and once again, comparison with the writer Walter Benjamin provides a useful way to think about the subject. Dylan does not introduce the Bible to his art systematically, nor does he offer direct commentary on the Scriptures in most instances. Instead, what we find in his songs is a montage, a compilation of biblical stories, characters, themes, and images that collectively reveal something unique and quite distinct from those individual parts on their own. He reads *The Book* and repeats quotations, creating a presentation of the Scriptures every bit as distinct as Woody Guthrie's vision of California in the 1930s (this section's epigraph) or Walter Benjamin's study of nineteenth-century Paris in *The Arcades Project*. All three pull together random bits and pieces to reveal a larger whole.

Sam Shepard includes a "monologue" by Bob Dylan in his *Logbook*, which opens with the words "I [Dylan] was lookin' for myself in this country store." During this surreal moment, Dylan asks the shopkeepers "if they'd seen [him]" suggesting perhaps that Dylan feels a sense of distance between the flesh and blood man standing in the store and his real self. This search for identity and reality then shifts to an unusual string of largely disconnected items as Dylan "start[s] listing things. . . . Everything the eyes could see and the ears could hear":

> Chain saws, hammers, cheese barrels, cracker barrels, crackers, rednecks, preachers, panthers, nails, jigsaws, horses, hobbyhorses, sawhorses, outboard motors, rain clouds, lightning, lumber trucks, pig meat, breakfast, teacups, dancers, Nijinsky, divers, deep seas, oceans, rivers, railroad, rapers, radio, waves, mothers, sons in battle, danger, ideas, magic. . . .[9]

This stream of consciousness, free association, or interior monologue identifies more than seventy-five people and things in this list, far more if we consider the various terms in the plural. At the very least, Shepard captures in the scene Dylan's love of wordplay. It also resembles this use of (apparently random) lists, evident in Guthrie and Benjamin.

Compare an example taken from Dylan's prose. In *Chronicles*, he not only takes time to describe the people he meets in detail but also the places he visits, often creating long lists of objects to provide some sense of the physical spaces he observes:

> The space was configured into a workshop with all kinds of paraphernalia piled up. Most things , , , *on a table.* . . . some iron flowers on a spiral vine painted white leaning in the corner. All kinds of tools lying around—hammers, hacksaws, screwdrivers, electricians' pliers, wire cutters and levers, claw chisels, boxes with gear wheels. . . . Soldering equipment and sketch pads, paint tubes and gauges, electric drill—cans of stuff that could make things either waterproof or fireproof.[10]

Nothing escapes his view, everything is potentially important, contributing in some way to the moment in question. What is striking about this fascination with minutiae is that it appears in a book characterized by startling gaps; in *Chronicles*, Dylan skips over whole decades of his career and yet still dedicates five pages to the contents of a friend's bookcase.[11] There are untold stories fans would love to hear, but he is obviously not writing to satisfy their curiosity. It remains that his frequent descents into detail serve a purpose. One thing we observe is how they often yield some flash of understanding, some revelation. For instance, soon after his list of objects in the room mentioned above (which continues beyond the excerpt cited), Dylan lands on an insight useful for a songwriter: "I needed to learn how to telescope things, ideas. Things were too big to see all at once, like the books in the library[12]— everything laying [*sic*] around *on all the tables.* You might be able to put it all into one paragraph or into one verse of a song if you could get it right."[13] As he seems to hold in mind this image of "things, ideas" scattered across tables, we suspect these pages provide a glimpse of a formative moment in the author's development as a songwriter, the skill of employing metonymy and synecdoche, of representing much in little, of encapsulating the whole in just a part, of montage. As with the *flâneur* strolling through the city streets, so too for Dylan taking in the objects in a cluttered room: "Things reveal themselves in their secret meaning."[14]

We find Dylan's endless curiosity, appetite for knowledge and insight, and willingness to consider everything available as a possible resource in this quest in the songs as well. Here he regularly positions his narrators and characters as spectators, travelers, readers, and listeners. Set the iPod to shuffle, and you will discover them listening to Neil Young one moment and Billy Joe Shaver the next; or they might be reading such disparate writers as Erica Jong and James Joyce.[15] We find a narrator standing in the rain waiting to see a Gregory Peck film, others citing lines from Humphrey Bogart movies.[16] You will also notice a dizzying array of named and imagined spaces, real and fantastic journeys,[17] and a seemingly endless cast of colorful characters populating his songs—as in "Desolation Row" (*Highway 61 Revisited*, 1965), for instance.

Bob Dylan and the Bible

Psalms and hymns were my first taste of inspirational music. I liked the words but I wasn't sure about the tunes—with the exception of Psalm 23, "The Lord is my Shepherd." I remember them as droned and chanted rather than sung. Still, in an odd way, they prepared me for the honesty of John Lennon, the baroque language of Bob Dylan and Leonard Cohen, the open throat of Al Green and Stevie Wonder—when I hear these singers, I am reconnected to a part of me I have no explanation for . . . my "soul" I guess.

Bono[18]

Bob Dylan's *John Wesley Harding* . . . sound[ed] like new acoustic psalms.

Stephen Davis[19]

By introducing the Bible to popular music, Bob Dylan engages material often overlooked by other songwriters.[20] His way of citing or alluding to its characters and themes resists structure. It is random, prizing the mingling of ideas more than order. The term *adaptation* describes well Bob Dylan's use of Scripture, a term defined by literary theorist Linda Hutcheon as "a form of repetition without replication"; a "derivation that is not derivative—a work that is second without being secondary."[21] Dylan adapts and recontextualizes biblical characters, themes, terms, and phrases, placing them into new settings, inevitably changing the meaning of those references. Despite this, many readers and listeners will recognize the canonical origins just the same. This is significant because as Hutcheon defines the term, adaptations usually announce the relationship with prior texts.[22] Dylan does this by typically invoking iconic stories and characters from the Bible familiar to most (the flood, the crucifixion; Abraham, Jesus, Judas, etc.). On other occasions, he explicitly identifies the Bible in songs, as in the reference to Leviticus and Deuteronomy in "Jokerman" (*Infidels*, 1983) and the Sermon on the Mount in "Up To Me" (*Biograph*, 1985). Someone quotes the Bible in "Man in the Long Black Coat" (*Oh Mercy*, 1989) and another reads it in "Quit Your Lowdown Ways" (Bootleg Series, Vols. 1–3, 1991). Hutcheon distinguishes works that include only brief echoes of source material, "short intertextual allusions," from those that involve "extended engagements,"[23] but her definition of *adaptation* is appropriate for Dylan's writing if we approach his works as a whole.

Also important is Dylan's tendency to look backwards as he writes, finding in stories from long ago a storehouse of imagery and wisdom that informs his own storytelling in the present. This fascination with received tradition extends to material from both recent memory and the distant past, including the disparate literature of the Bible. With reference to early songwriting, Michael Gray observes that Dylan "insists on the continued relevance of these voices from the past, and takes us so deeply among them that he frees us from the tyranny of the present."[24] Dylan's interpreters frequently note this fascination with received tradition, especially American roots music.[25] The title of Dylan's 2001 album *"Love and Theft"* speaks "directly to his love for all forms of American music, as well as to his tendency to express that love by direct quotation, borrowing, or 'theft'." That album, along with its predecessor *Time Out of Mind* (1997), "is saturated with quotations, both musical and verbal" and its "musical styles range over the whole history of twentieth-century American music."[26] As Larry "Ratso" Sloman puts it,

"Love and Theft" is rife with loving theft, right down to the album's title, an appropriation from an academic book about 19th century blackface minstrel shows.[27] The album is riddled with lines taken from both popular American culture (pre-1950)—Hemingway, Fitzgerald, Twain, and old bluesmen, as well as variations on Shakespeare, Donne, Virgil, Petrarch and the *Bible*. And of course the lines are all twisted out of shape, bounced on their head.[28]

Sloman is correct to include the Bible as one of the important sources behind Dylan's writing, and while some exaggerate its significance for his work, others are guilty of underestimating the ways it informs and gives atmosphere to the songs. It is interesting to observe where and how he introduces the Bible in his lyrics and poems, but there is much more to this subject than mere identification of allusions and quotations. Christopher Ricks observes that "Dylan not only opens his Bible; he opens up its radiations and its revelations."[29] This is high praise, an acknowledgement that this musician's incorporation of biblical literature is often insightful, involving reflection and frequent and deliberate irony.

Dylan uses the Bible in a variety of ways. For one thing, many biblical stories and themes are widely familiar to audiences and evoke predictable assumptions and emotions. Knowing this, Dylan can anticipate how audiences will respond to particular expressions, which allows him to introduce variations to his sources for rhetorical and artistic effect. The shocking and ironic declaration that even Jesus would not forgive the masters of war (in the song of that name on *The Freewheelin' Bob Dylan*, 1963) assumes audiences know the biblical backdrop (i.e., Jesus is someone who forgives sins). Indeed, this jeremiad against militarism is only effective to the degree that audiences recognize the source and the irony at play in the lyrics.

On other occasions, biblical terms and phrases may derive from nonbiblical sources, coming to Dylan's songs only indirectly. For instance, the Bible's influence on the English language and literature is immeasurable, and we cannot always determine if the songwriter is deliberately echoing a biblical passage or merely using a familiar turn of phrase with a biblical etymology, often specifically the King James Version. There are many examples of this kind of ambiguity in Dylan's lyrical imagery:

- A person said to be as innocent as a lamb ("Ballad in Plain D," *Another Side of Bob Dylan,* 1964; Exod. 12:5; Lev. 23:12; 1 Pet. 1:19)
- Conclusions written on a wall ("Love Minus Zero/No Limit," *Bringing It All Back Home,* 1965; Dan. 5:1–30)
- A willingness to sacrifice the world for another ("Wedding Song," *Planet Waves,* 1974; Matt. 19:27–29; Mark 10:28–30; Luke 18:28, 29b–30)
- "Forbidden fruit" ("Where Are You Tonight? [Journey Through Dark Heat]," *Street Legal,* 1978; also "T.V. Talkin' Song," *Under the Red Sky,* 1990; Gen. 3:1–6)
- Someone crying out in the wilderness ("Tight Connection to My Heart [Has Anybody Seen My Love?]," *Empire Burlesque,* 1985; Matt. 3:1–6; 11:7–11; Mark 1:2–6; Luke 3:2–4; 7:24–28; John 1:23)[30]

In cases like this, one suspects the songwriter is not attempting to evoke the biblical sources behind the terms so much as he is using well-known idioms. On still other occasions, biblical material may provide nothing more than a striking metaphor or, less profoundly still, language fitting a rhyme scheme. This may be the case with the following phrases:

- First now, last later ("The Times They Are A-Changin'," *The Times They Are A-Changin',* 1964; Matt. 19:30; Mark 10:31; Luke 13:30)
- Darkness at noon ("It's Alright, Ma [I'm Only Bleeding]," *Bringing It All Back Home,* 1965; Matt. 27:45; Mark 15:33; Luke 23:44)
- A growling wildcat ("All Along the Watchtower," *John Wesley Harding,* 1967; 1 Pet. 5:8)[31]

Biblical content also finds its way into Dylan's writing from musical sources, like folk songs, which he describes as "full of legend, myth, Bible, and ghosts."[32]

Occasionally, Dylan's employment of biblical imagery involves more sustained use of a particular text or image, unlike the passing glances at passages in these last examples. I suspect something of the kind in "Huck's Tune," from the soundtrack to the 2007 film *Lucky You* (released on Dylan's *Tell Tale Signs*, 2008). In describing the woman addressed in the song, the narrator celebrates her youth, compares her to fine wine, and likens her kisses to honey. The singer also calls on the wind to play its song as a backdrop for the moment captured in the scene. This imagery is remarkably similar to the story that unfolds in the biblical romance Song of Solomon. Here too we find a celebration of youth (e.g., 2:9, 17; 8:14) and a poet comparing his beloved to wine (4:10). Her lips "distill nectar . . . honey and milk are under [her] tongue" (4:11), and the winds inspire this poet as well, as he calls on them to blow beautiful fragrances in the garden for the woman's benefit (4:16). Dylan may base the song on a traditional Scottish ballad,[33] but the inspirations of Song of Solomon are also present. This is not a slavish retelling of that ancient story, because in Dylan's version there is a twist. Whereas the Hebrew poem presents unquestioned devotion between two lovers, the relationship described in Dylan's song is a stormy one. He might have no guile (compare "Behold an Israelite indeed, in whom is no guile!" [John 1:47 KJV]), but she "can't be nice." Despite his compliments and flattery, which owe much to the biblical poem, this woman is difficult to be with, and the singer needs to move on, at least for a while. (Of course, we only hear his side of the story!)

Bob Dylan's Bible often recalls the language of the King James (Authorized) Version, as in his use of the archaic "unto others" in lyrics recalling the Sermon on the Mount ("Ain't Talkin' "; *Modern Times*, 2006; Matt. 5:43–44) though he may read a variety of translations, and/or receive biblical imagery and phrases from any number of other sources. In the same song, his description of wheels flying in the heavens illustrates the most significant challenge for determining exactly what translation he uses. Here the obvious allusion to Ezekiel's vision (Ezek. 1:15–21) is a paraphrase and not dependent on any particular translation precursor. Bob Dylan's Bible is most often a unique rendition of Scripture because he shapes language for his own purposes, whether this means accommodating a rhyming pattern, changing terms, or weaving images together. There are many examples of his unique rendering of biblical material, such as the titular phrase "Spirit On the Water" (*Modern Times*, 2006), which alludes to Genesis 1:2 but without exact dependence on any particular translation (see, e.g., "a wind from God swept over the face of the waters" [NRSV]; "the Spirit of God moved upon the face of the waters" [KJV]).

There is a diverse bibliography commenting on Bob Dylan's use of the Bible and/or religious dimensions in his work. Bert Cartwright's seminal analysis of this topic deserves particular notice. He approaches this subject by connecting biblical themes to various phases of the songwriter's career, and, my earlier cautions about linking biography to song lyrics notwithstanding, this study remains the most important work on the subject (though unfortunately not widely available).

According to Cartwright, the first phase begins with Dylan's arrival in New York in 1961 and continues through to his motorcycle accident in 1966. During this time, Cartwright suggests, "Dylan saw the Bible as part of the poor white and black cultures of America with which he sought to identify." From 1966 through to 1973, a time of recovery from the accident and semiretirement with his young family, Dylan's writing "reveal[s] a more calculated use of the Bible," occasionally assuming a biblical perspective though it is not "personally claimed." In Dylan's work in the third phase (1974–1978) we see a writer using the Bible as "a sophisticated artist who had learned consciously to work simultaneously on several levels of meaning," whereas the fourth period (1979–1981) reveals Dylan's embrace of fundamentalist Christianity. The gospel songs during these years show Dylan's "desire to express in life and song what his fresh study of the Bible as a believer was telling him." Finally, Cartwright describes the fifth phase (1983 through to the publication of the book in 1992) as a time when Dylan's "biblical faith had been internalized sufficiently for it to serve subtly as [his] worldview."[34]

If pressed to follow Cartwright's approach and characterize Dylan's use of the Bible after 1992, I would highlight two tendencies. One is the recurring introduction of apocalyptic overtones, as in his Academy Award–winning "Things Have Changed," which announces that if indeed the Bible is right, "the world will explode" (*The Essential Bob Dylan*, 2000; 2 Pet. 3:7).[35] We find another example of this in "Cross the Green Mountain" from the Civil War film *Gods and Generals* (2002; the song appears on *Tell Tale Signs*, 2008). It includes an allusion to Revelation 13:1: "And I saw a beast rising out of the sea, having ten horns and seven heads." The narrator recalls dreaming about a monster rising out of the sea and sweeping through the land, adding the somber warning that "all must yield to the avenging God."[36]

A second tendency, and an unlikely companion to the first, is the blending of humor with biblical and religious overtones, as in the witty description of a "Po' Boy" (*"Love and Theft,"* 2001), who ends up feeding swine just like the prodigal son of Jesus' parable (Luke 15:15). Humor also emerges when we consider the previously mentioned public fascination with Dylan's spirituality and his reluctance to speak directly to this subject. One suspects Dylan plays into this persistent curiosity about his relationship to Judaism and Christianity when he sings tantalizingly about hiding his faith ("Dreamin' of You," *Tell Tale Signs*, 2008) or practicing one that was long-abandoned ("Ain't Talkin'," *Modern Times*, 2006). If read biographically, the latter begs the question of which faith he is referring to. Furthermore, there may be a joke at play here; the title suggests the songwriter is not revealing anything to anyone. This reminds us of the hazards of pulling isolated phrases like this out of context and reading them as biographical clues. Another lyric from approximately the same period reinforces the point because it makes a claim exactly opposite to the one put forward in "Ain't Talkin' ": "My faith is as cold as can be" ("Huck's Tune," *Tell Tale Signs*, 2008).

Organizational strategies that categorize artistic works along perceived trajectories of development (like Cartwright) are helpful to a degree, though attempts to compartmentalize artistic works rarely do justice to the entire canon in question. There are always exceptions to most boundaries analysts devise, and there is always the risk of oversimplification. Other models exist for approaching biblical and religious dimensions in Dylan's work. Christopher Ricks organizes his literary analysis of some of Dylan's songs around the traditional seven deadly sins (envy, covetousness, greed, sloth, lust, anger, pride), four cardinal virtues (justice, prudence, temperance, fortitude), and three heavenly graces (faith, hope, charity). My short look at Dylan's use of the Bible (*Tangled Up in the Bible*) focuses on themes, specifically the prophetic tradition, the Sermon on the Mount, apocalyptic thought, and redemption. There are also several books and articles commenting on Dylan's personal religiosity, usually from an explicitly Christian vantage point and/or with a focus on the gospel phase.[37] Others approach Dylan's spirituality from a Jewish perspective, among them Daniel Maoz, who proposes that "interpretive principles and methods of major kabbalistic interpreters have inspired Dylan, either directly or indirectly," a point he illustrates in a reading of Dylan's 1983 album *Infidels*. This album, according to Maoz, "holds the key to understanding what is the *crux interpretum* for Dylan's unique manner of expression and perception of life and [the] afterlife."[38] Seth Rogovoy reminds us that it is imperative "one consider the Jewish nature of so much of Dylan's life and work in order to appreciate it fully and to its truest and greatest extent."[39]

There are recurring patterns in Dylan's use of the Bible that deserve attention. For one thing, when he introduces biblical content to his songs, he usually goes beyond mere repetition of earlier texts and introduces poetic innovation to his source material. For instance, the song "You Changed My Life" (Bootleg Series, Vols. 1–3, 1991) refers to Jesus (presumably), with eyes of fire and feet of brass, and orphans waving palm branches as he passes, even though he remains an outcast in the very world he created.[40] The beautiful lyrics of this song bring together a cluster of biblical allusions (among them Matt. 21:8; Rev. 1:14; 2:18; John 1:10–11) without disrupting the original sense of the individual passages (i.e., each refers to Jesus, likely the "you" addressed by the singer). In this gospel-period song, Jesus is the object of a supplicant's poetic prayer.

Another tendency we find is his appropriation of biblical stories in "autobiographical" songs. What I mean by this are the first-person narratives noted earlier in which the storyteller applies to himself descriptions originating with biblical characters. This is a literary device, we should be clear, not a form of disclosure from Dylan about his religiosity, or worse, evidence of megalomania. In these first-person singular adaptations of biblical stories he places himself within those narratives, thus removing the sacred Other altogether. Not infrequently, such appropriations of the Bible integrate stories about the passion and resurrection of Christ, and so it is that a woman removes a "crown of thorns" from the singer's head in "Shelter from The Storm" while others gamble for his clothes (*Blood on the Tracks*, 1975; Matt. 27:29 and 35).[41] In "Spirit on the Water" (*Modern Times*, 2006), the narrator sweats blood while praying to the powers above, words alluding to Luke 22:44: "Being in an agony [Jesus] prayed more earnestly: and his sweat was as it were great drops of blood falling down to the ground" (KJV). It is also clear that the subject matter of the song has nothing to do with Jesus in the Garden of Gethsemane. The song opens with the narrator thinking about "you baby"; the image of Jesus' earnest prayer and garden solitude in the Gospel story illustrates the intensity of the singer's longing for an absent love.

Another example of this adoption of terms recalling Jesus' story occurs in "Ain't Talkin'" (*Modern Times*, 2006). While in the mystic garden the singer tells a woman that no one is around and the gardener has gone, words recalling the postresurrection encounter between Mary Magdalene and Jesus (John 20:15–16). In the Gospel story, Jesus brings clarity to the situation after Mary confuses him with the gardener; Dylan's narrator does a similar thing, mentioning the gardener's absence. He also refers to his ability to call for heavenly aid, something Jesus could also do (Matt. 26:53).

As Dylan takes on these biblical roles, he also brings the Scriptures into dialogue with other stories. The song "Sugar Baby," which closes the 2001 album *"Love and Theft,"* and "Thunder on The Mountain," which opens the 2006 album *Modern Times*, illustrate this phenomenon. I am assuming in what follows that Dylan deliberately plays one album off another, and one song off another, but even if not, these songs illustrate not only Dylan's habit of participating in biblical stories but also his ability to weave those stories into other narratives. We also observe in a comparison of "Sugar Baby" with "Thunder on The Mountain" how the sense of a single biblical image (in this case the angel Gabriel) can shift during migration[42] from one song and album to another. Bob Dylan's Bible, it follows, is not a stable, fixed point of reference but rather a storehouse of images that can morph into whatever he wants them to be in any given context.

The two songs in question follow one another in terms of album release dates (one closing an album, the other opening the next). The closing verse of *"Love and Theft"* warns a woman to seek her maker before the angel Gabriel sounds his horn ("Sugar Baby"[43]). These words allude to a cluster of biblical images (see e.g., Eccl. 12:1; Isa. 51:13; Job 35:10; 1 Thess. 4:16; Rev. 8:6). The first song of his next full-length studio album, *Modern Times*, also incorporates biblical themes, including the sound of thunder on a mountain and the sight of fire on the moon. The singer announces, "Today's the day, gonna grab my trombone and blow" ("Thunder on The Mountain").[44] The title phrase of this song recalls the divine presence at Mount Sinai (Exod. 19:16, 19) where the sound of thunder and trumpets causes the people to tremble. The moon is also a recurring image in Scripture, as in Ecclesiastes 12:2 (see also Isa. 13:10; Ezek. 32:7; Joel 2:10; Matt. 24:29; Mark 13:24; Luke 21:25; Rev. 8:12; whereas Dylan mentions [red] fire on the moon, biblical writers describe the moon turning to [red] blood, e.g., Acts 2:20; Rev. 6:12).

The sequence of "Sugar Baby" and "Thunder on The Mountain" —one follows the other with respect to album release dates— may involve a deliberately humorous segue. In the first song, the anticipated angelic figure Gabriel is coming to blow his horn (1 Thess. 4:16). In the second song, the singer assumes Gabriel's role himself, picking up his own horn (trombone). When Dylan uses the phrase "Today's the *day*" to indicate the time he will sound his horn, he may have in mind the biblical phrase "day of the Lord." Like Dylan, Joel links a horn blast, a mountain, and celestial phenomena, including the moon, in his prophecy about the day of the Lord: "Blow ye the trumpet in Zion, and sound an alarm in my holy mountain: let all the inhabitants of the land tremble: for the day of the LORD cometh, for it *is* nigh at hand. . . . The sun and moon shall be dark, and the stars shall withdraw their shining" (Joel 2:1, 10 KJV). All these elements—horn, day, mountain, moon—appear also in the "Sugar Baby"–"Thunder on The Mountain" dyad.

In both songs, biblical imagery contributes to the singer's commentary about the women in question. In "Sugar Baby," the singer speaks to a brainless woman who has abandoned the singer. He is a spurned lover, understandably angry with one whose "charms" have broken many hearts. We could plausibly read his warning to watch out for the avenging angel Gabriel as the hyperbolic vitriol of the singer whose own heart was broken. By contrast, the narrator of "Thunder on The Mountain" tells a very different story. He is actively pursuing this female—Alicia Keys—and deeply sympathetic about *her* plight (not his own as in the earlier song), even shedding sympathetic tears on her behalf. When asked about this reference to Alicia Keys in an interview, Dylan said, "I remember seeing her on the Grammys. I think I was on the show with her; I didn't meet her or anything. But I said to myself, 'There's *nothing* about that girl I don't like.' "[45] She clearly stands apart from the brainless heartbreaker of "Sugar Baby." In one song, the horn-blowing Gabriel is an image expressing the singer's anger and heartbreak, and in the other, the singer himself is a horn-blowing angel, seeking to rescue a damsel in distress. Both songs draw inspiration from a biblical precursor.

However, the Bible is not the only inspiration here. Dylan opens *Modern Times* with a search for Alicia Keys, who was born, he tells us, in Hell's Kitchen.[46] Does this image allude to the Orpheus myth? If so, Dylan's musical, trombone-blowing narrator searches for the hell-bound Alicia Keys in the same way Orpheus searches for Eurydice in the underworld (there is even a remote resemblance between the names Alicia and Eurydice, with their soft "c" sounds). In the Orpheus myth, the poet/musician journeys to the underworld in an effort to convince Hades and Persephone to let Eurydice return to the living. They allow her to return with him on the condition that he walk in front of her and not look back until they both reach the world of the living. Orpheus looks back, however, and consequently Eurydice disappears to the realm of the dead, this time forever. Here we see another dimension of Dylan's use of biblical material. He weaves Scripture into songs alongside other sources that inform the stories he tells.

Dylan's use of the Bible is endlessly flexible. To some extent, we can generalize about broad tendencies and patterns characterizing his use of Scripture at points in his career (Cartwright) but beyond this, rigid definitions do not help. Readers with even a passing knowledge of the Bible will recognize in Bob Dylan a songwriter who adapts the Bible with endless creativity and wit, or, to return to Hutcheon's phrase, one who repeats its stories without replicating them.[47]

Chapter Six

"Searchin' High, Searchin' Low" for Religious Meaning in Bob Dylan's Music

> Reminiscences, even extensive ones, do not always amount to an autobiography. And these quite certainly do not. . . . For autobiography has to do with time, with sequence and what makes up the continuous flow of life. Here, I am talking of a space, of moments and discontinuities.
>
> Walter Benjamin, "A Berlin Chronicle"[1]

*B*ob Dylan spends considerable space (eleven or so pages) in *Chronicles* describing the contents of a friend's bookcase. Fiction, poetry, philosophy, history, religion, psychology, politics . . . it is all there.[2] His account of thumbing through this material emphasizes the randomness of his encounters with a wide representation of art and learning as well as an insatiable curiosity and desire to absorb all he can. We saw in the last chapter that he is a sponge, soaking up music, literature, film, fine art, and anything else that nourishes, but how does he go about finding that which feeds his art and his spirit? This chapter considers the songwriter's modus operandi and its relation to meaning making. More specifically, I look at the significance of artistic collaboration and randomness in Bob Dylan's artistic endeavors and search for inspiration.

Artistic Collaboration and a Musical Resurrection
in Bob Dylan's *Chronicles*

Just as Ruby welcomes the restless narrator of "Brownsville Girl" to "the land of the living dead," so also critics seem to delight in announcing Bob Dylan's latest arrival to the land of artistic obscurity and irrelevance, the equivalent of a musical death.[3] However, as fans of George A. Romero's films know—I assume Dylan alludes here to *Night of the Living Dead* (1968)[4] but even if not, it still makes for a catchy hook—the dead do not lie still for long. Dylan rises from the graves assigned to him by critics as often as they try to bury him. Using a similarly morbid analogy, *The Encyclopedia of Popular Music* entry on Dylan describes him as "a devil for hopping out of the hearse on the way to the cemetery."[5]

Eulogies about Dylan's career are common enough in the popular and critical literature, typically lauding past accomplishments and lamenting the most recent output—whatever and whenever it happens to be—as subpar, at best, or proof of his decline, at worst. Concert reviews regularly raise the issue of Dylan's continued relevance and inevitably compare his recent performances and albums with earlier work, unreasonably expecting the artist to remain static and ageless. The supposed signs of his professional downfall vary from decade to decade: the perceived betrayal of the folk community in the 1960s; the turn toward gospel music in the 1970s; awkward forays into the video generation in the 1980s; stripped-down studio efforts in the early 1990s; and selling out to Victoria's Secret in 2004,[6] to name but a few examples. Some claimed the muses no longer cast their dancing spell his way because of specific projects as well. Again, the list of artistic missteps varies widely but often includes, among others, the album *Self Portrait* (1970), the film *Renaldo and Clara* (1978), and the performance at Live Aid (1985). Everyone has his or her own opinion about what constitutes the peaks and valleys of the man's career, but one thing is certain—the celebrations of those highs and the complaints about those lows are intense and vociferous.

Dylan rarely seems deterred by the fickleness of his audiences and appears to respond playfully to negative reactions directed at his work. I am thinking here of his on-screen performances in 1987's *Hearts of Fire* and 2003's *Masked and Anonymous* (the first of which almost universally appears on the valley side of the ledger sheet). In both films, Dylan plays the part of a musical icon long past his prime, the washed-up Billy Parker and Jack Fate, respectively. It is striking that a singer regularly accused of being yesterday's news unabashedly takes on such parts without any apparent self-consciousness, bringing instead a knowing wink and playful touch of irony to the roles. Audiences of both films inevitably conflate Bob Dylan the actor-musician with the has-beens Billy Parker and Jack Fate. Naturally, Dylan knows this, which makes the decision to play these parts—and even write the part in the case of the later film—so fascinating. Few others would be so audacious. To engage in what amounts to a self-deprecating, tongue-in-cheek disavowal of his musical prowess is bold, witty, and, to my mind, brilliant.

I wonder if those watching *Hearts of Fire* in 1987, conflating the pathetic Billy Parker with Bob Dylan, appreciated that performance even more for the remarkable turnaround Dylan's career enjoyed soon after? It is as though the film put on screen the faded condition of the mid-1980s Dylan, thus offering a bleak backdrop against which the brilliance of *Oh Mercy* would shine out less than two years later, bringing an artistically uneven decade to a close with strong, critically well-received work. *Oh Mercy* was not the only sign of resurgence at this time. A year after *Hearts of Fire*'s disappointing release in October 1987, Dylan would enjoy high sales and positive reviews with the Traveling Wilburys' first album (*The Traveling Wilburys*, vol. 1, October 1988). The other collaborative work of the period, *Dylan & The Dead* (1989), also put him back on the charts. Dylan expressed some surprise at the favorable reception of these albums in *Chronicles*.[7]

Masked and Anonymous (2003) also depicts an artist living in the shadow of his own legacy, only this time Dylan was in the midst of a late-career resurgence as the film came out. *Time Out of Mind* (in 1997) and *"Love and Theft"* (in 2001) silenced the naysayers who dismissed *Under the Red Sky* (1990) as sloppy, the sparse covers in *Good As I Been to You* (1992) and *World*

Gone Wrong (1993) as bland, and *Bob Dylan: MTV Unplugged* (1995) as formulaic. The 1997 and 2001 albums earned Grammy recognition and high praise from all corners. Coming after these successes, and shortly before the magnificent *Modern Times* (2006), we find in *Masked and Anonymous* another reminder of the range of reactions generated by Dylan's artistic output. One character refers to Jack Fate as "Jack Nobody," whereas others are in raptures over his importance. To repeat a great line, when asked about Fate's declining popularity, Uncle Sweetheart (John Goodman) responds, "Did Jesus have to walk on water twice to make his point?" Unlike *Hearts of Fire*, however, the later film forces us to ask *why* some dismiss Jack Fate as washed up. Rather than record sales, commercial success, and fame (things offered to Jack Fate by the likeable but sinister Sweetheart), the film celebrates artistic integrity, authenticity, and tradition. Jack Fate follows his own musical path and refuses to compromise for the oppressive "Network" and its demand for songs that simply appease the masses. His inspirations reach to the heart of music that matters, symbolized by Blind Lemon's guitar, a gift given to him by Bobby Cupid (Luke Wilson).

When introduced at concerts in recent years, the announcer's scripted remarks include the statement that Bob Dylan was "written off as a has-been in the late eighties." This sounds oddly harsh, but as Larry "Ratso" Sloman observes in his liner notes to *Tell Tale Signs*, Dylan is an even harsher critic of the period in his memoir *Chronicles*.[8] The *Chronicles* chapter "Oh Mercy" includes disparaging and despairing remarks about the sorry state of the author's somewhat Billy Parker–like professional life in the 1980s. The very words of the chapter and album titles suggest prayer, a cry for relief. As we read "Oh Mercy" (the chapter) with *Oh Mercy* (the album) playing in the background, we hear a plea for renewed inspiration directed to . . . whom? A lover? The absent muse perhaps? His audience? God? (Though shouting to God is problematic, as we learn in "Political World." What name should one use?). What we have in "Oh Mercy"/*Oh Mercy* is the substance of a prayer—a cry for assistance and relief—without any vocative attached.

To speak of the phrase "Oh Mercy" as a prayer is in keeping with the general tenor of this chapter of *Chronicles*, haunted as it is with a mysterious and vague mysticism. There is the prostitute doomed to wander the hallway of a hotel for a thousand years; the angels who communicate to the singer's psyche; the undefined something that guides the recording of a song, as if "Joan of Arc was out there"; and those "watching gods" who witness the *Oh Mercy* sessions. Added to these vaguely spiritual experiences are those unexpected inspirations for songs arriving out of the blue: for "Political World," "What Good Am I?" "Dignity," "Disease of Conceit," "What Was It You Wanted?"[9] and "Where Teardrops Fall." Indeed, Dylan has a tendency throughout *Chronicles* to slip in and out of straightforward realism into quasi-dreamlike moments. These transitions are seamless and not the least bit self-conscious. He describes the Bull's Head Tavern where John Wilkes Booth used to drink, for instance, adding the detail that he once "saw [Booth's] ghost in the mirror—an ill spirit."[10]

The intended recipient of the oh-mercy prayer is ambiguous, but the crisis motivating this cry for help is not. Music and sound are clearly on his mind with these songs. Angels sing ("Political World"); crickets chirp ("Man in the Long Black Coat"); and there is an invitation to heathen and saints alike to provide musical accompaniment ("Ring Them Bells"). Unfortunately, the references to music reveal an unnerving silence or disruption of beautiful sound. Broken (lyrical) lines and (guitar) strings appear first in the long list of problems announced in "Everything Is Broken," and the needle skips on a broken record in "What Was It You Wanted?" Time and tempo fly (out of control?) in "Series of Dreams" and more subtly, the lack of distinction between the tongues of angels and men in "Dignity" alludes to the cacophony of sound described by St. Paul: "If I speak in the tongues of mortals and of angels, but do not have love, I am a noisy gong or a clanging cymbal" (1 Cor. 13:1). That will not sell records or garner favorable reviews.[11]

Dylan laments the sorry state of his 1980s musical output in the "Oh Mercy" chapter, and occasionally we suspect hearing allusions to this professional crisis in the album's songs as well. However, in both the book and the songs there are notes of optimism and hints of recovery. For instance, in "What Was It You Wanted?" the singer directs a series of questions at an unspecified "you." Are there moments in the song when he means us, his audience? Let's allow for the moment there are no mistakes in life and agree to see it this way. If we do, we can here imagine Dylan engaging his audience in conversation—the same audience he describes sympathetically as going through deserted orchards and dead grass when attending recent performances.[12] He seems to ask, in effect, "What do you, as an audience, want from me, a singer?"

The optimism emerges when he assures listeners the invitation to speak is genuine and sincere: "What was it you wanted / You can tell me, I'm back."[13] He's back. What a relief to hear. Musically rejuvenated, newly inspired to reconnect with old songs and write new ones. This is the story he tells in "Oh Mercy," and the results in *Oh Mercy* prove the claim. He started with a "cacophony of ideas" and spent all he had "under the watching gods," accomplishing what he set out to do. To be sure, Dylan is surprisingly modest about the album. Producer Daniel Lanois wanted songs like "Masters of War," "Girl from the North Country," and "Gates of Eden" but did not get them, and in the end, Dylan admits, "It's not the record either of us wanted."[14] Still, many critics refer to *Oh Mercy* as an impressive comeback album, even if Dylan considers *The Traveling Wilburys*, Vol. 1, and *Dylan & The Dead* more significant at this moment of his career, at least in terms of sales.[15] Some agree with this cautious, understated assessment: "[*Oh Mercy* is] an honorable minor work, well-received by the public and reviewers, and marred only by the feeling that Dylan has one eye on that public approbation: that he is asking if this is the sort of album people want from him."[16]

The fourth chapter of Bob Dylan's *Chronicles* provides the only sustained reflection on the artist's activities in the recording studio,[17] focusing on the circumstances resulting in *Oh Mercy* and this marvelous return from artistic oblivion. This is interesting in itself. One might expect the first volume of an autobiography (of sorts) to focus on one of the apogees of the artist's career, or at least one of the early seminal works. Instead, it treats an artistic low point; Dylan admits repeatedly in the chapter that he is long past his professional prime. *Oh Mercy* is strong, but it is not *Blonde on Blonde*. There is "something magical" about the album, but Lanois did not get "Masters of War," "Hard Rain," or "Gates of Eden."[18] If I had my choice, I would rather hear Dylan tell the story behind *Blood on the Tracks*, including his reasons for rerecording that masterpiece, or maybe his reflections on the writing and recording of *Highway 61 Revisited* and the epic "Like A Rolling Stone."[19] As autobiographical writing goes, *Chronicles* rarely conforms to expectations.

So if Dylan's chapter "Oh Mercy" is not a celebration of a professional highlight or concerned to address questions readers want answered, what is it? The chapter follows a trajectory that begins with professional and artistic death and ends with a musical rebirth occurring in New Orleans, the birthplace of so much American music, that place where everything is "a good idea."[20]

Before proceeding further, it deserves notice that fact and fiction sit together comfortably in Bob Dylan's songs, populated as they are with a colorful cast of characters and narrators who are clearly born out his fertile imagination and others we know to be actual people, both past and present. The same blending of the real and unreal occurs in *Chronicles*. The book permits some annotation; we recognize plenty of the names given, can verify dates of events mentioned, and point to geographical references on a map. There are other moments in this lively prose, however, where we either suspect, or know for certain, that things have changed as the author slips back and forth between memory and creativity. I am not convinced that characters like "Sun Pie" and a host of others in the book are real people, yet they play as important a part in the story as Bono or Daniel Lanois. I do not bother trying to distinguish authentic recollection from fiction in these notes. If Dylan wanted to write a straightforward autobiography, we would have a very different—and for that reason certainly less interesting—tale. Instead, we have *Chronicles*, with its curious mix of fact and fantasy. For what follows, I simply read the book on its own terms with little interest in historical verisimilitude, accepting that Sun Pie and Lanois are no more than characters in a great story.

As said already, the phrase "Oh Mercy" suggests prayer uttered by one in desperate need. Two times in this section of *Chronicles* the mysterious shop owner Sun Pie asks the singer if he is a praying man,[21] and both times Dylan answers in the affirmative. If the album title is a prayer, the album itself is a partial answer to that prayer in this story of musical collaboration and resurrection. The story begins with remarks about the slow "regeneration" of the guitar player's injured hand in 1987, an image that parallels the serious injury to and recovery of his career. That it was a time of artistic death for the songwriter and performer is a conclusion forced on readers through a relentless string of self-deprecating remarks: "faded out"; audiences face "deserted orchards and dead grass"; "whitewashed and wasted out professionally"; "done for"; "burned-out wreck"; "couldn't overcome the odds"; "over the hill"; music that is "archaic." Dylan insists that all connection with inspiration disappeared, that spontaneity was blind, that he lost all ability to understand and creatively perform his own songs, that he lost all feeling for them. As if this were not enough to convince readers of the severity of the crisis, he adds that the "instinct and intuition" that served him so well in the past were gone: "These ladies had turned into vultures and were sucking me dry." If circling vultures are a harbinger of death, feeding vultures are confirmation of its arrival. Dylan sings of vultures in "Dignity." This song also mentions "hollow" men, an adjective used in the same section of *Chronicles*.[22]

But death is not the end. The author of *Chronicles* looks back on the demise of his career *and* celebrates renewed creativity and confidence. Things have changed, he tells us, and the language of the chapter shifts from a litany of terms outlining the loss and death of artistic energy to one announcing its rebirth and rediscovery: "transformed"; "the veil had lifted"; "something internal came unhinged"; "metamorphosis." Earlier on, "everything was smashed," but now "everything came back." Earlier on he was planning his retirement, but now he would put the "decision to retire on hold." Formerly there was no connection to inspiration, but now the angels communicate. What the performer experiences amounts to a resurrection, an ability to call his songs "up from the grave."[23]

The remarkable reversal outlined in *Chronicles* is the result of a series of epiphanies and inspirations, most of them encounters with musicians, though other characters contribute to Dylan's recovery in their own way, such as the shopkeeper Sun Pie (described as "inspiring") and the female disc jockey Brown Sugar (credited with bringing inner peace and serenity). The first of these epiphanies occurs during rehearsals with the Grateful Dead. He mentions collaborations with both Tom Petty and the Heartbreakers and the Dead in this section of the chapter, and in each case, the creative energies they brought to his songs proved overwhelming. The resulting tension culminates when he walks out of rehearsals and finds himself in a tiny bar listening to live jazz music. In a scene reminiscent of Jack Kerouac's *On the Road*, a jazz performer finds "an open window to [Dylan's] soul," just as another jazz performer did for Dean Moriarty in the novel. Dylan does not gush quite like Moriarty, but the effects of this encounter remain significant. It reenergizes the songwriter, who, newly inspired and confident, returns to rehearsals with the Grateful Dead. This sets up what might be a vague but delightful pun. He has "that old jazz singer to thank," he is *grateful* that he pointed the way out of an artistic *death*.[24]

Another similarly inspiring scene occurs when Dylan watches a saxophone player who was "the spitting image of Blind Gary Davis," a bluesman long dead by the time of the events Dylan here describes (d. 1972). The scene amounts to an epiphany for Dylan, who asks (himself, I hope!), "What was he doing here?" The encounter with "Blind Gary Davis" has a profound effect on Dylan and the *Oh Mercy* sessions. Dylan believes the musician is throwing him a lifeline to grip and soon feels everything coming together for him: "All of a sudden I know that I'm in the right place doing the right thing at the right time and Lanois is the right cat. Felt like I had turned a corner and was seeing the sight of a god's face."[25]

Dylan also acknowledges the important inspiration of blues guitarist Lonnie Johnson. Dylan met Johnson in the 1960s and credits him with showing a "way of playing" that until now he did not use. Now, "all of a sudden," this system of playing came back to him, a technique that would "revitalize" his world. Dylan suspected the blues player was revealing a secret when they met back in the sixties, but he did not understand it then. Now in the eighties, "it all clicked" and Dylan had at his disposal all the technical theory he would ever need. Dylan expresses relief and renewed enthusiasm for his music as a result, with energy to play each night.[26]

U2's Bono and a case of Guinness provide a third inspiration for the beleaguered Dylan, whose account of their boozy meeting offers one of the most intriguing scenes in *Chronicles*. This visit represents the genesis of a chain of events resulting in *Oh Mercy*.

> Spending time with Bono was like eating dinner on a train—feels like you're moving, going somewhere. Bono's got the soul of an ancient poet and you have to be careful around him. He can roar 'til the earth shakes. He's also a closet philosopher. He brought a case of Guinness with him. . . . Bono says things that can sway anybody. He's like that guy in the old movie, the one who beats up a rat with his bare hands and wrings a confession out of him.[27]

As they drink and talk about Jack Kerouac, the conversation eventually turns to music, at which point Bono asks about new songs, pressing Dylan to record them. Continuing this momentum, Bono then calls up Canadian producer Daniel Lanois (responsible for U2's *Joshua Tree* [1987]) on the spot, insisting he and Dylan meet to discuss a possible project.[28]

One gets the sense Dylan needed an encounter with such a personality, to be with someone constantly "moving" and forceful enough to make things happen. Dylan is somewhat lethargic heading into his meetings with Bono and Lanois. He has some songs hidden away in a box but no energy to make anything of them: "[Bono] said I should record them. I said that I wasn't so sure about that, thought that maybe I should pour lighter fluid over them—said that I had been having a hard time making records."[29] An evening with the ever-moving Bono obviously stirred up something, and we can be glad he prevented Dylan from leaving those songs in a box, or worse.

Lanois and Dylan worked together on both *Oh Mercy* (1989) and *Time Out of Mind* (1997), and I wonder if we catch subtle allusions to his positive influence in "Where the Teardrops Fall." The singer bangs a drum and plays a fife with someone who not only knows about the songs hidden away in his heart but also has the means to retrieve them. This person can provide "a new place to start."[30] This multi-instrumentalist companion who brings out hidden music sounds remarkably like Lanois, who not only plays several instruments but insists Dylan has a good album in him. The singer is doubtful, but Lanois is insistent: " 'You can make a great record, you know, if you really want to.' "[31]

The importance of collaboration emerges as an important leit-motif in this chapter, the key (or at least *a* key) to Dylan's artistic resurgence. Tom Petty, the Grateful Dead, and the Traveling Wilburys, not to mention the inspirations and lessons coming from Lonnie Johnson and nameless players in New Orleans' jazz clubs, lift Dylan out his creative fog. The collaboration with Daniel Lanois in particular stands out; it is something fated, and the producer enters his recording life "like something foretold in the scriptures." Bob Dylan finds new life in music and musicians, and remarkably, as suggested earlier, he gestures toward the audience to participate in his artistic resurrection, to collaborate with him as well.[32] He does not always extend such invitations. To press the sense of his pronouns a little, there are times he pushes us away, telling us to go away from his window, reminding us that he needs solitude, and warning us against trusting him.[33] However, for a brief moment in 1989, he called out to us: What is it you want from me? You can tell me, *I'm back.*

"Drifting from Scene to Scene": The Wandering Observer

I memorized Poe's poem "The Bells" and strummed it to a melody on my guitar.

Bob Dylan[34]

There was a lot of action and people on the street and I watched them go by.

Bob Dylan[35]

Dylan is well aware that one's identity is inscrutable and ever shifting, and he distinguishes his artistic, public persona from what we might call his private and real self. In remarks included with the liner notes to the *Biograph* collection (1985), he says, "I don't think of myself as Bob Dylan. It's like Rimbaud said, 'I is another.' " Dylan also comments on his discovery of French Symbolist Arthur Rimbaud in *Chronicles*, noting that his first encounter with the poet "was a big deal. . . . I came across one of his letters called 'Je est un autre,' which translates into 'I is someone else.' When I read those words the bells went off. It made perfect sense."[36] Appropriately, given his fascination with identity, he plays a character named "Alias" in Sam Peckinpah's 1973 film *Pat Garrett and Billy the Kid*, and in his own 1978 film *Renaldo and Clara*, he plays the role of Renaldo while musician Ronnie Hawkins plays "Bob Dylan." He also hides behind literal masks on occasion, wearing makeup during his 1975 tour, dark sunglasses for an indoor concert for the MTV Unplugged series (which first aired in December of 1994), and a fake beard at the Newport Folk Festival in 2002. (This is the same beard used for the "Cross the Green Mountain" video, featured in the Ronald F. Maxwell film *Gods and Generals*, 2003.)

The Todd Haynes film *I'm Not There* (2007) illustrates the insuperable distance between the persona and the artist. Six different actors play the part of Bob Dylan, the most discussed among them being Cate Blanchett. This clever break with notions of singularity, the idea that a single actor could capture the essence of his or her subject, is insightful. Bob Dylan has spent nearly fifty years as a public figure, hiding behind masks and resisting efforts to encapsulate him and his art in biography and criticism. The autobiographical *Chronicles* is one more mask. This book is not a typical celebrity memoir, having far more in common with Woody Guthrie's *Bound for Glory* (1943) and Jack Kerouac's *On the Road* (1957) than any rock-star tell-alls of recent vintage. A remark in the book about topical songs provides a fitting description of *Chronicles* itself: "The writer doesn't have to be accurate, could tell you anything and you're going to believe it."[37] Bob Dylan's memoir is a grab bag, a curious, highly random (by appearance) rummaging through his personal memories mingled with pure fiction.

At one point, he describes spending time in the New York Public Library, reading "articles in newspapers on microfilm from 1855 to about 1865 to see what daily life was like." What intrigued him was "the language and rhetoric of the times" in this diverse collection of articles about such things as slavery, reform movements, anti-gambling leagues, rising crime, child labor, and temperance movements. It is interesting to observe Dylan shift immediately from this story about random perusal of nineteenth-century reportage to remarks about his own writing technique as a topical songwriter in the 1960s. Here too we find the artist Bob Dylan operating without any rigid, predetermined methodology. Sitting in a coffee shop with his friend Len Chandler, Dylan tells us he would "drink coffee and look through the daily newspapers left behind on the counter to see if there was song material in any of it." After seeing the newspapers at the New York Public Library, he continues, "These papers seemed almost threadbare and dull." He mentions stories in the news: France's nuclear capabilities, Vietnam's independence from colonial power, psychiatric theories about phobias, women's rights, and even the score from a New York Rangers vs. Chicago Black Hawks hockey game.[38] One thing is clear. Dylan looks to the past, not the present, to escape the threadbare and dull.

In *Chronicles*, he habitually circles back to origins and explores earlier times, to the point that this backward-looking perspective even structures the book itself. *Chronicles* ends where it begins, the closing pages referring again to people and places (New York; Columbia Records) first introduced in the opening ones.[39] There is clear repetition of various individuals and situations, suggesting a return to the people and places that are most important to the author. The names John Hammond and David Van Ronk are prominent within this pattern, as the following lines illustrate, first with reference to John Hammond:

- [beginning] [He] was legendary, pure American aristocracy; [end] . . . a true American aristocrat.
- [beginning] John Hammond, who had brought me to Columbia Records. . . . [end] Hammond . . . told me that he'd like me to record for Columbia Records.

- [beginning] [John Hammond's] mother was an original Vanderbilt. . . . . [end] One of his forebears, Cornelius Vanderbilt, had stated somewhere . . .
- [beginning] John had been raised in the upper world, in comfort and ease—but he wasn't satisfied and had followed his own heart's love. [end] Money didn't make much of an impression on him.
- [beginning] He put a contract in front of me, the standard one, and I signed it right then and there . . . didn't need a lawyer, advisor or anybody looking over my shoulder. I would have gladly signed whatever form he put in front of me. [end] John Hammond put a contract down in front of me—the standard one they gave to any new artist. . . . I wrote my name down with a steady hand. I trusted him.
- [beginning] He looked at the calendar, picked out a date for me to start recording. [end] John picked out a date on the calendar for me to come back and start recording.

This return to the start pattern appears again when the author celebrates folk musician David Van Ronk for a second time:

- [beginning] He was passionate and stinging, sang like a soldier of fortune and sounded like he paid the price. [end] Van Ronk seemed ancient, battle tested.
- [beginning] Van Ronk could . . . turn blues into ballads and ballads into blues. [end] He turned every folk song into a surreal melodrama.
- [beginning] David Van Ronk . . . a mass of bristling hair . . . [end] . . . long brown straight hair which flew down covering half his face.
- [beginning] He looked like he'd come from the Russian embassy. [end] Dave was reading the Daily News. . . . The Russians were testing nuclear weapons.
- [beginning] I told him . . . could I play something for him? He said, "Sure." [end] "I got a record I want to play for Dave."[40]

Both Hammond and Van Ronk provided pivotal opportunities for the young Dylan. Van Ronk invited Dylan to the Gaslight to "play a couple of songs,"[41] and Hammond launched the singer's recording career with Columbia.

The picture emerging from *Chronicles* suggests that the discovery of meaning and fulfillment involves collaboration with other artists—as we see in the *Oh Mercy* work of the late 1980s and in the Rolling Thunder Revue of the 1970s. There is also a rich world of wisdom and authenticity in the people, music, and stories of the past that Dylan returns to constantly. Bono once confessed to Dylan that he did not pay much attention to traditional music, and Dylan told him this was a mistake: "You've gotta go back."[42]

There is yet another distinguishing feature of Dylan's approach to learning that is particularly instructive as we consider his interests in religion and spirituality. In *Chronicles* and elsewhere we discover that meaning and fulfillment are not byproducts of conformity or rigid adherence to predetermined paths. Structure stifles, but liberation is illuminating. Booksellers categorize *Chronicles* as "Biography & Autobiography" (according to the notice placed above the barcode on the back cover of my copy), but as noted already, the book fits these labels only awkwardly. The author writes about the inspirations that give his art meaning but does not provide the expected chronological exactitude or a recital of mere mundane facts.

Instead, *Chronicles* is truer because of its near mysticism than any simpler prose could hope to achieve. By not claiming or pretending to provide a straightforward account of his past life, the book claims an honesty and authenticity not possible in other forms of memoir, which can potentially distort. Memory is unreliable and subject to deliberate and unintended adjustments. Lists of facts involve selection, and all omissions and inclusions shape the narrative in one way or another. It follows that a pure, unadulterated, unmediated history is not possible. *Chronicles* is a different kind of autobiographical writing, one that explores the author's artistic instincts and imagination and provides glimpses into the kinds of inspirations that fuel his music. The book, like the education Dylan describes at various points in it (rummaging through a friend's bookcase, etc.), is random and episodic, jumping constantly from scene to scene. To understand this approach to storytelling and meaning making, I appeal to analogy once again and compare the artist/writer to a character exemplifying a similar curiosity and approach to life.

Just Walkin' with Edgar Allan Poe

Like Woody Guthrie in *Bound for Glory*, like the *flâneur* who appears periodically in Walter Benjamin's writings, like the Rolling Thunder Revue described by Sam Shepard, and like many characters in his songs, Bob Dylan is a wandering observer. The religious content of his work reflects this, suggesting a spirituality that defies narrow, restrictive definition and cultivates an openness to whatever nourishes. This includes the biblical canon but other canons as well. The Bible reveals, but so do the blues. Beauty, meaning, and truth exist inside the usual sites of religious inquiry (like his "Bible school") but also in unexpected places (like Woody Guthrie's hospital room). Just as the discovery of meaning is not limited spatially, as though only available in particular places, it also lacks chronological fixity. Revelations occur in modern times but also in the music, texts, and memories of the past. As noted, when he tells stories (as in *Chronicles*), Dylan moves back and forth across the decades, recalling moments that matter.

While much has been said so far on Dylan's preference for serendipity, chance encounters, unanticipated experience, and spontaneity, emphasizing an unscripted approach to meaning making and discovery, a few words on the deliberateness of Dylan's "search" are in order.

Edgar Allan Poe's short story "The Man of the Crowd," first published in 1840, begins with a nameless individual sitting in a coffee house with a cigar in his mouth and a newspaper in his lap, "peering through the smoky panes into the street." He is watching the crowds walk along the busy sidewalk, observing details of their dress and behavior, speculating about their careers and habits. Though he describes a wide variety of people, his gaze gradually shifts from respectable, business-minded folk to those "descending in the scale of what is termed gentility."[43] He is increasingly fascinated by less savory individuals: peddlers, street beggars, feeble and ghastly invalids, drunkards innumerable and indescribable, coal-heavers, sweeps, organ-grinders, monkey exhibitors, and ragged artisans . . . here we go again with lists. While "scrutinizing the mob," this narrator finds himself completely fixated with one individual in particular walking along the road. He describes "a countenance which at once arrested and absorbed my whole attention, on account of the absolute idiosyncrasy of its expression." The viewer is so enthralled he gets up from his comfortable café seat in order to follow this person, admitting to "a craving desire to keep the man in view—to know more of him." After hurriedly putting on an overcoat and seizing his hat and cane, this narrator makes his way "into the street," pushing his way through the crowd in the direction the stranger walks. Through fog and rain, this voyeur pursues him through the streets of London, but not just any streets. Most people avoid these areas of the city. This perambulator heads toward "the most noisome quarter" of the city, "where everything wore the worst impress of the most deplorable poverty, and of the most desperate crime."[44]

When I read Poe's story, I cannot help but think of Bob Dylan. In my mind's eye, I conflate various images of Dylan and his characters: his top hat–wearing, nineteenth-century, mortician-looking appearance in the "Blood in My Eyes" video, strolling along crowded city sidewalks; the solitary narrator of "Standing in the Doorway" smoking a cheap cigar; a photograph of the singer with walking stick in hand.[45] What really interests me, though, is the resemblance of temperament between Dylan and Poe's character. Poe's short story serves as a parable about an onlooker interested in the human condition, both its public respectability and its hidden, sinister qualities. Dylan is just such a spectator.

This short story presents us with an instructive analogy as we consider Bob Dylan's artistic life. As we read his prose, look at his sketches,[46] and listen to the songs or episodes of *Theme Time Radio Hour*, we soon discover Dylan is an observer of people and their activities. He is particularly fascinated with an array of dangerous, sinister folks who populate the imagined worlds of his musical stories: a Bible-quoting stranger wearing a long black coat; the opportunist Uncle Sweetheart; the money-waving Judas Priest; the violent William Zanzinger.[47] There are drunks and gangsters, political ideologues and cruel women.[48] Like Poe's narrator, Dylan seems drawn to those "descending in the scale of what is termed gentility." On many occasions, he gets up from the café, as it were, and follows these unsavory characters into the night, tracing their individual stories in song. Also like Poe's narrator, Bob Dylan has an insatiable curiosity about the world around him.

What is more, to press this analogy further, we might add that the characters and places Poe and Dylan describe are those easily overlooked by others. We might not want to leave the café to roam the rainy streets in the rougher parts of town, but artists can force us to do so, to look at things we would not otherwise see. Said differently, Dylan often presents us with subjects we might rather ignore: militarism, racism, poverty, struggling faith, and so on.[49] This is no empty exercise, however. The highly motivated voyeur in Poe's story ambles into the streets—a deliberate choice—but follows no preconceived route because he does not know where the man will go. As a result, he sees things he would not normally see and in the process gains insights that are completely unanticipated.

In the closing pages of Poe's story, this narrator claims, "A blaze of light burst upon my sight." What is intriguing about this scene is that he does not explain this burst of light in any literal sense. Poe writes that it was "*nearly* daybreak" at that moment, so it cannot refer to the sunrise, which he mentions later.[50] This suggests a more symbolic meaning. The burst of light indicates illumination, an unexpected insight or a revelation. This too, many Dylan fans know, is a quality of Bob Dylan's art. No matter how dark and dreary the destination, some "blaze of light" usually bursts upon our senses.

Edgar Allan Poe's "The Man in the Crowd" intrigued German philosopher and culture critic Walter Benjamin, who refers to the story on several occasions,[51] and this brings us back to the image of the *flâneur* first mentioned in chapter 1. Benjamin saw in Poe's story a model of an ideal thinker, the *flâneur* wandering through the city streets observing everything. For Benjamin, "the case in which the *flâneur* completely distances himself from the type of the philosophical promenader, and takes on the features of the werewolf restlessly roaming a social wilderness, was fixed for the first time and forever afterward by Poe in his story 'The Man of the Crowd.' "[52] The *flâneur* is an idler, strolling through the city by choice but without apparent aim.

Poe's character loses himself in the pursuit of the old man, and his compulsiveness borders on a kind of intoxication. Poe goes to great lengths to develop this aspect of his character, who has "a craving desire to keep the man in view"; feels "a calm but inquisitive interest in everything"; and is "absorbed in contemplation," "occupied in scrutinizing the mob," and fascinated with "an interest all-absorbing." This story is, on one level, a celebration of intellectual curiosity. This intoxication with knowledge motivates a compulsive pursuit, which only ends once it is clear he will "learn no more of him, nor of his deeds."[53]

The narrator's study of the mysterious pedestrian involves a willingness to go wherever the evidence leads. He chases the man all night, through fog and rain, resolving to "follow the stranger whithersoever he should go" even though the man wanders "without apparent aim."[54] The picture provided by Edgar Allan Poe suggests a thinker who does not slavishly follow a previously choreographed route. There is no predetermined destination, no anticipated return to the start, and no dialectic promising a synthesis and forward progress. Here in Poe's story, he finds an alternative way to think, an unstructured, somewhat random pursuit of knowledge that serves as a safeguard against mindless ideological commitments. There is liberty in this. Such a thinker is free to consider the people, places, and evidence easily overlooked by others. As an allegory of the ideal thinker, this story presents a search for knowledge that is open to new sources of information. This is a fitting description of Dylan and his art. This singer-songwriter's curiosity takes him everywhere in his search for religious meaning, for truth, for "IT" (as Kerouac's Dean Moriarty would put it).

This inquisitive nature characterizes Bob Dylan's dialogues

with spiritual themes. The religious, often biblical, content in his songs does not indicate an arrival at a fixed destination so much as the delight of a seeker on a journey. When we think of religious content in Bob Dylan's art—even in his so-called gospel phase—he never allows himself to be confined by, say, the limitations imposed by dogma or creed. Instead, religion becomes art, mingled in with all the scatter of other people, things, and ideas he comes across.

Finding Dylan's Gospel in Narrative Bits and Pieces

Two delightful readings of "Lily, Rosemary and the Jack of Hearts" (*Blood on the Tracks*, 1975)—one by Wendy Lesser, the other by Stephen Scobie—discuss the numerous narrative ambiguities in the story Dylan tells in this song.[55] Mystery, gaps, and plot twists abound in this tale, a song Andy Gill and Kevin Odegard describe as "a Wild West movie, sketched with verve and ambiguity, in broad mythic strokes akin to old folk ballads, but delivered like saloon-bar gossip."[56]

The basic plot includes the following elements. The setting is a bar and cabaret. The Jack of Hearts and his companions are in the process of robbing a bank, and while his partners drill through the wall in a room linking the cabaret and the adjacent bank, the Jack of Hearts enters the saloon to drink and watch the show. Lily is in the back room playing cards when the wealthy Big Jim enters the saloon. Soon afterwards, Rosemary arrives at the bar. She may be Big Jim's wife, but he takes no notice of her because he is busy looking across the barroom at the Jack of Hearts, trying to figure out why he looks so familiar. Both of these men also stare at Lily, who is now performing in the cabaret. At this point listeners begin to piece together the complicated love triangle that lies at the heart of the story. Rosemary plays "the role of Big Jim's wife" (but is she actually his wife?), but Lily has his ring (is she Big Jim's mistress?). At the same time, Lily is in love with the Jack of Hearts. It is possible she knows him already, something made explicit in the version of the story printed in *Lyrics* ("'I've missed you so,' she said to him, and he felt she was sincere"[57]), but this remains ambiguous in the *Blood on the Tracks* recording of the song, which omits this stanza. After the show, the Jack of Hearts meets Lily in her dressing room as ominous footsteps are "comin' for the Jack of Hearts," and violence erupts. Big Jim is dead, killed by Rosemary—or at least "the hangin' judge" accuses her of doing so—and she now faces the gallows. The Jack of Hearts disappears, presumably with his companions, who succeeded in cleaning out the bank's vault, though his absence could also indicate he is dead. The story (and the cabaret) closes, leaving Lily alone with her thoughts about the Jack of Hearts.

The song opens in the midst of a story not explained to listeners. We know that a festival is over and that people are leaving town, but we have no idea if or how either bit of context informs the narrative that follows. Furthermore, the details of the story "go by in a rapid succession of cinematic cuts, omitting sections of the narrative, which the listener must attempt to reconstruct in retrospect."[58] As a result, even though we can list various "facts" about the major characters, the story raises more questions than it answers. Is the Jack of Hearts an actual man or a playing card? Does Big Jim kill the Jack of Hearts, or does the Jack of Hearts kill Big Jim (and leave Rosemary to take the blame)? Did Lily know the Jack of Hearts before she became Big Jim's mistress? Why does Lily's wall have a new coat of paint, and why does she bury her dress after the show? Who is "the leading actor" disguised as a monk? There are no certain answers for these and other plot questions the song presents, and what is more, Wendy Lesser observes an intriguing "gap between what we feel we know and what we actually know." The song wants us to hope that the Jack of Hearts survives the events at the cabaret, but "whether it wants us to *believe* that is less clear."[59]

Significantly, we should note that Dylan's ambiguity is deliberate. As Big Jim bursts in on the Jack of Hearts and Lily in her dressing room, the narrator admits, "No one knew the circumstance but they said that it happened pretty quick." With these words, Dylan accepts a "limited viewpoint"; he is deliberately ambiguous, refusing "the stance of the omniscient narrator."[60]

This one line should mute our expectations about deciphering a definitive reading of the song. It is an intentionally mysterious story, and the storyteller appears to enjoy spinning a yarn that puzzles as much as it delights.

Interpreters wanting to make sense of events unfolding at the cabaret face other challenges as well. For one thing, "Lily, Rosemary, and the Jack of Hearts" has various hallmarks of traditional balladry—love and betrayal, death and martyrdom—yet the song confounds those hoping to piece together the narrative in light of other songs within that form. Traditional ballads often omit details from stories because "the audience is presumed to know the story already and can therefore be depended upon to fill the gaps itself." If this were the case, one would reasonably expect to find answers to narrative questions by tracing the story's ancestry back through other incarnations of the tale. The strategy fails in this case, however, because this particular story has "no clear antecedent in American literature or history" and questions raised by the song "cannot be quelled by a diligent scrutiny of history or legend." Even when there are echoes of earlier ballads, Dylan appears to take stock characters and rework them thoroughly. The betraying female Lily is a familiar character in balladry, but this particular incarnation has "a rather mixed-up background."[61]

Exacerbating the issue of interpretation further is the existence of different versions of Dylan's story. As mentioned above, one stanza included in an earlier recording of the song, and printed in *Lyrics*, is not part of the officially released *Blood on the Tracks* recording. The stanza in question makes it clear that Lily and the Jack of Hearts had an earlier romance and that he returned the love she clearly feels for him.[62] Lesser and Scobie agree that the omission of these lines is significant,[63] so which "text" should interpreters follow? Related to this last point, Dylan's actual performance of the song on the album deserves notice. We read in the printed lyrics, "she'd never met anyone quite like the Jack of Hearts,"[64] which indicates Lily had an earlier encounter with the man (i.e., she *had* never met . . .). However, Lesser observes that Dylan sings the line differently on *Blood on the Tracks*: "When our master of ambiguity records the song, he drops the 'd' ('she never met . . .'), managing to imply that perhaps she never did [know the Jack of Hearts], even now."[65] The mysteries remain, and there is little chance we will find consensus on questions left to us by the song.

There are of course many examples of ambiguity in Dylan's writing. Songs like "Subterranean Homesick Blues" and "Desolation Row" (*Bringing It All Back Home*, 1965); "Visions of Johanna" (*Blonde on Blonde*, 1966); "Every Grain of Sand" (*Shot of Love*, 1981); and "Jokerman" (*Infidels*, 1983) baffle those seeking to organize characters and imagery into a coherent, simple statement. Confusion, however, is part of the fun. No one knows the circumstances, even the songwriter, so we must be wary of reducing chaos to order, mystery to definition.

A song like "Lily, Rosemary, and the Jack of Hearts" illustrates a quality of the religious language in Dylan's songs. Just as this song leaves us puzzling over possible meanings, so it is with Bob Dylan's gospel. As Scobie says of "Lily, Rosemary, and the Jack of Hearts," Dylan refuses the role of the omniscient narrator. Scattered throughout Dylan's work we find Moses and Jesus, preachers and church bells, devils and prayers, but in the religious sphere there are as many mysteries as there are in the cabaret.

Concluding Thoughts

My stuff were songs, you know? They weren't sermons. If you examine the songs, I don't believe you're gonna find anything in there that says that I'm a spokesman for anybody or anything really.

Bob Dylan[1]

A bunch of years from now, all these people . . . are gonna be writing about all this shit I write. I don't know where the fuck it comes from, I don't know what the fuck it's about, and they're gonna write about what it's about.

Bob Dylan, as remembered by Joan Baez[2]

*T*he first comment is from a sixty-three-year-old Bob Dylan spoken to Ed Bradley on the CBS program *60 Minutes*, suggesting his songs do not include any particular messages or profound meanings. In the second, Joan Baez represents the impressions of a twenty-something-year-old Dylan whose sentiments look pretty much the same. It begs the question, Where does meaning reside? Dylan knew early on that his lyrics would come under intense scrutiny and his comments (or are they Baez's?) proved to be prescient—people have been writing about this shit ever since and no doubt will for generations to come.

We are fortunate to have such an impressive bibliography of skilled commentary treating Bob Dylan's work, and this body of amateur and scholarly analysis will only grow as time passes, proving the lasting merits of the Dylan canon. Such secondary literature is useful. Dylan's sentiments notwithstanding, careful readers can open up his songs by helping us recognize and understand literary devices and techniques used, by showing us how his songs dialogue with one another and with other texts, by identifying allusions and quotations, and by highlighting relevant contextual matters, such as sociopolitical environments. On occasion, they even identify biographical details that help us understand something of the mood and the moment captured in a recording. Commentary, however, has limits.

Whether writing about art or religious texts, our attempts to explain and articulate meaning are always partial and selective. For instance, what does Psalm 23 mean? "The LORD is my shepherd, I shall not want. . . ." For individual readers, the experience of this poem will differ infinitely. All might appreciate the pastoral simplicity of the scene and its comforting promise of peace and abundance, but someone young and in good health will not hear the promise of God's presence in the valley of the shadow of death (v. 4) in quite the same way as one who is old, sick, or in danger.[3] Our circumstances determine where our eyes land on the page and what images, ideas, and themes capture our imagination and spirit.

The same is true with music. When we hear a song for the first time, it matters whether we are in love at that moment or brokenhearted, spiritually hungry or indifferent to matters of faith, looking to be entertained or forced to think, angry at the world or motivated to make it a better place—all such contexts and a thousand others determine our experience of songs and *perception* of meaning in the sounds and words we encounter. Chances are those words and sounds did not mean the same thing to the songwriter when composing, recording, and performing them in concert, but it does not matter. Nor does it matter if other audience members hear and respond to music differently. Their encounters and ours are inimitable.

John Barlow, onetime lyricist for the Grateful Dead, tells a great story about a confused music fan who came to him praising his song about the "watchtowers and stuff." After explaining that Bob Dylan wrote the song in question (i.e., "All Along the Watchtower," *John Wesley Harding*, 1967), this young Deadhead asked, "Who's Bob Dylan?" The experience proved illuminating for Barlow:

> This was a great moment for me. I realized, as I should have known all along, that if the song is any good, it detaches from its apparent source and enters into the hearts and minds of those who hear it to make its own home there.[4]

In a sense, the song was no longer Bob Dylan's but rather part of the unique experience of this misinformed music fan. Barlow does not leave it with confusion over the authorship of a great song. He goes on to reflect on the ways that meaning—not just an author's name—separates individual listeners from lyricists and musicians as it takes root in the mind and soul of audiences:

> As Deadheads [and, I add, Bobheads] know, these songs are continuously growing and revealing themselves. Resonating with frequencies unheard at the time of their writing. Being imbued with all that received belief, collateral and yet vital as anything that happened in the silence of our minds or in the hugeness of two hundred thousand people dancing.[5]

Meaning, including religious meaning, is a construction, crafted by the listener out of the raw materials provided by musicians.[6] Because this is the nature of popular music, I approach the topic of the gospel according to Bob Dylan with an emphasis on the audience's reception of his work. The presence or absence of religious meaning in Bob Dylan's music is something that rests largely with the listener. For the most part, we are not accustomed to this kind of language in the context of religious discourse. It is far more common for discussions of religion to be prescriptive: this is what the Bible, the Koran, or the Bhagavad Gita means; this is what a Jew, a Christian, a Muslim, a Hindu should do; this is right, that is wrong; and so on. The kind of religiosity that resides in popular culture is more individualistic, and so reflections on the subject must remain descriptive in nature. This is not to deny that Bob Dylan is a serious religious thinker, a "musical theologian" to use

Webb's term,[7] and I argue this point elsewhere. My concern here is to balance Dylan's lyrical genius with the inventive and idiosyncratic assimilation of that art into private spiritual reflection. My particular approach to religious dimensions in Dylan's songs and the possible ways people respond to this art identifies two major assumptions held by his vast and diverse fans. One considers the religious content in Dylan's music to be primarily *artistic*. Religion, particularly the Jewish and Christian traditions, is part of the songwriter's cultural inheritance as an English-speaking North American. Religion is an inevitable precursor for Western artists and audiences, regardless of their personal attachments to or intolerance of this material. It is just there. Dylan's language and culture, including the literary and musical influences that inform his writing and thinking, introduce a great deal of religious content to his art. He dialogues creatively with this material, often commenting on religious traditions, people, institutions, and texts. The second assumption many fans bring to the subject of religion and Bob Dylan is *experiential* in focus. Some find an oxymoronic secular spirituality in the man and his music, one that substitutes Dylan for traditional religious experiences (i.e., he meets the needs traditionally found in God and prophets). For others, Dylan's art points beyond itself to traditional religion or some notion of God.

So, what is so good about Bob Dylan's good news? I conclude with words from literary critic Harold Bloom and suggest that Dylan provides audiences with what he calls "a difficult pleasure." As soon as we begin thinking about the song lyrics, we discover that Bob Dylan's music is not easy. The songs are puzzling and make us think. They are emotional and make us feel. They address questions we carry with us and help us articulate our anxieties, anger, fears, joys, attitudes, and impressions of the world around us. The songs are demanding. This affords us pleasures analogous to those we experience when we persist with good but challenging literature. "There is a reader's Sublime," Bloom writes, "and it seems the only secular transcendence we can ever attain, except for the even more precarious transcendence we call 'falling in love.'" A thoughtful engagement with Bob Dylan's songs accomplishes the same thing, I suggest, and with that body of work in mind, Bloom's exhortation to his readers serves Dylan's listeners well:

> I urge you to find what truly comes near to you, that can be used for weighing and for considering. Read deeply, not to believe, not to accept, not to contradict, but to learn to share in that one nature that writes and reads.[8]

We do not all agree on what constitutes religious truth, nor do we all agree about the interpretation of Bob Dylan's lyrics. However, his fans do agree that his music "comes near" in some profound sense, causing us to weigh and consider. His songs deserve deep reading, and engagement with this challenging work always rewards those who persist. Bob Dylan's music points us toward a vague but tantalizing vision of "that one nature," a common spirit or authenticity—"IT," as Dean Moriarty would say—that we all long for. Dylan has his Mr. Tambourine Man to follow, a muse chasing that shadow. Thank God we have Bob Dylan to do the same for us.

Appendix

Bob Dylan's Career in Stolen Moments

You could put his whole life on trial," says Nina Veronica (Jessica Lange) with reference to Jack Fate (*Masked and Anonymous*, 2003), and so it is with Bob Dylan as well. One reason this is possible is accessibility. There is an enormous amount of Dylan material available for the curious to peruse. His official Web site (http://www.bobdylan.com) posts set lists ("Dylan Geo") for more than forty years of touring, including many photos and videos. His song lyrics are available at the same Web site and in print form, through an ever-expanding and changing collection (called *Lyrics: 1962–2001* [2004] in the latest incarnation). He published a collection of poetry early in his career (*Tarantula: Poems*, written in 1966; first released in 1971), and as I write this, one volume of his memoir *Chronicles* is available. He was the creative force behind three films (*Eat the Document* [1971]; *Renaldo and Clara* [1978]; *Masked and Anonymous* [2003]); appeared in others (e.g., *Hearts of Fire* [1987]); and released a collection of sketches in 1994 with the title *Drawn Blank*. There are music videos, like the one for "'Cross the Green Mountain," commissioned for the film *Gods and Generals* (2003), and documentary films, like D. A. Pennebaker's *Dont [sic] Look Back* (1967) and Martin Scorsese's *No Direction Home* (2005). There are plenty of interviews as well, many of which appear in Jonathan Cott's *Bob Dylan: The Essential Interviews*.[1] Artists find creative ways to depict him and his work, as in the Todd Haynes film *I'm Not There* (2007) and poet Stephen Scobie's *And Forget My Name: A Speculative Biography of Bob Dylan*.[2] Countless musicians cover his songs, thus offering their own interpretation of his work. And there is the seemingly endless popular and academic literature that scrutinizes every aspect of his private and public life. A new print journal dedicated to Bob Dylan's work was launched in 2009 (*Montague Street: The Art of Bob Dylan*).[3]

Several biographers[4] ably document Bob Dylan's personal and professional story, and there is no need to repeat this work here. There is also no attempt at thoroughness in what follows. What I offer instead is merely a list of highlights and points of interest from Dylan's long and varied career. Similar compilations appear elsewhere, each unique in the selection of items selected for inclusion.[5]

I list all officially released albums (in bold print) and other published material (books, movies, and drawings), awards, and significant appearances. With respect to albums, I include here only official releases though numerous impressive bootleg collections are available. (See the Web site http://www.bobsboots.com for extensive information.) I list only American releases and American titles of those releases. In various instances, collections appear with other names in other markets (e.g., *Greatest Hits Vol. II* has the title *More Bob Dylan Greatest Hits* in the U.K.), and there are other collections not released within the United States, for example, the Japanese greatest hits package *Masterpieces* (1978). Release dates also vary in different parts of the world. I use the American release dates, providing as much detail as possible, though gaps remain.

1941, May 24, born Robert Allen Zimmerman, in Duluth, Minnesota

1955–59, high school years during which Dylan begins playing music with friends as part of such groups as the Golden Chords and Elston Gunn and the Rock Boppers

1959, enrolls at the University of Minnesota; while in Minneapolis as a student, becomes part of the folk music scene in the coffee houses of the Dinkytown area; changes his name to Bob Dylan during this time

1960, summer, spends time in Denver, where he adopts a Woody Guthrie–like persona and a new voice; speaking in an Okie twang, he begins playing guitar and harmonica together with the help of a harp rack, something learned from blues performer Jesse "Lone Cat" Fuller[6]

1961, January 24, arrives in New York City; "At last I was here . . . . to find singers, the ones I'd heard on record";[7] meets his hero Woody Guthrie soon after and becomes part of the Greenwich Village folk scene, playing in such coffeehouses as the Cafe Wha?, the Commons, and Gerde's Folk City

1961, April, secures a supporting slot during a two-week John Lee Hooker residency at Gerde's Folk City; Dylan's sets included "a new arrangement of 'House of the Rising Sun' taught to him by Dave Van Ronk, and the first song he had written on his arrival in New York, 'Song to Woody' "[8]

1961, September 29, Robert Shelton writes a favorable review of a Dylan performance for the *New York Times*, an important boost to the singer's career[9]

1961, October 26, signs contract offered to him by John Hammond of Columbia Records; Dylan speaks affectionately of Hammond in *Chronicles* (4–6, 277–81), writing that he "had vision and foresight, had seen and heard me, felt my thoughts and had faith in the things to come" (5)

1962, March 19, *Bob Dylan*

1962, October, a coffee-house set was recorded, eventually released as *Live At the Gaslight 1962* (2005); this recording includes the earliest extant recordings of "A Hard Rain's A-Gonna Fall" and "Don't Think Twice, It's All Right" (both eventually released on *The Freewheelin' Bob Dylan*, 1963)[10]

1962, December 30, and January 4, 1963, Dylan acts a small part in the BBC television drama *The Madhouse on Castle Street*, which aired January 13[11]

1963, May 12, Dylan is scheduled to perform on the *Ed Sullivan Show* but cancels when told he could not perform "Talkin' John Birch Paranoid Blues"; Dylan gets a laugh when he prefaces a later performance of the song by remarking, "There ain't nothing wrong with this song" (included in Bootleg Series, Vols. 1–3)

1963, May 27, *The Freewheelin' Bob Dylan*

1963, July 6, performs "Only a Pawn in Their Game," about the killing of civil rights activist Medgar Evers, at a voter registration rally in Greenwood, Mississippi, organized by the Student Nonviolent Coordinating Committee (SNCC)[12]

1963, July 26–28, debut performances at the Newport Folk Festival[13]

1963, August 28, performs at the March on Washington for Jobs and Freedom

1964, January 13, *The Times They Are A-Changin'*

1964, July 24–26, Newport Folk Festival appearance

1964, August 8, *Another Side of Bob Dylan*

1964, August 28, meets the Beatles in New York

1964, October 31, performs at the Philharmonic Hall in New York City; Columbia released a recording of the performance forty years later as *Bob Dylan, Live 1964*, Bootleg Series, Vol. 6 (2004)

1965, March 22, *Bringing It All Back Home*

1965, July 22–25, Newport Folk Festival, including Dylan's (in)famous electric set with members of the Paul Butterfield Blues Band and keyboardist Al Kooper

1965, August 30, *Highway 61 Revisited*

1966, May 16, *Blonde On Blonde*

1966, May 17, an audience member famously shouts "Judas" just before Dylan performs "Like a Rolling Stone"; the moment encapsulates many fans' discontent over Dylan's turn away from traditional, acoustic folk music and toward electric rock and roll[14]

1966, July 29, hurt in a motorcycle accident, resulting in a temporary withdrawal from public life

1967, March 27, *Bob Dylan's Greatest Hits*

1967, May 17, D. A. Pennebaker documentary *Dont* [*sic*] *Look Back*, which follows Dylan on his spring 1965 tour of England

1967, June–October, records songs at Big Pink, a house rented by members of The Band in West Saugerties, New York; twenty-four of these songs were released in 1975 as Bob Dylan and The Band, *The Basement Tapes*, though many of the songs began circulating in 1969 as the bootleg album *Great White Wonder*[15]

1967, December 27, *John Wesley Harding*

1968, January 20, performs with the Crackers (formerly the Hawks, later known as The Band) at the Woody Guthrie Memorial Concert at Carnegie Hall in New York

1969, April 9, *Nashville Skyline*

1969, August 31, performs at the Isle of Wight Festival

1970, June 8, *Self Portrait*

1970, June, honorary Doctor of Music, Princeton University; Dylan's song "Day of the Locusts" (*New Morning*, 1970) refers to the event

1970, October 21, *New Morning*

1971, premiere of the film *Eat the Document* at the New York Academy of Music and the Whitney Museum of American Art[16]

1971, August 1, performs at George Harrison's Concert for Bangladesh[17]

1971, publication of the book *Tarantula* (New York: Macmillan & London)

1971, November 17, *Bob Dylan's Greatest Hits Vol. II*

1973, July 13, *Pat Garrett & Billy the Kid*

1973, July 26, publication of *Writings and Drawings by Bob Dylan* (New York: Alfred A. Knopf)

1973, August 31, release of the Sam Peckinpah film *Pat Garrett & Billy the Kid*; in addition to contributing to the soundtrack, Dylan plays the part of Alias

1973, November 16, *Dylan*; released by Columbia Records after Dylan signed with the Asylum Records label, this unusual album "of out-takes and warm-ups, presumably intend[ed] either to embarrass Dylan beyond endurance or to steal some of the thunder from his Asylum album, *Planet Waves*"[18]

1974, January 17, *Planet Waves*

1974, January–February, tours with The Band; the first major tour since 1966

1974, June 20, *Before the Flood*; live album documenting Dylan's tour with The Band[19]

1975, January 17, *Blood on the Tracks*

1975, June 26, *The Basement Tapes*, with The Band (recorded June–November, 1967)

1975, December 8, Dylan and the Rolling Thunder Revue perform at "The Night of the Hurricane" in support of boxer Rubin Carter

1976, January 16, *Desire*

1976, January 25, Dylan and the Rolling Thunder Revue perform a second benefit concert for Rubin "Hurricane" Carter, this time in Houston, Texas

1976, September 10, *Hard Rain*

1976, September 14, the television special *Hard Rain* airs on NBC

1976, November 25, Dylan joins The Band for their final performance, along with other musical guests; Martin Scorsese films the concert, releasing it in 1978 as *The Last Waltz*

1978, January 25, release of the film *Renaldo and Clara*; Dylan directs, edits (with Howard Alk), and stars in the film

1978, June 15, *Street Legal*

1979, approximately January through March, attends Bible classes at the Vineyard Fellowship's School of Discipleship in Reseda, California;[20] in Dylan's own words, "I went to Bible school"[21]

1979, April, *Bob Dylan at Budokan*

1979, August 18, *Slow Train Coming*

1979, October 20, performs songs from his first gospel album, *Slow Train Coming,* on NBC's *Saturday Night Live*; for many, it is the first time they learn of Dylan's interest in Christianity as he performs "Gotta Serve Somebody," "I Believe in You," and "When You Gonna Wake Up"

1980, February 20, wins Grammy Award, Best Rock Vocal Performance, Male, for "Gotta Serve Somebody" (*Slow Train Coming*)

1980, wins Dove Award for *Slow Train Coming*, in the category Album by a Secular Artist (shared with Jerry Wexler and Barry Beckett)

1980, June 20, *Saved*

1981, August 12, *Shot Of Love*

1982, March 15, inducted into the Songwriters Hall of Fame

1983, November 1, *Infidels*

1984, March 22, appears on *The Late Show with David Letterman*, performing with the Cruzados

1984, April, puts out "Jokerman" video in support of *Infidels*[22]

1984, November or December, *Real Live*

1985, March 11, release of "We Are the World" (by Michael Jackson and Lionel Richie) in support of famine aid to Africa; Dylan contributes vocals

1985, June 8, *Empire Burlesque*

1985, July 13, performs in Philadelphia as part of Live Aid, with Ron Wood and Keith Richards

1985, September 22, performs at Farm Aid, a benefit for struggling American farmers, backed by Tom Petty and the Heartbreakers and, on a few numbers, Willie Nelson

1985, October 12, publication of *Lyrics: 1962–1985* (New York: Alfred A. Knopf), an expanded version of *Writings and Drawings by Bob Dylan* (1973)

1985, October or November, *Biograph*

1986, February 5, begins touring with Tom Petty and the Heartbreakers, a partnership that would last for much of 1986–1987[23]

1986, July 2 and 7, performs on a double bill with the Grateful Dead in Akron, Ohio, and Washington, D.C. (with Tom Petty and the Heartbreakers in support)

1986, August 8, *Knocked Out Loaded*

1987, July, tours with the Grateful Dead, recordings of which appear on *Dylan & The Dead* (1989)

1987, October 9, appears in director Richard Marquand's film *Hearts Of Fire*[24]

1988, January 20, inducted to the Rock and Roll Hall of Fame; in his induction speech, Bruce Springsteen observes that "wherever great rock music is being made, there is the shadow of Bob Dylan"[25]

1988, May 31, *Down in the Groove*

1988, October 18, *Traveling Wilburys, Vol. 1*, as Lucky Wilbury, along with George Harrison, Jeff Lynne, Roy Orbison, and Tom Petty

1989, February, *Dylan & The Dead*, with the Grateful Dead

1989, September 22, *Oh Mercy*

1990, September 11, *Under the Red Sky*

1990, October 23, *Traveling Wilburys, Vol. 3*, as Boo Wilbury, along with George Harrison, Jeff Lynne, and Tom Petty

1990, France names Dylan a *Commandeur dans l'Ordre des Artes et des Lettres*, the country's highest cultural award

1991, February 20, honored with a Lifetime Achievement Award at the Grammys

1991, March 26, Bootleg Series Vols. 1–3: *Rare and Unreleased, 1961–1991*

1992, October 16, concert in honor of Bob Dylan's thirty-year career, featuring a wide array of performers; recordings of the event released as *Bob Dylan: The 30th Anniversary Concert Celebration* (1993)

1992, November 3, *Good As I Been to You*

1993, August, release of *Bob Dylan: The 30th Anniversary Concert Celebration*, in audio and video format

1993, October 26, *World Gone Wrong*

1994, November 15, publication of a collection of sketches with the title *Drawn Blank* (New York: Random House); an enhanced version of these drawings, along with essays by various contributors, was published later as *Bob Dylan: The Drawn Blank Series*, with contributions from Frank Zollner, Ingrid Mossinger, and Kerstin Dreschel (New York: Prestel USA; released March 30, 2008)

1994, *Bob Dylan's Greatest Hits Volume 3*

1995, Grammy Award, Best Traditional Folk Album, for *World Gone Wrong*

1995, release of *Highway 61 Interactive CD-ROM*

1995, April 25, release of video *Bob Dylan: MTV Unplugged*

1995, June 30, *MTV Unplugged*

1996, September 28, nominated for the (1997) Nobel Prize for Literature by Prof. Gordon Ball (for details, see his 2007 essay "Dylan and the Nobel"[26])

1997, May 25, hospitalized for pericarditis resulting from histoplasmosis (an infection of the heart); in words widely cited, Dylan quipped, "I really thought I'd be seeing Elvis soon"

1997, September, *Time Out of Mind*

1997, September 27, performs for Pope John Paul II at the World Eucharist Congress in Bologna, Italy; John Paul's successor (Cardinal Ratzinger, Pope Benedict XVI) would later admit his disapproval of Dylan's participation in this event in his book *John Paul II: My Beloved Predecessor*[27]

1997, October 16, receives Dorothy and Lillian Gish Prize

1997, December 7, receives Kennedy Center Award

1998, February 25, receives Grammy Award, Album of the Year, for *Time Out of Mind*; Grammy Award, Best Male Rock Vocal Performance, for "Cold Irons Bound" (*Time Out of Mind*); Grammy Award, Best Contemporary Folk Album, for *Time Out of Mind*

1998, October 13, Bootleg Series, Vol. 4: *Bob Dylan Live 1966: The "Royal Albert Hall" Concert*

2000, May 15, receives Sweden's Polar Music Prize

2001, January 21, Golden Globe Award, Best Original Song—Motion Picture, for "Things Have Changed," featured in the film *Wonder Boys* (2000)

2001, March 25, Academy Award, Best Music, Original Song, for "Things Have Changed," featured in the film *Wonder Boys* (2000)

2001, September 11, *"Love And Theft"*

2002, Grammy Award, Best Contemporary Folk Album, for *"Love And Theft"*

2002, August 3, Newport Folk Festival appearance

2002, November 26, Bootleg Series, Vol. 5: *Bob Dylan Live 1975: The Rolling Thunder Revue*

2003, January 22, premiere of *Masked and Anonymous* at the Sundance Film Festival (DVD release, February 17, 2004); written by Bob Dylan and Larry Charles under the pseudonyms Sergei Petrov and Rene Fontaine, and starring Bob Dylan as Jack Fate

2004, March 30, Bootleg Series, Vol. 6: *Bob Dylan Live 1964: Concert at Philharmonic Hall*

2004, April, appearance in a Victoria's Secret television ad; Victoria's Secret also sells a compilation album of nine songs with the title *Lovesick*

2004, June 23, receives honorary Doctorate of Music from the University of St. Andrews

2004, October, publication of the autobiographical *Chronicles*, vol. 1 (New York: Simon & Schuster)

2004, October, publication of *Lyrics: 1962–2001* (New York: Simon & Schuster), an expanded and revised version of *Lyrics: 1962–1985*

2005, *Bob Dylan: Live at the Gaslight, 1962*; originally distributed through Starbucks

2005, July 21, subject of Martin Scorsese's documentary *No Direction Home*, part of PBS's American Masters series; the DVD released September 2005

2005, August 30, Bootleg Series, Vol. 7: *No Direction Home: The Soundtrack*

2005, September, publication of *The Bob Dylan Scrapbook: An American Journey 1956–1966* (New York: Simon & Schuster); compiled by Bob Santelli in association with Bob Dylan, this book compiles various items, including handwritten lyrics, photographs, and facsimiles of programs and tickets

2005, November 15, *The Best Of Bob Dylan*

2006, May 3, launch of Bob Dylan's *Theme Time Radio Hour* on XM Satellite Radio

2006, summer, the Experience Project exhibition "Bob Dylan's American Journey, 1956–1966" on display at the Rock and Roll Hall of Fame

2006, August 29, *Modern Times*

2006, October 26, opening of the Broadway Show *The Times They Are A-Changin'*, choreographed by Twyla Tharp

2007, February 11, receives Grammy Award, Best Solo Rock Vocal Performance, for "Someday Baby" (*Modern Times*); Grammy Award, Best Contemporary Folk/Americana Album, for *Modern Times*

2007, October 2, *Dylan* (one- and three-disk versions)

2007, October 28, opening of the first of several exhibitions of Dylan's art, held in Chemnitz, Germany; the pictures have since toured various galleries around the world

2007, November 28, release of Todd Haynes's film *I'm Not There*, inspired by Bob Dylan

2007, June 12 and November 20 (deluxe ed.), *The Traveling Wilburys*; a rerelease of the earlier albums with audio and video bonus material

2008, April, wins Pulitzer Prize, "Special Citation: A Special Citation to Bob Dylan for his profound impact on popular music and American culture, marked by lyrical compositions of extraordinary poetic power"[28]

2008, October 7, Bootleg Series, Vol. 8: *Tell Tale Signs: Rare and Unreleased 1989–2006*

2009, April 28, *Together Through Life*

2009, October 13, *Christmas in the Heart*

2010, February 9, performs at the White House as part of "A Celebration of Music of the Civil Rights Movement," a concert celebrating Black History Month

2010, October 19, Bootleg Series, Vol. 9: *The Witmark Demos: 1962–1964*

2010, October 19, *Bob Dylan: The Original Mono Recordings*

Notes

Preface

1. Walter Benjamin, *One-Way Street*, in *Reflections: Essays, Aphorisms, Autobiographical Writings*, trans. Edmund Jephcott, ed. Peter Demetz (New York: Schocken, 1978), 61.
2. Ibid., 61.
3. Bob Dylan, "My Life in a Stolen Moment," in *Lyrics: 1962–1985* (New York: Alfred A. Knopf, 1985), 72.
4. Walter Benjamin, *The Arcades Project*, trans. Howard Eiland and Kevin McLaughlin (Cambridge, MA: Belknap Press of Harvard University Press, 1999).
5. Benjamin, *One-Way Street*, 61.
6. Ibid., 61.
7. Dylan, "My Life in a Stolen Moment," 72.

Introduction

1. Salman Rushdie, *The Enchantress of Florence* (Toronto: Alfred A. Knopf Canada, 2008), 43. I comment on Rushdie's insights into the power of music in Michael J. Gilmour, *Gods and Guitars: Seeking the Sacred in Post-1960s Popular Music* (Waco, TX: Baylor University Press, 2009), 6–8, 37–41. Rushdie occasionally alludes to Bob Dylan in his fictional writings. For instance, there is a character named Sara (the same spelling as Dylan's first wife's name) in his novel *Fury*, described as a "Sly-eyed lady of the Fenlands," a phrase obviously alluding to the song "Sad-Eyed Lady of the Lowlands" (*Blonde On Blonde*, 1966). In the same novel, someone mentions a "Woman name of Hatty, Carole Hatty," a playful echo of Dylan's "The Lonesome Death of Hattie Carroll" (*The Times They Are A-Changin'*, 1964). See Salman Rushdie, *Fury* (Toronto: Vintage, 2001), 31, 121.
2. Lyrics posted at the band's official Web site (www.thehip.com).
3. Lyrics taken from the album liner notes.
4. Bob Dylan, *Lyrics: 1962–2001* (New York: Simon & Schuster, 2004), 510–12 (hereafter referred to as *Lyrics*). I take most lyrics from this source. For

lyrics and poems not in this volume, including songs on *Modern Times* (2006), *Tell Tale Signs: Rare and Unreleased 1989–2006*, Vol. 8 of the Bootleg Series (2008), and *Together through Life* (2009), I use either Dylan's *Lyrics: 1962–1985* (New York: Alfred A. Knopf, 1985), http://www.bobdylan.com, or my own transcriptions. I clarify the source used in endnotes.

5. T. S. Eliot, "The Love Song of J. Alfred Prufrock," in Stephen Greenblatt, M. H. Abrams, et al., eds., *The Norton Anthology of English Literature*, vol. 2, *The Romantic Period through the Twentieth Century*, 8th ed. (New York: Norton, 2006), 2289-92.

6. "Slow Train," *Slow Train Coming*, 1979; *Lyrics*, 406–07.

7. The term "train" is actually a common one in Bob Dylan's songs, carrying both literal and figurative levels of meaning. See, e.g., Bryan Cheyette, "On the 'D' Train: Bob Dylan's Conversions," in *Do You Mr Jones? Bob Dylan with the Poets and Professors*, ed. Neil Corcoran (London: Pimlico, 2003), 221–52.

8. Woody Guthrie, *Bound for Glory* (New York: Plume, 1983; first published 1943), 36.

9. Dylan used white face paint during these concerts.

10. Sam Shepard, *The Rolling Thunder Logbook* (Cambridge, MA: Da Capo Press, 2004 [original publication, 1977]), 79.

11. Stephen Scobie, *Alias Bob Dylan Revisited* (Calgary: Red Deer Press, 2003) and *And Forget My Name: A Speculative Biography of Bob Dylan* (Victoria, BC: Ekstasis, 1999); Paul Williams, e.g., *Bob Dylan, Performing Artist: The Early Years, 1960–1973* (London: Omnibus Press, 2004); *Bob Dylan Performing Artist 1974–1986: The Middle Years* (London: Omnibus Press, 1994); *Bob Dylan, Performing Artist,* Vol. 3, *Mind Out of Time, 1986 and Beyond* (London: Omnibus Press, 2004).

12. The challenges facing literary critics with their emphasis on the texts of Dylan's songs are a recurring subject in the essays in Corcoran, *Do You Mr Jones?* See, e.g., the editorial remarks, 10–14.

13. Louis P. Masur, " 'Famous Long Ago': Bob Dylan Revisited," *American Quarterly* 59, no.1 (2007): 168.

14. Ibid., 177.

15. Simon Frith, *Music for Pleasure: Essays in the Sociology of Pop* (Cambridge: Polity, 1988), 107.

16. Robin Sylvan, *Traces of the Spirit: The Religious Dimensions of Popular Music* (New York: New York University Press, 2002), 114.

17. Jeremy S. Begbie, *Resounding Truth: Christian Wisdom in the World of Music* (Grand Rapids: Baker, 2007), 24. The term "content analysis" is Frith's, as in *Music for Pleasure*, 106.

18. Gordon Ball, "Dylan and the Nobel," *Oral Tradition* 22, no. 1 (2007): 25; see too 15–18.

19. Ezra Pound, *Literary Essays of Ezra Pound*, ed. and intro. T. S. Eliot (New York: New Directions, 1954), 91; cited in Ball, "Dylan and the Nobel," 16.

20. Ball, "Dylan and the Nobel," 18.

21. Ibid., 18–20.

22. See Bob Dylan, *Tarantula* (New York: St. Martin's Press, 1994; first published 1971).

23. Referring here to the 1985 edition, *Lyrics 1962–1985*. See 32–36, 78–85, and 106–16.

24. For a recent publication resembling early editions of *Lyrics* in this respect, see, e.g., Alicia Keys's *Tears for Water: Songbook of Poems and Lyrics* (New York: Penguin, 2004). This seems like a suitable example to choose since Dylan mentions Keys in "Thunder on the Mountain," *Modern Times* (2006).

25. See "Legionnaire's Disease," in Dylan, *Lyrics*, 396; Clinton Heylin, *Bob Dylan: Behind the Shades, Take Two* (London: Penguin, 2001), 738.

26. "Long Ago, Far Away" (Dylan, *Lyrics*, 23–24; see too Heylin, *Behind the Shades*, 738–39); "Long Time Gone" (Dylan, *Lyrics*, 28–29; Heylin, ibid.).

27. See *Lyrics*, 434. Dylan first performed this song in San Francisco on November 10, 1980 (Heylin, *Behind the Shades*, 733). Of course, we know of other songs still, either recorded or performed, that do not appear in *Lyrics* (see Heylin, *Behind the Shades*, 730–47 for examples of copyrighted songs falling into this category, and 748–50 for noncopyrighted songs, many of which "have been recorded in some form"). One interesting example of a song not available in an officially released form or in *Lyrics*, one rich in religious content, is "Ain't Gonna Go to Hell for Anybody," which Dylan performed in Toronto on April 17, 1980. An unofficial recording of this concert circulates widely, as does a grainy video of the concert.

Chapter 1: The *Flâneur* Plays Guitar

1. Ken Regan took the photograph, which appears in Sam Shepard's *The Rolling Thunder Logbook* (Cambridge, MA: Da Capo Press, 2004 [original publication, 1977]), 95. I take the first epigraph for this chapter from p. 71.

2. See, e.g., Larry "Ratso" Sloman's liner notes to *Bob Dylan Live 1975: The Rolling Thunder Revue*, Bootleg Series, Vol. 5 (2002), 48. This colored photograph shows Dylan in dark sunglasses and Ginsberg pointing to lines in Kerouac's 1959 poem *Mexico City Blues* (for the detail about which book this is, see Sloman's notes, 32). Shepard's *Logbook* also includes a picture of the two poets at the grave, with Dylan strumming a guitar (92). Dylan stands alone graveside in another (90). The pictures in *Logbook* are black and white.

3. For discussion about this incident, both the context of the remark and subsequent reactions, see Steve Turner, *The Gospel according to the Beatles* (Louisville, KY: Westminster John Knox Press, 2006), chap. 2. Turner cites Lennon's phrase on p. 22.

4. Whether he is one of the twelve disciples or another devoted follower is not clear, but he was definitely present during Jesus' ministry as John relates it. Some argue that the beloved disciple is a literary construct, but this does not

detract from the point I make here. I am concerned with the story John tells, not the historical veracity of the account.

5. This implies Mary was by this time a widow. Responsibility for her well-being fell to her eldest son, Jesus, who, knowing his own death was imminent, left her to the care of this close friend.

6. Albert Schweitzer, *The Quest of the Historical Jesus*, trans. W. Montgomery, J. R. Coates, Susan Cupitt, and John Bowden (Minneapolis: Fortress Press, 2001; original German publication, 1906), 5.

7. Ibid., 6.

8. Ibid. Italics added.

9. Woody Guthrie, *Bound for Glory* (New York: Plume, 1983; first published 1943), 100.

10. James S. Spiegel, "With God (and Socrates and Augustine) on Our Side," in *Bob Dylan and Philosophy: It's Alright, Ma (I'm Only Thinking)*, Popular Culture and Philosophy 17, ed. Peter Vernezze and Carl J. Porter (Chicago: Open Court, 2006), 134.

11. Robert Santelli, *The Bob Dylan Scrapbook: 1956–1966* (New York: Simon & Schuster, 2005), 60.

12. Kelton Cobb, *The Blackwell Guide to Theology and Popular Culture*, Blackwell Guides to Theology (Malden, MA: Blackwell, 2005), 292.

13. See esp. Paul Tillich, *What Is Religion?* trans. William Baillie Green, ed. James Luther Adams (New York: Harper & Row, 1969).

14. Cobb, *Theology and Popular Culture*, 127–28.

15. Ibid., 128.

16. The term obviously indicates musicians who write and perform their own songs. In defining this label, Roy Shuker adds, "An emphasis on lyrics has resulted in the work of such performers often being referred to as song poems, accorded auteur status, and made the subject of intensive lyrics analysis" (*Popular Music: The Key Concepts*, 2d ed. [London: Routledge, 2005], 248). I have this literary sense in mind as I use the term throughout.

17. Shepard finds it ironic that Bob Dylan, who spends much of his time hiding from people and seeking privacy, at the same time hires people to follow him with cameras and document his every move during the Rolling Thunder Revue (*Logbook*, 47). Shepard also describes occasions when Dylan makes efforts to escape the cameras and publicity (48; 171 [he is an "escape artist"]; 176).

18. Shepard, *Logbook*, 98, 63. Note also Dylan's song "I Feel a Change Comin' On" (*Together Through Life*, 2009) in which the narrator is said to have the blood of the land in his voice.

19. Shepard, *Logbook*, 71, 79 (emphasis added).

20. Bob Dylan, *Chronicles*, vol. 1 (New York: Simon & Schuster, 2004), 8.

21. Michael Gray, *The Bob Dylan Encyclopedia* (New York: Continuum, 2006), 137. Gray credits this observation to Paul Baragona, a contributor to his Web site.

22. For a list see, e.g., Daniel Maoz, "Shekhinah as Woman: Kabbalistic

References in Dylan's *Infidels*," in *Call Me the Seeker: Listening to Religion in Popular Music*, ed. Michael J. Gilmour (New York: Continuum, 2005), 8.

23. Louis P. Masur, " 'Famous Long Ago': Bob Dylan Revisited," *American Quarterly* 59, no. 1 (2007): 171.

24. Anthony DeCurtis, "6 Characters in Search of an Artist," *The Chronicle Review*, Section B of *The Chronicle of Higher Education* 54, no. 13 (2007): 14–15. Dylan makes an interesting comment in *Chronicles* that anticipates (or inspires) one creative element of the film: "I wondered if Denzel [Washington] could play Woody Guthrie. In my dimension of reality, he certainly could have" (187). In *I'm Not There*, a black child actor (Marcus Carl Franklin) plays the character Woody.

25. See the lyrics to "It Ain't Me, Babe," *Another Side of Bob Dylan* (1964), and "Trust Yourself," *Empire Burlesque* (1985), in Bob Dylan, *Lyrics: 1962–2001* (New York: Simon & Schuster, 2004), 131, 497. See also Dylan, *Chronicles*, 78–79 (name change and pseudonyms), and 7–8 (fabricated stories of origin).

26. Mikal Gilmore, taken from Jonathan Cott, ed., *Bob Dylan: The Essential Interviews* (New York: Wenner Books, 2006), xiii.

27. Dylan, *Chronicles*, 4–6, 277–81.

28. This is the emphasis found in the artistic *Logbook* and to some extent *Renaldo and Clara*. In fact, the tour included stops in several major centers, including Boston, Hartford, and New York City.

29. Shepard, *Logbook*, 6, 15 (italics added). The phrase "on the road" recalls Jack Kerouac's novel of that name.

30. Wayne Robins, *A Brief History of Rock, Off the Record* (New York: Routledge, 2008), 45.

31. Shepard, *Logbook*, 170.

32. Ibid., 152.

33. For an account of Dylan's first encounter with Guthrie's *Bound for Glory* and its contributions to the musician's songwriting, see, e.g., Howard Sounes, *Down the Highway: The Life of Bob Dylan* (New York: Grove Press, 2001), 63–65.

34. Guthrie, *Bound for Glory*, 191.

35. Ibid., 242.

36. Compare comments on Edgar Allan Poe's "Man of the Crowd" in chapter 6.

37. Guthrie, *Bound for Glory*, 243.

38. Ibid., 244.

39. Shepard, *Logbook*, v.

40. Ibid., 87–97. At times, U2's film *Rattle and Hum* reminds me of the Rolling Thunder Revue and *Renaldo and Clara*. Dylan's tribute at Kerouac's grave parallels U2's visit to Elvis's Graceland burial site. Both tours/movies involve a musical journey through various symbolic American places, and U2 performs Dylan's "All Along the Watchtower." On the CD *Rattle and Hum*, Dylan sings

with Bono on "Love Rescue Me," which they cowrote, and plays organ on "Hawkmoon 269."

41. See, e.g., *Chronicles*, 48, 114, 174, 235.

42. Shepard, *Logbook*, 8, 26, 64–70 (strangers); 60, 70 (out-of-the-way places); 6, 8 (a random encounter between Shepard and a stranger); 22, 130 (Dylan's camper).

43. Bryan Cheyette, "On the 'D' Train: Bob Dylan's Conversions," in *Do You Mr Jones? Bob Dylan with the Poets and Professors*, ed. Neil Corcoran (London: Pimlico, 2003), 237.

44. Walter Benjamin, "Some Motifs in Baudelaire," in *Illuminations: Essays and Reflections*, trans. Harry Zohn, ed. Hannah Arendt (New York: Schocken Books, 1968), 172–73.

45. A striking example of the latter is the fact that Dylan managed to keep his second marriage a secret for several years. See Sounes, *Down the Highway*, xii, 371–72.

46. "Is Your Love in Vain?" *Street Legal* (1978); Dylan, *Lyrics*, 389.

47. Hannah Arendt, "Walter Benjamin: 1892–1940," editorial introduction to Benjamin, *Illuminations*, 12 (italics added).

48. S. Brent Plate, *Walter Benjamin, Religion, and Aesthetics: Rethinking Religion through the Arts* (New York: Routledge, 2005), 131 (italics added).

49. Dylan, *Chronicles*, 203, 209.

50. Ibid., 61 (first two citations), 69.

51. About which see Emmanuel Désveaux's "Amerindian Roots of Bob Dylan's Poetry," trans. Valerie Burling, *Oral Tradition* 22, no. 1 (2007): 134–50.

52. See the 2004 preface (Shepard, *Logbook,* v).

53. See Charters's introduction to Jack Kerouac's *On the Road* (London: Penguin, 1991), xxi; see also Kerouac's definition of "Beat" cited on viii.

54. Shepard, *Logbook*, 71.

55. Walter Benjamin, *The Arcades Project*, trans. Howard Eiland and Kevin McLaughlin (Cambridge, MA: Belknap Press of Harvard University Press, 1999), M1,5; also M1a,2; M1,3; M2,4; M3a,5; M17a,4–5.

56. Ibid., O12a,2; H1a,2.

57. Howard Eiland, "Reception in Distraction," in *Walter Benjamin and Art*, ed. Andrew Benjamin (London: Continuum, 2005), 6. Later in the same article, still speaking of the *flâneur*, gambler, and collector, Eiland adds, "All three are at home, relatively speaking, in the world's scatter. They are touched and inspired by it. They spend themselves and expand themselves in being dispersed to the current of objects. And their reception in distraction, like that of the movie audience, is not merely visual but tactile, or visceral; it involves their whole sensorium, as illuminated by memory" (11).

58. Plate, *Walter Benjamin*, 131.

59. Benjamin, *Arcades Project*, H2,7; H1a,2.

60. Kerouac, *On the Road,* 256, 259. The Mexican odyssey provides them

with a symbolically poignant place of unencumbered freedom, where the police lack "swagger" (249) and leave visitors to their own devices (250, 261, 265). This contrasts with American authority figures (e.g., "the mean cop" who harasses Dean [122–23]).

61. Dylan, *Chronicles*, 61–62, 69–71.

62. Ibid., 174–76.

63. Ibid., 7.

64. Dylan, "My Life in a Stolen Moment," in *Lyrics 1962–1985* (New York: Alfred A. Knopf, 1985), 71. See the whole poem, 70–72 for examples.

Chapter 2: The Gospel according to Bob Dylan: Are You Serious?

1. See "Shelter from the Storm" (*Blood on the Tracks*, 1975; Bob Dylan, *Lyrics: 1962–2001* [New York: Simon & Schuster, 2004], 345–46), and "When the Deal Goes Down" (*Modern Times*, 2006; http://www.bobdylan.com).

2. R. Clifton Spargo and Anne K. Ream, "Bob Dylan and Religion," in *The Cambridge Companion to Bob Dylan*, Cambridge Companions to American Studies, ed. Kevin J. H. Dettmar (Cambridge: Cambridge University Press, 2009), 93.

3. For examples of Dylan-Christ betrayal and temptation parallels, see Michael Gray, *Song and Dance Man III: The Art of Bob Dylan* (London: Continuum, 2000), 210–11, 217, 220, 224.

4. The first citation about Dylan's Christlike appearance is from Gray, *Song and Dance*, 502, and the second from Michael Gray, *The Bob Dylan Encyclopedia* (New York: Continuum, 2006), 296.

5. Mark Allan Powell, *Encyclopedia of Contemporary Christian Music* (Peabody, MA: Hendrickson, 2002), 286.

6. Comment made during an interview in *Bob Dylan World Tours 1966–1974: Through the Camera of Barry Feinstein*, directed by Joel Gilbert (Highway 61 Entertainment, 2004). Author's transcription.

7. T-Bone Burnett, foreword to Sam Shepard's *The Rolling Thunder Logbook* (Cambridge, MA: Da Capo Press, 2004 [original publication, 1977]), ix.

8. Taken from Tom Russell and Sylvia Tyson, *And Then I Wrote: The Songwriter Speaks* (Vancouver: Arsenal Pulp Press, 1995), 70.

9. Colin Larkin, compiler and ed., *The Encyclopedia of Popular Music*, 5th concise ed. (London: Omnibus Press, 2007), 471.

10. Louis P. Masur, " 'Famous Long Ago': Bob Dylan Revisited," *American Quarterly* 59, no. 1 (2007): 167.

11. Bruce Springsteen, induction speech delivered for the Rock and Roll Hall of Fame in New York City, January 20, 1988, taken from Elizabeth Thomson and David Gutman, eds., *The Dylan Companion*, updated and expanded ed. (Cambridge, MA: Da Capo Press, 2001), 287.

12. Neil Young, in Jimmy McDonough, *Shakey: Neil Young's Biography* (New York: Random House, 2002), 143. Italics original.

13. Taken from Sean Michaels, "Arcade Fire: Inside the Church of Arcade Fire," *Paste Magazine* 30 (Published online, April 11, 2007; http//www.pastemagazine.com).

14. Woody Guthrie, *Bound for Glory* (New York: Plume, 1983; first published 1943), 178.

15. Eric Clapton comments on this phenomenon in his book *Clapton: The Autobiography* (New York: Broadway Books, 2007), 64.

16. Taken from John Barlow's afterword in *The Complete Annotated Grateful Dead Lyrics*, ed. Alan Trist and David Dodd (New York: Free Press, 2005), 419.

17. Taken from Howard Sounes, *Down the Highway: The Life of Bob Dylan* (New York: Grove Press, 2001), 184. Johnston produced some of Dylan's albums during the 1960s and 1970s.

18. Shepard, *Logbook*, 115.

19. Feinstein makes this comment in the documentary *Bob Dylan World Tours 1966–1974*. Author's transcription.

20. You can hear the (in)famous moment when an audience member shouted "Judas" at Dylan during a 1966 performance on *Bob Dylan Live 1966: "The Royal Albert Hall" Concert*, Bootleg Series, Vol. 4 (1998). Video footage of this incident appears in the Martin Scorsese documentary *No Direction Home: Bob Dylan* (2005). See too Mickey Jones's home videos of that tour for reflections on the incident (*1966 World Tour [The Home Movies]: Through the Camera of Bob Dylan's Drummer Mickey Jones,* directed by Joel Gilbert; Highway 61 Entertainment, 2006). Numerous commentaries remark on the significance of this episode in music history. See, e.g., Greil Marcus, *Like a Rolling Stone: Bob Dylan at the Crossroads* (New York: Public Affairs, 2005), 182–84.

21. Dylan, *Lyrics*, 29. Dylan recorded this song in 1963, but there is no official release.

22. Powell, *Encyclopedia*, 277.

23. My transcription. The program originally aired December 5, 2004. During one of the gospel concerts, Dylan said, "That's right, they want the old stuff, but ah, the old stuff's not gonna save you, and um, *I'm not gonna save you*, neither is anybody else that follows gonna save you. They can boogie all night; it's not gonna work" (taken from the documentary *Bob Dylan 1975–1981: Rolling Thunder and the Gospel Years* [Highway 61 Entertainment, 2006]; my transcription).

24. Posted at http://www.bobdylan.com. The interview is largely a discussion of *Together through Life* (2009) (accessed August 12, 2010).

25. Radio interview with Studs Terkel of WFMT, Chicago (May 1963), taken from Jonathan Cott, ed., *Bob Dylan: The Essential Interviews* (New York: Wenner Books, 2006), 12.

26. Guthrie, *Bound for Glory*, 182.

27. Ibid., 188–89.

28. Bobbie Ann Mason, *Elvis Presley* (New York: Penguin, 2003), 158.

29. Dylan, *Lyrics*, 512.

30. For his remarks on the "potentially lethal nature of the rock star's audience," see Stephen Scobie, *Alias Bob Dylan Revisited* (Calgary: Red Deer Press, 2003), 275–80; the citation is from 279. Scobie also points out that Shepard explores this idea of a lethal audience in his *Rolling Thunder Logbook* (see, e.g., 113, 115).

31. Shepard, *Logbook*, 61.

32. Bob Dylan, *Chronicles,* vol. 1 (New York: Simon & Schuster, 2004), 115–16.

33. Ibid., 9, 22.

34. Taken from Cott, *Essential Interviews*, ix.

35. Joseph Ratzinger, Benedict XVI, *John Paul II: My Beloved Predecessor*, ed. Elio Guerriero, trans. Matthew Sherry and the Vatican (Boston: Pauline Books & Media, 2007), 20.

36. In his foreword to Ratzinger's book, John L. Allen Jr. highlights the differences between John Paul II and Benedict XVI. If their lives had taken different directions, Karol Wojtyla would likely have been an actor, and Joseph Ratzinger, a university professor. "By the standards of pop culture, John Paul was also 'hip'," he adds, "an adjective few would dare apply to Benedict XVI" (x). When Allen refers to Cardinal Ratzinger's concerns about having Dylan on stage, he points out that "John Paul had no such reservations, even quoting Dylan that night to roars from his young audience. Another rock star, Bono of the Irish band U2, once allowed John Paul to playfully don his trademark sunglasses, upon which Bono pronounced him 'history's first funky pontiff.' It seems deeply improbable that anyone will nominate Benedict XVI as the second" (xi).

37. Taken from Andrew Muir, *Razor's Edge: Bob Dylan and the Never Ending Tour* (London: Helter Skelter, 2001), 157. See 156–58 for description of and reflections on the event.

38. Taken from *Bono in Conversation with Michka Assayas* (New York: Penguin, 2005), 308.

39. Dwyer makes this remark during an interview included in the documentary *Bob Dylan 1975–1981*. Author's transcription.

40. Both excerpts taken from *Bob Dylan 1975–1981*. Author's transcription.

41. Clinton Heylin, *Bob Dylan: Behind the Shades, Take Two* (London: Penguin, 2001), 512–13. Heylin also cites backup singer Helena Springs in this context, who recalls a lot of people "pressuring him about a lot of things" (513). Reporter Joel Selvin also tells this story about Wasserman, in an interview included in the documentary *Bob Dylan 1975–1981*.

42. Deena Weinstein, "Progressive Rock as Text: The Lyrics of Roger Waters," in *Progressive Rock Reconsidered*, ed. Kevin Holm-Hudson (New York: Routledge, 2002), 98.

43. Ibid.

44. Umberto Eco, "On Symbolism," in *On Literature*, trans. Martin McLaughlin (Orlando: Harcourt, 2004), 157.

45. Ibid., 159 and 160.

46. Greil Marcus, liner notes to Bob Dylan and The Band, *The Basement Tapes* (1975), 6–7.

47. Stanley Fish, *Is There a Text in This Class? The Authority of Interpretive Communities* (Cambridge, MA: Harvard University Press, 1980), vii.

48. Ibid., 21.

49. Ibid., 32.

50. Ibid., 28 (italics in original).

51. Ibid., 13, 163.

52. Ibid., 3, 21, 172–73.

53. In fact, Osbourne denies having any interest in the occult (see, e.g., Pete Ward, "The Eucharist and the Turn to Culture," in *Between Sacred and Profane: Researching Religion and Popular Culture*, ed. Gordon Lynch [London: I.B. Tauris, 2007], 91).

54. Alice Cooper, with Keith and Kent Zimmerman, *Alice Cooper, Golf Monster: A Rock 'N' Roller's 12 Steps to Becoming a Golf Addict* (New York: Crown Publishers, 2007), esp. 231–33. Incidentally, Alice Cooper includes among "three compliments in [his] life [he] will always cherish" a remark by Bob Dylan made in a *Rolling Stone* interview: "I think Alice Cooper is an overlooked songwriter" (73; see also 93). The other compliments come from Groucho Marx, who said that Alice Cooper was the last hope for vaudeville, and Tiger Woods, who said he would not give Alice "two a side."

55. Comments made in Martin Scorsese's *No Direction Home: Bob Dylan*, 2005. Author's transcription.

56. Stephen H. Webb comments on the tendency to speculate about Dylan's beliefs in *Dylan Redeemed: From* Highway 61 *to* Saved (New York: Continuum, 2006), 155–61.

57. Dylan made this statement during a 1997 interview with *Newsweek*. I take this excerpt from Kevin J. H. Dettmar's introduction to *The Cambridge Companion to Bob Dylan*, ed. Kevin J. H. Dettmar, Cambridge Companions to American Studies (Cambridge: Cambridge University Press, 2009), 8, though it is widely cited. See also, e.g., Larry "Ratso" Sloman's liner notes to *Tell Tale Signs*, 22.

58. Dylan, *Chronicles*, 81.

59. Guthrie, *Bound for Glory*, 299.

60. Toronto, April 17, 1980. Author's transcription.

61. See, e.g., Seth Rogovoy, *Bob Dylan: Prophet, Mystic, Poet* (New York: Scribner, 2009), 254–56.

62. Don E. Saliers, *Music and Theology*, Horizons in Theology (Nashville: Abingdon Press, 2007), ix.

63. Ibid., 60, 61. On the collapse of the distinction of high and low art, see, e.g., Derek B. Scott, "Postmodernism and Music," in *The Routledge Companion to Postmodernism*, ed. Stuart Sim (London: Routledge, 1998), 123–24.

64. Webb, *Dylan Redeemed*, 11.

65. Spargo and Ream, "Bob Dylan and Religion," 98.

66. Note also remarks by François Gauthier: "Opposing the social studies secularization theory and other modern views holding religion to be doomed to history's burial ground, the idea that religion and the religious experience do not end with the dwindling of traditional forms of instituted religion is becoming widespread." Indeed, "far from dying out, religion can be found thriving in contemporary quests for meaning and ritual, although in a more *instituant* and fragmented manner (and thus shunning dogmas, credos and institutions)" ("Rapturous Ruptures: The 'Instituant' Religious Experience of Rave," in *Race, Culture, and Religion*, ed. Graham St. John, Routledge Advances in Sociology 8 [London: Routledge, 2004], 66, 80). On the term "instituant," as distinct from "instituted," see esp. 66–67.

67. Robin Sylvan, *Traces of the Spirit: The Religious Dimensions of Popular Music* (New York: New York University Press, 2002), 78.

68. Cobb, *Theology and Popular Culture*, 291–92.

69. See also Simon Frith, *Music for Pleasure: Essays in the Sociology of Pop* (Cambridge: Polity, 1988), 164–65.

70. Bruce David Forbes, "Finding Religion in Unexpected Places," editorial introduction to *Religion and Popular Culture in America*, ed. Bruce David Forbes and Jeffrey H. Mahan (Berkeley: University of California Press, 2000), 10. He defines these categories in pp. 10–17. The essays in the book illustrate each of these phenomena.

71. Ibid., 10.

72. Ibid., 12.

73. Ibid., 14.

74. Sylvan, *Traces of the Spirit*, 215.

75. Gregory L. Reece, *Elvis Religion: The Cult of the King* (London: I. B. Tauris, 2006), 19.

76. Susan Fast, *In the Houses of the Holy: Led Zeppelin and the Power of Rock Music* (New York: Oxford University Press, 2001), 60; also 35–36.

77. Forbes, "Finding Religion," 15–16.

78. Forbes and Mahan, *Religion and Popular Culture*, 242.

79. See, e.g., Bert Cartwright, *The Bible in the Lyrics of Bob Dylan*, rev. and updated, Wanted Man Study Series 4 (Bury, Lancashire: Wanted Man, 1992); and Michael J. Gilmour, *Tangled Up in the Bible: Bob Dylan and Scripture* (New York: Continuum, 2004).

80. See Scott M. Marshall, with Marcia Ford, *Restless Pilgrim: The Spiritual Journey of Bob Dylan* (Lake Mary, FL: Relevant Books, 2002); Steve Stockman, *The Rock Cries Out: Discovering Eternal Truth in Unlikely Music* (Lake Mary, FL: Relevant Books, 2004). For gospel musicians covering Dylan's songs, see, e.g., *Gotta Serve Somebody: The Gospel Songs of Bob Dylan* (2003), which includes covers by a variety of artists and a Bob Dylan–Mavis Staples duet of "Gonna Change My Way of Thinking."

81. Dylan, *Chronicles*, 191.

82. See note 57.

83. See, e.g., Heylin, *Behind the Shades*, 548.

84. Taken from Bill Flanagan, *U2 at the End of the World* (New York: Delta, 1995), 163.

85. Taken from Cott, *Essential Interviews*, 396. Jon Pareles interviewed Dylan on September 28, 1997, following the release of *Time Out of Mind*.

86. Dylan, *Chronicles*, 18, 236.

87. See, e.g., David Yaffe, "Bob Dylan and the Anglo-American Tradition," in *The Cambridge Companion to Bob Dylan*, ed. Kevin J. H. Dettmar, Cambridge Companions to American Studies (Cambridge: Cambridge University Press, 2009), 15–27; Gray, *Song and Dance Man III*, throughout, but especially chaps. 1 and 15; Sean Wilentz, "American Recordings: On *'Love and Theft'* and the Minstrel Boy," in *Do You Mr Jones? Bob Dylan with the Poets and Professors*, ed. Neil Corcoran (London: Pimlico, 2003), 295–305; and Greil Marcus, *The Old, Weird America: The World of Bob Dylan's Basement Tapes* (New York: Picador USA, 1997). Dylan refers to the latter book under its original title (*The Invisible Republic*) in *Chronicles*, 34–35.

88. Taken from Cott, *Essential Interviews*, 431. Robert Hilburn interviewed Dylan for *The Los Angeles Times*, April 4, 2004.

89. Comments made in an interview with Jon Pareles, taken from Cott, *Essential Interviews*, 396.

90. This album is the soundtrack to Lanois's film *Here Is What Is* (2008). I explore connections between music and notions of space in "Going Back to the Prairies: Neil Young's Heterotopia in the Post-9/11 World," in *West of Eden: New Approaches in Canadian Prairie Literature*, ed. Sue Sorensen (Winnipeg: Canadian Mennonite University Press, 2008), 205–18. I take some cues for that chapter from David B. Knight's *Landscapes in Music: Space, Place, and Time in the World's Great Music* (Lanham, MD: Rowman & Littlefield, 2006).

91. Bono, introduction to *Selections from the Book of Psalms*, Pocket Canon (New York: Grove Press, 1999), x–xi (ellipses original).

92. Taken from Cott, *Essential Interviews*, 432.

Chapter 3: Not a Prophet or Savior . . . Elvis Maybe: Bob Dylan's Devoted Disciples

1. See, e.g., http://www.cbc.ca/canada/manitoba/story/2008/11/10/dylan-young.html (accessed August 13, 2010). Dylan mentions listening to Neil Young in "Highlands" (*Time Out of Mind*, 1997).

2. Taken from Jonathan Demme's film *Neil Young: Heart of Gold* (Paramount Classics, 2006). My transcription. Young makes the first comments cited just before his performance of "It's a Dream" (also from the album *Prairie Wind*, 2005).

3. William Echard, *Neil Young and the Poetics of Energy* (Bloomington: Indiana University Press, 2005), 79; also 51–52. Echard draws on Paul Thé-

berge's *Any Sound You Can Imagine: Making Music/Consuming Technology* (Hanover, NH: Wesleyan University Press, 1997), 120.

4. We see another illustration of this sense of sacred musical space in U2's performances at the old Ed Sullivan Theater as part of *The Late Show with David Letterman* in March 2009. They acknowledged the significance of performing on the very stage where the Beatles sang years earlier, and on the last night of the five-day run, part of their launch for *No Line on the Horizon*, Bono closed "Get On Your Boots" with the Beatles' famous lyric "She loves you, yeah, yeah, yeah."

5. Bob Dylan, *Chronicles,* vol. 1 (New York: Simon & Schuster, 2004), 4–5.

6. Ibid., 5.

7. Ibid., 282.

8. Ibid., 285.

9. See Bob Dylan, *Lyrics: 1962–2001* (New York: Simon & Schuster, 2004), 579, 591.

10. Dylan, *Chronicles*, 285.

11. Dylan visited Woody Guthrie in the Greystone Park Hospital (Morris Plains, New Jersey). Prior to Greystone, Guthrie also stayed briefly at the Brooklyn State Hospital. We find God in church and Woody Guthrie in the Brooklyn State Hospital, according to Bob Dylan's poem "Last Thoughts on Woody Guthrie" (*Lyrics 1962–1985* [New York: Alfred A. Knopf, 1985], 36). This poem does not appear in the more recent *Lyrics 1962–2001*.

12. Comments made in Martin Scorsese's *No Direction Home: Bob Dylan*, 2005. My transcription.

13. Bob Dylan, "Last Thoughts on Woody Guthrie," in *Lyrics 1962–1985*, 32–36. There is a recording of Dylan reading "Last Thoughts on Woody Guthrie" on the Bootleg Series, Vols. 1–3.

14. Stephen Davis provides another interesting example of Dylan's high opinion of a contemporary artist. In the mid-1960s, he reports, "Dylan was said to be obsessed with charismatic Brian Jones [of the Rolling Stones] and wanted to meet him on Dylan's upcoming English tour in May" (*Old Gods Almost Dead: The 40-Year Odyssey of the Rolling Stones* [New York: Broadway Books, 2001], 119–20). Despite his fascination with Jones, Dylan (with Bob Neuwirth) was apparently not beyond exploiting the musician's paranoia for comedic effect. After suggesting the Stones would eventually fire Jones, "Brian cracked like an egg" and "broke into drunken tears." " 'Aw, come on, Brian,' Dylan finally drawled. 'You can always join *my* band' " (146).

15. Ellis Cashmore, *Celebrity/Culture* (New York: Routledge, 2006), 78.

16. Ibid.

17. For comments on the tendency to treat celebrities in quasi-religious ways, see too Robin Sylvan, *Traces of the Spirit: The Religious Dimensions of Popular Music* (New York: New York University Press, 2002), 72–73.

18. See, e.g., Ted Harrison, *Elvis People: The Cult of the King* (London: Fount, 1992); John Strausbaugh, *E: Reflections of the Birth of the Elvis Faith*

(New York: Blast Books, 1995); Erika Doss, *Elvis Culture: Fans, Faith, and Image* (Lawrence, KS: University Press of Kansas, 1999).

19. Gregory L. Reece, *Elvis Religion: The Cult of the King* (London: I.B. Tauris, 2006), 21.

20. M. H. Abrams, with Geoffrey Galt Harpham, *A Glossary of Literary Terms*, 8th ed. (Boston: Thomson Wadsworth, 2005), 27.

21. Linda Hutcheon, *A Theory of Parody: The Teachings of Twentieth-Century Art Forms* (Urbana, IL: University of Illinois Press, 2000), 20.

22. Ibid., 115.

23. Similarly, in the film *Eat the Document* (1971), which records Dylan's 1966 tour of Britain, the camera lingers on a sidewalk prophet wearing a sandwich board with the words "IT IS APPOINTED UNTO MEN ONCE TO DIE" on the front and "AFTER DEATH THE JUDGMENT" on the back (cf. Heb. 9:27). He is standing near Dylan while the singer watches a parade with a bagpipe band.

24. According to Clinton Heylin, Dylan recorded the song between October and November 28, 1975 (*Bob Dylan: The Recording Sessions 1960–1994* [New York: St. Martin's Griffin, 1995], 117); see too Clinton Heylin, *Bob Dylan: Behind the Shades, Take Two* (London: Penguin, 2001), 746, which narrows the recording date to October 1975). The film version is the only release of the song. Dylan performed it during the Rolling Thunder Revue tour (Mark Allan Powell, *Encyclopedia of Contemporary Christian Music* [Peabody, MA: Hendrickson, 2002], 279). *Lyrics* does not include the song.

25. Dylan, *Lyrics*, 406.

26. Dylan, *Chronicles*, 216.

27. Christopher Butler, "Dylan and the Academics," in *Do You, Mr Jones? Bob Dylan with the Poets and Professors*, ed. Neil Corcoran (London: Pimlico, 2003), 63–64. See too Michael Roos and Don O'Meara, "Is Your Love in Vain—Dialectical Dilemmas in Bob Dylan's Recent Love-Songs," in *The Dylan Companion*, ed. Elizabeth Thomson and David Gutman (Cambridge, MA: Da Capo Press, 2001), 47 (cited by Butler).

28. Dylan, *Lyrics*, 149.

29. Ibid., 345–46.

30. Ibid., 509.

31. Taken from Jonathan Cott, ed., *Bob Dylan: The Essential Interviews* (New York: Wenner Books, 2006), 75. Italics original.

32. Do these words lie behind the title of Dylan's Bootleg Series album *Tell Tale Signs* (2008)?

33. Note that Matt. 24:3–8, cited earlier, warns against following other messiahs. If the preacher and scenes of destruction at the beginning of the film indeed allude to this passage, Jack Fate would then be one of the failed Christs referred to in the Gospel passage.

34. Note also the Shakespearean allusion in the name Prospero, mentioned above.

35. For analysis of the film, see Lucas Stensland's "Scatter Shots: Reading *Masked and Anonymous*," *Montague Street* 1 (2009): 80–103.

Chapter Four: "He's the Property of Jesus": The Gospel Period

1. Taken from the documentary *Bob Dylan 1975–1981: Rolling Thunder and the Gospel Years* (Highway 61 Entertainment, 2006). My transcription.

2. In recent years, Yusuf Islam has returned to the recording studio, releasing the albums *An Other Cup* (2006) and *Roadsinger* (2009).

3. Dale C. Allison Jr., *The Love There That's Sleeping: The Art and Spirituality of George Harrison* (New York: Continuum, 2006), 3. I have expressed my own appreciation for Harrison's religious reflections in *"Brainwashed,* by George Harrison and the *Bhagavad Gita,"* *Journal of Religion and Popular Culture* 8 (2004): http://www.usask.ca/relst/jrpc. See too Joshua M. Greene, *Here Comes the Sun: The Spiritual and Musical Journey of George Harrison* (Hoboken, NJ: John Wiley & Sons, 2006).

4. For various perspectives on Bob Dylan's gospel period, see in addition to other items listed in notes, Scott M. Marshall, with Marcia Ford, *Restless Pilgrim: The Spiritual Journey of Bob Dylan* (Lake Mary, FL: Relevant, 2002), esp. chaps. 2 and 3; Marshall, "Talkin' Religion," in *Isis: A Bob Dylan Anthology*, ed. Derek Barker (London: Helter Skelter, 2001), 171–76; Mark Allan Powell, *Encyclopedia of Contemporary Christian Music* (Peabody, MA: Hendrickson, 2002), 277–86; Stephen H. Webb, *Dylan Redeemed: From* Highway 61 *to* Saved (New York: Continuum, 2006); John J. Thompson, *The Story of Christian Rock & Roll* (Toronto: ECW, 2000), 73–75; and Mark Joseph, *The Rock & Roll Rebellion* (Nashville: Broadman & Holman, 1999), 101–11.

5. See Bob Dylan, *Lyrics: 1962–2001* (New York: Simon & Schuster, 2004), 442–43.

6. Allison, *The Love There That's Sleeping*, 52.

7. George Harrison, "Awaiting On You All," *All Things Must Pass*, 1970, as quoted in George Harrison, *I Me Mine* (San Francisco: Chronicle Books, 2002 [originally published 1980]), 204. For full lyrics, see pp. 203–4.

8. Yusuf Islam responds to various criticisms directed at him in his Web site, prefacing a section (called "Chinese Whiskers") of questions and answers with the following statement: "Over the years, since becoming a Muslim, I have been accused of saying and doing things I have neither said nor done. Stories spread from person to person, whether intentionally or not; the result is that some people are led into thinking I am connected to causes I don't believe in or subscribe to. Now that I've decided to sing again, I'm sure it will attract a whole new wave of articles and allegations to diminish my work for peace and better understanding. So to avoid relying on whispers or hearsay, here's a chance to glance at what I have to say first-hand about some of those controversial issues people tried to tag me with—past and present—as well as a chance to reprise some of my old lyrics" (http://www.yusufislam.org.uk) (accessed August 13, 2010).

9. Ron Rosenbaum, "Born-again Bob: Four Theories," in *The Dylan Companion*, ed. Elizabeth Thomson and David Gutman (Cambridge, MA: Da Capo Press, 2001), 233.

10. "Precious Angel," *Slow Train Coming*, 1979; Dylan, *Lyrics*, 403.

11. This issue emerges in attempts to explain his name change from Zimmerman to Dylan as well, on which, see Daniel Karlin, "Bob Dylan's Names," in *Do You Mr Jones? Bob Dylan with the Poets and Professors*, ed. Neil Corcoran (London: Pimlico, 2003), 41–42, 338 n. 16.

12. Rosenbaum, "Born-again Bob," 235.

13. Paul Williams reprinted "Dylan—What Happened?" in *Bob Dylan: Watching the River Flow, Observations on His Art-In-Progress 1966–1995* (London: Omnibus Press, 1996), 63–133. He mentions Dylan's purchase of copies of the booklet on the first, unnumbered page after the front cover.

14. This article also appears in Williams's *Bob Dylan: Watching the River Flow*, 158–61. This excerpt is from 158.

15. Ibid., 159.

16. Lyrics available at http://www.bobdylan.com.

17. R. Clifton Spargo and Anne K. Ream, "Bob Dylan and Religion," in *The Cambridge Companion to Bob Dylan*, Cambridge Companions to American Studies, ed. Kevin J. H. Dettmar (Cambridge: Cambridge University Press, 2009), 96.

18. See Dylan, *Lyrics*, 383–84 for "Changing of the Guards"; 386–87 for "No Time to Think"; and 394–95 for "Where Are You Tonight? (Journey through Dark Heat)."

19. Ibid., 396. I am not aware of any recording of this song by Dylan, but it appears on the album *Up Front* (1981) by Billy Cross and the Delta Cross Band.

20. Anthony Varesi, *The Bob Dylan Albums: A Critical Study* (Toronto: Guernica, 2002), 143.

21. Howard Sounes, *Down the Highway: The Life of Bob Dylan* (New York: Grove Press, 2001), 319.

22. Ibid., 324.

23. Dylan, *Lyrics*, 383–84.

24. Ibid., 389.

25. Ibid., 390.

26. Ibid., 417, 432.

27. Ibid., 394–95.

28. Compare the language of "Up to Me" (*Biograph*, 1985), where we hear that Jesus' Sermon on the Mount (Matt. 5–7) is "too complex." See Bob Dylan, *Lyrics: 1962–1985* (New York: Alfred A. Knopf, 1985), 371–72.

29. Dylan, *Lyrics*, 394.

30. As the last song on *Street Legal*, this song occupies a conspicuous position as "closest" to the first song on *Slow Train Coming*, chronologically speaking. I discuss another significant transition from one album to the next—*"Love and Theft"* (2001) to *Modern Times* (2006)—in chapter 5.

31. Walter Benjamin, "The Work of Art in the Age of Mechanical Reproduction," in *Illuminations: Essays and Reflections*, trans. Harry Zohn, ed. Hannah Arendt (New York: Schocken Books, 1968), 234.

32. For reflections on this album, see Mark Allan Powell, *Encyclopedia of Contemporary Christian Music* (Peabody, MA: Hendrickson, 2002), 195–96; and Michael J. Gilmour, *Gods and Guitars: Seeking the Sacred in Post-1960s Popular Music* (Waco, TX: Baylor University Press, 2009), 119–22.

33. Alice Cooper's real name is Vince Damon Furnier. He usually refers to his stage alter ego, Alice Cooper, in the third person.

34. Alice Cooper, with Keith and Kent Zimmerman, *Alice Cooper, Golf Monster: A Rock 'N' Roller's 12 Steps to Becoming a Golf Addict* (New York: Crown Publishers, 2007), 198.

35. *The Simpsons*, "She Used To Be My Girl" (episode number 339, 16th season) first aired Sunday, December 5, 2004. CBS aired Ed Bradley's interview with Bob Dylan on *60 Minutes* the same evening.

36. Bryan Cheyette, "On the 'D' Train: Bob Dylan's Conversions," in *Do You Mr Jones? Bob Dylan with the Poets and Professors*, ed. Neil Corcoran (London: Pimlico, 2003), 251, 246, 248, 249–50.

37. See, e.g., Marshall, *Restless Pilgrim*, 175–80, and throughout.

38. Sounes, *Down the Highway*, 335, with notes 489.

39. Ibid., 335.

40. My transcription.

41. For an introduction to Steve Taylor and his music, see Powell, *Encyclopedia*, 928–33.

42. Dan Peters and Steve Peters, with Cher Merrill, *Why Knock Rock?* (Minneapolis: Bethany House, 1984), 23.

43. Ibid., 220.

44. For discussion of this album from a Jewish perspective, see Daniel Maoz, "Shekhinah as Woman: Kabbalistic References in Dylan's *Infidels*," in *Call Me the Seeker: Listening to Religion in Popular Music*, ed. Michael J. Gilmour (New York: Continuum, 2005), 3–16.

45. Sounes, *Down the Highway*, 355–56.

46. Colin Larkin, compiler and ed., *The Encyclopedia of Popular Music*, 5th concise ed. (London: Omnibus Press, 2007), 470.

47. C. S. Lewis, *The Four Loves* (Glasgow: William Collins Sons & Co., 1960), 45–46.

48. Powell, *Encyclopedia*, 279.

49. Lewis, *Four Loves*, 46.

50. Greil Marcus, "Amazing Chutzpah," in *The Dylan Companion*, ed. Elizabeth Thomson and David Gutman, updated and expanded ed. (Cambridge, MA: Da Capo Press, 2001), 237. Italics in original.

51. Fran Landesman, "Sorry, Bobby," in Thomson and Gutman, *Dylan Companion*, 242.

52. Lewis, *Four Loves*, 46.

53. Melody Green, with David Hazard, *No Compromise: The Life Story of Keith Green*, rev. and expanded ed. (Eugene, OR: Harvest, 2000), 291. Powell claims Dylan spoke to them about the lyrics for *Saved* (*Encyclopedia*, 382).

54. Green, *No Compromise*, 290–91.

55. Lewis, *Four Loves*, 46.

56. Green, *No Compromise*, 291. Emphasis original.

57. Dylan, *Lyrics*, 403.

58. Ibid., 125–26.

59. Ruvik Danieli and Anat Biletzki, "We Call It a Snake: Dylan Reclaims the Creative Word," in *Bob Dylan and Philosophy: It's Alright, Ma (I'm Only Thinking)*, Popular Culture and Philosophy 17, ed. Peter Vernezze and Carl J. Porter (Chicago: Open Court, 2006), 90. On this song, see too Karlin, "Bob Dylan's Names," 37–38.

60. Allison, *The Love There That's Sleeping*, 3.

61. Dylan, *Lyrics*, 389.

62. See esp. Hal Lindsey, with C. C. Carlson, *The Late Great Planet Earth* (Grand Rapids: Zondervan, 1970).

63. Green, *No Compromise*, 290.

64. http://www.bobdylan.com (accessed August 16, 2010). Italics added.

65. "Brownsville Girl," *Knocked Out Loaded*, 1986 (Dylan, *Lyrics*, 511).

66. Taken from Jonathan Cott, ed., *Bob Dylan: The Essential Interviews* (New York: Wenner Books, 2006), xii.

67. For the contents of these sermons, see Clinton Heylin, ed., *Saved: The Gospel Speeches of Bob Dylan* (New York: Hanuman Books, 1990).

68. This is also true of Dylan's Christmas album, released in fall 2009. The arrival of *Christmas in the Heart* was a delightful surprise for many. Seasonal music by popular artists, like other genres Dylan dabbles in, has a diverse and venerable history, and it seems only fitting he should pay tribute to the genre. For a few remarks on Christmas songs and albums by pop artists, see my *Gods and Guitars*, 181–82, n. 9.

69. Dylan, *Chronicles*, 199, 221.

70. Powell, *Encyclopedia*, 283.

71. Steve Stockman, *The Rock Cries Out: Discovering Eternal Truth in Unlikely Music* (Lake Mary, FL: Relevant, 2004), 15.

72. See also Francis J. Beckwith, "Busy Being Born Again: Bob Dylan's Christian Philosophy," in Vernezze and Porter, *Bob Dylan and Philosophy*, 145; and Spargo and Ream, "Bob Dylan and Religion," 87–88.

Chapter 5: That Most Serious of Subjects: The Good Book, the Testaments Both Old and New

1. Bob Dylan dedicated an episode of his *Theme Time Radio Hour* to the Bible (September 6, 2006), and I take this chapter title from his opening remarks. I illustrate Dylan's career-long use of the Scriptures in Michael J. Gilmour, *Tan-*

gled Up in the Bible: Bob Dylan and Scripture (New York: Continuum, 2004), particularly in the appendix, which lists parallels between the songs and biblical passages chronologically according to album release dates (105–41).

2. Bob Dylan, *Chronicles,* vol. 1 (New York: Simon & Schuster, 2004), 71.

3. Linda Hutcheon, *A Theory of Adaptation* (New York and London: Routledge, 2006), xvi, 16.

4. Woody Guthrie, *Bound for Glory* (New York: Plume, 1983; first published 1943), 258.

5. Walter Benjamin, *The Arcades Project*, trans. Howard Eiland and Kevin McLaughlin (Cambridge, MA.: Belknap Press of Harvard University Press, 1999), N1, 10.

6. Ibid., N2, 6; N1a, 8.

7. Walter Benjamin, "One-Way Street," in *Reflections: Essays, Aphorisms, Autobiographical Writings*, trans. Edmund Jephcott, ed. Peter Demetz (New York: Schocken, 1978), 69.

8. Gerhard Richter, "Acts of Self-Portraiture: Benjamin's Confessional and Literary Writings," in *The Cambridge Companion to Walter Benjamin*, ed. David S. Ferris (Cambridge: Cambridge University Press, 2004), 233.

9. Sam Shepard, *The Rolling Thunder Logbook* (Cambridge, MA: Da Capo Press, 2004 [original publication, 1977], 156.

10. Dylan, *Chronicles*, 58 (emphasis added).

11. Ibid., 36–41. Compare a young Woody Guthrie poring over the books in the library: "I went to the town library and scratched around in the books. I carried them home by the dozens and by the armloads, on any subject, I didn't care which. I wanted to look into everything a little bit, and pick out something, something that would turn me into a human being of some kind—free to work for my own self, and free to work for everybody" (Guthrie, *Bound for Glory*, 174).

12. The phrase is reminiscent of one in "Talkin' John Birch Paranoid Blues" where the narrator investigates "all the books in the library" (Bootleg Series, Vols. 1–3, *Rare and Unreleased*, 1991; see Bob Dylan, *Lyrics: 1962–2001* [New York: Simon & Schuster, 2004], 17–18).

13. Dylan, *Chronicles*, 61 (emphasis added). Note the repetition of items on a table on 58 and 61, perhaps suggesting those scenes provide similar illuminations.

14. Hannah Arendt, "Walter Benjamin: 1892–1940," editorial introduction to *Illuminations: Essays and Reflections*, trans. Harry Zohn, ed. Hannah Arendt (New York: Schocken Books, 1968), 12 (italics added).

15. For these examples, listen to "Highlands," *Time Out of Mind*, 1999; and "I Feel A Change Coming On," *Together through Life*, 2009.

16. "Brownsville Girl," *Knocked Out Loaded*, 1986. For discussion of movie influences on Dylan's lyrics, see Gray's entry "Film Dialogue in Dylan's Lyrics," in Michael Gray, *The Bob Dylan Encyclopedia* (New York: Continuum, 2006), 225–31. See p. 226 for examples of Humphrey Bogart lines cited in songs.

17. On the spaces and journeys in Bob Dylan's songs, see Richard Brown, "Highway 61 and Other American States of Mind," in *Do You, Mr Jones? Bob Dylan with the Poets and Professors*, ed. Neil Corcoran (London: Pimlico, 2003), 193–220; and Bryan Cheyette, "On the 'D' Train: Bob Dylan's Conversions," in Corcoran, *Do You, Mr Jones?* 221–52.

18. Bono, introduction to *Selections from the Book of Psalms*, Pocket Canon (New York: Grove Press, 1999), viii–ix (ellipses original).

19. Stephen Davis, *Old Gods Almost Dead: The 40-Year Odyssey of the Rolling Stones* (New York: Broadway Books, 2001), 237.

20. For this section, I draw largely on my chapter "Bob Dylan's Bible," which appears in *The Oxford Handbook of Reception History of the Bible*, ed. Michael Lieb, Emma Mason, Christopher Rowland, and Jonathan Roberts (Oxford: Oxford University Press, forthcoming).

21. Hutcheon, *Adaptation*, xvi and 9; see too 4, 7, 149, 173, 176.

22. Ibid., xiv, 3, 8.

23. Ibid., 170, 9.

24. Michael Gray, *Song and Dance Man III: The Art of Bob Dylan* (London: Continuum, 2000), 15.

25. See, e.g., Gray, *Song and Dance Man III*, 17–44; Greil Marcus, *The Old, Weird America: The World of Bob Dylan's Basement Tapes* (New York: Picador USA, 1997); and Sean Wilentz, "American Recordings: On *'Love and Theft'* and the Minstrel Boy," in *Do You, Mr Jones? Bob Dylan with the Poets and Professors*, ed. Neil Corcoran (London: Pimlico, 2003), 295–305.

26. Stephen Scobie, *Alias Bob Dylan Revisited* (Calgary: Red Deer Press, 2003), 305, 306.

27. The book in question is Eric Lott's *Love and Theft: Blackface Minstrelsy and the American Working Class* (1993), which is itself a riff (Lott's term) off Leslie Fielder's *Love and Death in the American Novel* (1966). Lott includes an essay on Dylan's album *"Love and Theft"* in *The Cambridge Companion to Bob Dylan*, ed. Kevin J. H. Dettmar (Cambridge: Cambridge University Press, 2009), 167–73, in which he speculates about reasons why his title caught the singer's attention: "I suspect Dylan liked my title for its general resonance, in which stolen hearts and emotional misdemeanors stalk the sweetness of love, as they usually do in Dylan's songs. More particularly, though, he knows full well the cross-cultural indebtedness of music in the Americas, his included, and alludes to it in the songs as well as the title, itself stolen, of *'Love and Theft'*" (167–68).

28. Sloman, liner notes to *Tell Tale Signs*, 34.

29. Christopher Ricks, *Dylan's Visions of Sin* (New York: HarperCollins, 2003), 210–11.

30. See Dylan, *Lyrics*, 129, 145, 326, 395, 549, and 490.

31. Ibid., 81, 156, and 224.

32. Taken from Jonathan Cott, ed., *Bob Dylan: The Essential Interviews* (New York: Wenner Books, 2006), 50.

33. Sloman, *Tell Tale Signs* liner notes, 44.

34. Bert Cartwright, *The Bible in the Lyrics of Bob Dylan*, rev. and updated, Wanted Man Study Series 4 (Bury, Lancashire: Wanted Man, 1992), 15.

35. Dylan, *Lyrics*, 574.

36. Author's transcription.

37. See, e.g., Scott M. Marshall, with Marcia Ford, *Restless Pilgrim: The Spiritual Journey of Bob Dylan* (Lake Mary, FL: Relevant, 2002); Mark Allan Powell, *Encyclopedia of Contemporary Christian Music* (Peabody, MA: Hendrickson, 2002), 277–86; Stephen H. Webb, *Dylan Redeemed: From* Highway 61 *to* Saved (New York: Continuum, 2006); cf. Paul Williams, *Bob Dylan: Watching the River Flow, Observations on His Art-In-Progress 1966–1995* (London: Omnibus Press, 1996), 63–151.

38. Daniel Maoz, "Shekhinah as Woman: Kabbalistic References in Dylan's *Infidels*," in *Call Me the Seeker: Listening to Religion in Popular Music*, ed. Michael J. Gilmour (New York: Continuum, 2005), 4.

39. Seth Rogovoy, *Bob Dylan: Prophet, Mystic, Poet* (New York: Scribner, 2009), 13. For further discussion, see also Michael Billig, *Rock n' Roll Jews, Judaic Traditions in Literature, Music and Art* (Syracuse, NY: Syracuse University Press, 2001), 118–31.

40. Dylan, *Lyrics*, 458.

41. Ibid., 345–46.

42. I take this term from Hutcheon, *Adaptation*, xvi.

43. Dylan, *Lyrics*, 598.

44. Taken from http://www.bobdylan.com.

45. Taken from Jonathan Lethem, "The Genius of Bob Dylan," *Rolling Stone* 1008 (September 7, 2006): 76.

46. This is literally true, as Keys was born in Hell's Kitchen, an area in Manhattan, New York.

47. Hutcheon, *Adaptation*, xvi, 4, 7, 149, 173, 176.

Chapter 6: "Searchin' High, Searchin' Low" for Religious Meaning in Bob Dylan's Music

1. Walter Benjamin, "A Berlin Chronicle," in *Reflections: Essays, Aphorisms, Autobiographical Writings*, trans. Edmund Jephcott, ed. Peter Demetz (New York: Schocken, 1978), 28.

2. Bob Dylan, *Chronicles*, vol. 1 (New York: Simon & Schuster, 2004), 35–46.

3. This section of the chapter first appeared as "Death Is Not the End: Artistic Collaboration and a Musical Resurrection in Dylan's *Chronicles*," *Montague Street* 1 (Winter 2009): 24–31. I am grateful to editor Nina Goss for her many helpful suggestions and permission to reprint, slightly edited, in this context.

4. See too Christopher Ricks, *Dylan's Visions of Sin* (New York: HarperCollins, 2003), 27.

5. Colin Larkin, compiler and ed., *The Encyclopedia of Popular Music*, 5th concise ed. (London: Omnibus Press, 2007), 471.

6. Victoria's Secret sold a limited edition CD of Dylan songs under the title *Lovesick*, and he appeared in one of the company's commercials.

7. Dylan, *Chronicles*, 218.

8. Sloman, liner notes to *Tell Tale Signs*, 12–13.

9. The song title does not have a question mark on the album itself, or at http://www.bobdylan.com, but does include one in Bob Dylan, *Lyrics: 1962–2001* (New York: Simon & Schuster, 2004), 536–37. I follow *Lyrics* here.

10. Dylan, *Chronicles*, 210 (prostitute), 146 (angels), 213 (Joan of Arc), 217 ("watching gods"), 165 ("Political World"), 167 ("What Good Am I?"), 169 ("Dignity"), 171 ("Disease of Conceit"), 172 ("What Was It You Wanted?"), 191 ("Where Teardrops Fall"), 25 (John Wilkes Booth).

11. Dylan recorded the last two songs mentioned during the *Oh Mercy* sessions but cut them from the album. Versions of both appear on later releases, including 2008's *Tell Tale Signs*.

12. Dylan, *Chronicles*, 146.

13. "What Was It You Wanted?" *Oh Mercy* (1989); Dylan, *Lyrics*, 536.

14. Dylan, *Chronicles*, 218, 195.

15. Ibid., 218.

16. Michael Gray, *The Bob Dylan Encyclopedia* (New York: Continuum, 2006), 515.

17. The "New Morning" chapter is different in kind from "Oh Mercy."

18. Dylan, *Chronicles*, 220, 218.

19. For now we will need to settle for accounts of these stories by others. See, e.g., Andy Gill and Kevin Odegard's informative *A Simple Twist of Fate: Bob Dylan and the Making of* Blood on the Tracks (Cambridge, MA: Da Capo Press, 2004), and Greil Marcus, *Like a Rolling Stone: Bob Dylan at the Crossroads* (New York: Public Affairs, 2005).

20. Dylan, *Chronicles*, 143–221, 181. Dylan, with Canadian producer and musician Daniel Lanois, recorded *Oh Mercy* between March 7 and March 24, 1989 (see Clinton Heylin, *Bob Dylan: The Recording Sessions 1960–1994* [New York: St. Martin's Griffin, 1995], 175). The chapter begins with events leading up to those productive sessions.

21. Dylan, *Chronicles*, 204, 206.

22. Ibid., 145–49, 219. The phrase may allude to the 1925 T. S. Eliot poem of that name.

23. Ibid., 146, 151, 153, 148, 152 (for *Chronicles* page citations, numbers are listed in the order in which quotes appear within the paragraph).

24. Ibid., 209, 188, 148–51.

25. Ibid., 191.

26. Ibid., 157, 161.

27. Ibid., 174.

28. Among other professional contacts, U2 performs an energized version of

"All Along the Watchtower" in their film and CD *Rattle and Hum* (1988). Dylan accompanies Bono on the *Rattle and Hum* CD in the song "Love Rescue Me," which the two cowrote.

29. Dylan, *Chronicles*, 176.
30. Dylan, *Lyrics*, 527.
31. Dylan, *Chronicles*, 182, 177.
32. Ibid., 179, 146.
33. "It Ain't Me, Babe," *Another Side of Bob Dylan* (1964); "Is Your Love in Vain?" *Street Legal* (1978); "Trust Yourself," *Empire Burlesque* (1985).
34. Dylan, *Chronicles*, 37.
35. Ibid., 72.
36. Ibid., 288.
37. Ibid., 82.
38. Ibid., 84, 87, 88–89.
39. Woody Guthrie does the same in *Bound for Glory*, which starts and finishes with the author riding on a freight train, on the same journey, in chapters 1 and 19. In between he tells a series of stories about his life, beginning with childhood.
40. Dylan, *Chronicles*, 4–7, 15, 21, 22, 261, 279–82.
41. Ibid., 22.
42. Taken from Bill Flanagan, *U2 at the End of the World* (New York: Delta, 1995), 159.
43. Edgar Allan Poe, "The Man of the Crowd," in *Tales of Mystery and Imagination*, Wordsworth Classics (Hertfordshire: Wordsworth, 1993), 387, 390.
44. Ibid., 392, 393, 396.
45. The song "Blood in My Eyes" is on the album *World Gone Wrong*, 1993. One edition of *Modern Times* (2006) includes a DVD with the video for this song. "Standing in the Doorway" is on *Time Out of Mind*, 1997. The walking-stick picture I have in mind appears in the liner notes to *Tell Tale Signs* (2008).
46. See esp. Bob Dylan, *Drawn Blank* (New York: Random House, 1994). Dylan introduces this collection of sketches in his foreword this way: "They were done over a two- or three-year period from about 1989 to about 1991 or '92 in various locations mainly to relax and refocus a restless mind. My drawing instructor in high school lectured and demonstrated continuously to 'draw only what you can see' so that if you were at a loss for words, something could be explained and even more importantly, not misunderstood. Rather than fantasize, be real and draw it only if it is in front of you and if it's not there, put it there and by making the lines connect, we can vaguely get at something other than the world we know" (n.p.).
47. In order: "Man in the Long Black Coat" (*Oh Mercy*, 1989); the film *Masked and Anonymous* (2003; played by John Goodman); "The Ballad of Frankie Lee and Judas Priest" (*John Wesley Harding*, 1967); "The Lonesome Death of Hattie Carroll" (*The Times They Are A-Changin'*, 1964).

48. E.g., in order: "Only a Hobo" (Bootleg Series, Vols. 1–3, 1991); "Joey" (*Desire*, 1976); "Talkin' John Birch Paranoid Blues" (Bootleg Series, Vols. 1–3, 1991); "Leopard-Skin Pill-Box Hat" (*Blonde on Blonde*, 1966).

49. E.g., in order: "Masters of War" (*The Freewheelin' Bob Dylan*, 1963); "Hurricane" (*Desire*, 1976); "Who Killed Davey Moore?" (Bootleg Series, Vols. 1–3, 1991), "Every Grain of Sand" (*Shot of Love*, 1981).

50. Poe, "The Man of the Crowd," 397 (emphasis added).

51. See Walter Benjamin, "Some Motifs in Baudelaire," in *Illuminations: Essays and Reflections*, trans. Harry Zohn, ed. Hannah Arendt (New York: Schocken Books, 1968), esp. 170–76; *The Arcades Project*, trans. Howard Eiland and Kevin McLaughlin (Cambridge, MA: Belknap Press of Harvard University Press, 1999), M1, 6; M2, 8; M12a, 1–3; M14, 1; M15a, 2; M16, 1; and "The Return of the *Flâneur*," in *Selected Writings, Volume 2 1927–1934*, trans. Rodney Livingstone et al., ed. Michael W. Jennings, Howard Eiland, and Gary Smith (Cambridge, MA: Belknap Press of Harvard University Press, 1999), 262–67.

52. Benjamin, *Arcades Project*, M1, 6.

53. Poe, "Man of the Crowd," 393, 387, 388, 392, 397, 398.

54. Ibid., 393, 394. Hannah Arendt describes the *flâneur* as "aimlessly strolling through the crowds in the big cities in studied contrast to their hurried, purposeful activity," and it is to him "that things reveal themselves in their secret meaning" (editorial introduction to Benjamin, *Illuminations*, 12). For S. Brent Plate, the *flâneur* "wanders the streets, ambling through its passages, and revealing undisclosed secrets" (*Walter Benjamin, Religion, and Aesthetics: Rethinking Religion through the Arts* [New York: Routledge, 2005], 131).

55. Wendy Lesser, "Dancing with Dylan," in *The Rose & The Briar: Death, Love and Liberty in the American Ballad*, ed. Sean Wilentz and Greil Marcus (New York: W. W. Norton, 2005), 317–25; Scobie, *Alias*, esp. 159–63. Note also Nicholas Roe, "Playing Time," in *Do You, Mr Jones? Bob Dylan with the Poets and Professors*, ed. Neil Corcoran (London: Pimlico, 2003), 97–102. For "Lily, Rosemary and the Jack of Hearts," see Dylan, *Lyrics*, 341–43.

56. Gill and Odegard, *Simple Twist of Fate*, 160.

57. Dylan, *Lyrics*, 342.

58. Scobie, *Alias*, 159.

59. Lesser, "Dancing," 323–24 (emphasis original).

60. Scobie, *Alias*, 162.

61. Lesser, "Dancing," 319, 320–21.

62. See Dylan, *Lyrics*, 342.

63. Lesser, "Dancing," 322; Scobie, *Alias*, 326, n. 29

64. Dylan, *Lyrics*, 341.

65. Lesser, "Dancing," 322. There seem to be other vocal jokes at play as well. Scobie hears the singer slurring the *r* in "drillin' " with the result we almost hear "Dylan" (*Alias*, 326, n. 30). Nicholas Roe hears the phrase "a cold revolver" (*Lyrics*, 342) as "Colt revolver," which is plausibly a deliberate pun ("Playing Time," 99).

Concluding Thoughts

1. Comments made during an interview with Ed Bradley, for the CBS program *60 Minutes*. The program originally aired December 5, 2004. Author's transcription.

2. Comments made by Joan Baez regarding (and presumably paraphrasing) words spoken by Bob Dylan early in his career, in Martin Scorsese's documentary *No Direction Home* (2005).

3. I choose this example at random, but it is a psalm Dylan knows well. We hear it in "Love Rescue Me," coauthored with Bono, which appears on U2's album *Rattle and Hum* (1988). The song includes obvious allusions to this biblical poem.

4. John Barlow's afterword in *The Complete Annotated Grateful Dead Lyrics*, ed. Alan Trist and David Dodd (New York: Free Press, 2005), 420.

5. Ibid., 421.

6. For theoretical perspectives, a classic statement on this phenomenon is Roland Barthes's *The Death of the Author*, trans. Stephen Heath (New York: Hill, 1977).

7. Stephen H. Webb, *Dylan Redeemed: From* Highway 61 *to* Saved (New York: Continuum, 2006), 11, etc.

8. Harold Bloom, *How to Read and Why* (New York: Touchstone, 2000), 29.

Appendix: Bob Dylan's Career in Stolen Moments

1. Jonathan Cott, ed., *Bob Dylan: The Essential Interviews* (New York: Wenner Books, 2006).

2. Stephen Scobie, *And Forget My Name: A Speculative Biography of Bob Dylan* (Victoria, BC: Ekstasis, 1999). Note also Allen Ginsberg's poems "Postcard to D," "Blue Gossip," and "On Reading Dylan's Writings," all included in *The Dylan Companion*, ed. Elizabeth Thomson and David Gutman (Cambridge, MA: Da Capo Press, 2001), 145–48.

3. For information, see http://www.montaguestreetjournal.com.

4. For biographical considerations, see, for instance, Clinton Heylin, *Bob Dylan: Behind the Shades, Take Two* (London: Penguin, 2001); Howard Sounes, *Down the Highway: The Life of Bob Dylan* (New York: Grove Press, 2001); and Michael Gray, *The Bob Dylan Encyclopedia* (New York: Continuum, 2006).

5. See, e.g., Kevin J. H. Dettmar, "Chronology of Dylan's Life," in *The Cambridge Companion to Bob Dylan*, ed. Kevin J. H. Dettmar, Cambridge Companions to American Studies (Cambridge: Cambridge University Press, 2009), xii–xvii. Note also Gray's "Introduction: An Album-by-Album Guide to Dylan's Work," in Michael Gray, *Song and Dance Man III: The Art of Bob Dylan* (London: Continuum, 2000), 1–16 (releases up to 1998, with short commentary).

6. Colin Larkin, compiler and ed., *The Encyclopedia of Popular Music*, 5th concise ed. (London: Omnibus Press, 2007), 467.

7. Bob Dylan, *Chronicles,* vol. 1 (New York: Simon & Schuster, 2004), 9.

8. Heylin, *Behind the Shades*, 64.

9. On the significance of this review, see, e.g., ibid., 74–77.

10. See Sean Wilentz's liner notes to *Bob Dylan Live at the Gaslight 1962* (2005) for an introduction to this long-in-coming release.

11. For various details, see Gray, *Encylopedia*, 447–49.

12. For details, see Andy Gill, *Classic Bob Dylan 1962–69: My Back Pages* (London: Carlton, 1998), 47–48; Sounes, *Down the Highway*, 133–35.

13. For footage of Dylan's early Newport appearances, see *Bob Dylan: The Other Side of the Mirror: Live at Newport Folk Festival 1963–65* (produced and directed by Murray Lerner, 2007).

14. Martin Scorsese's documentary *No Direction Home* includes footage of the moment.

15. See Greil Marcus's liner notes to *The Basement Tapes* for various details about the circumstances and the nature of these recordings. For interesting reflections on the circulation of unofficial recordings, see James C. Klagge, "*Great White Wonder*: The Morality of Bootlegging Bob," in *Bob Dylan and Philosophy: It's Alright, Ma (I'm Only Thinking)*, Popular Culture and Philosophy, ed. Peter Vernezze and Carl J. Porter (Chicago: Open Court, 2006), 40–52.

16. Gray, *Encyclopedia*, 204. "It's not much of a movie," Greil Marcus writes. There is "a lot of travelogue, endless shots of crowds gathering outside the Albert Hall, much hotel-room composing and playing between Dylan and Robertson; the fundamental text seems to be a variation on the theme of the betrayed fan . . . and the artist-who-to-himself-must-be-true" (*Mystery Train: Images of America in Rock 'N' Roll Music*, 4th rev. ed. [New York: Plume, 1997], 218).

17. The album recording these two concerts earned a Grammy Award for Album of the Year in 1973.

18. Larkin, *Encyclopedia*, 469.

19. Paul Williams's review captures the genius of these performances and deserves a reading by anyone listening to this album: "Impact? After a dozen times through, I feel I'm just *starting* to hear this album"; "That singer, that guitar, those drums . . . oh God" (*Bob Dylan: Watching the River Flow, Observations on His Art-In-Progress 1966–1995* [London: Omnibus Press, 1996], 34, 35 [italics and ellipses original]). See too Marcus, *Mystery Train*, 221.

20. See, e.g., Sounes, *Down the Highway*, 325.

21. See the liner notes to *Biograph* (1985) for comments on "Gotta Serve Somebody."

22. Sounes notes how important an up-to-date sound and video presence was for Dylan in the early 1980s, with the advent of compact discs and music television: "MTV had more than sixteen million subscribers within two years of its launch in 1981. When Bob resumed his career in 1983, to make the album *Infidels*, he had to take into account these notable changes" (*Down the Highway*, 354).

23. Other collaborations with Petty include the cowriting and recording of "Got My Mind Made Up" (*Knocked Out Loaded*, 1986), and "Band of the Hand

(It's Hell Time Man!)" (lyrics by Dylan only), part of the soundtrack for the Paul Michael Glaser film *Band of the Hand* (1986). Both were also part of the supergroup the Traveling Wilburys.

24. The soundtrack for the film, released October 20, 1987, features three songs by Dylan: "The Usual," "Had a Dream about You Baby," and "Night After Night." In the film, Dylan also sings "A Couple More Years." For details and discussion, see Clinton Heylin, *Bob Dylan: The Recording Sessions 1960–1994* (New York: St. Martin's Griffin, 1995), 165–70.

25. The full speech appears in Elizabeth Thomson and David Gutman, eds., *The Dylan Companion*, updated and expanded ed. (Cambridge, MA: Da Capo Press, 2001), 286–88. The citation is from 287.

26. Gordon Ball, "Dylan and the Nobel," *Oral Tradition* 22.1 (2007): 14-29.

27. Joseph Ratzinger, Benedict XVI, *John Paul II: My Beloved Predecessor*, ed. Elio Guerriero, trans. Matthew Sherry and the Vatican (Boston: Pauline Books & Media, 2007), 20.

28. The Pulitzer Prizes, "The 2008 Pulitzer Prize Winners: Special Awards and Citations," Columbia University, http://www.pulitzer.org (accessed August 24, 2010).

Selected Bibliography

Cartwright, Bert. *The Bible in the Lyrics of Bob Dylan.* Rev. and updated. Wanted Man Study Series 4. Bury, Lancashire: Wanted Man, 1992.

Corcoran, Neil, ed. *Do You Mr Jones? Bob Dylan with the Poets and Professors.* London: Pimlico, 2003.

Cott, Jonathan, ed. *Bob Dylan: The Essential Interviews.* New York: Wenner Books, 2006.

Dettmar, Kevin J. H., ed. *The Cambridge Companion to Bob Dylan.* Cambridge Companions to American Studies. Cambridge: Cambridge University Press, 2009.

Dylan, Bob. *Chronicles,* Vol. 1. New York: Simon & Schuster, 2004.

———. *Drawn Blank.* New York: Random House, 1994.

———. *Lyrics: 1962–1985.* New York: Alfred A. Knopf, 1985.

———. *Lyrics: 1962–2001.* New York: Simon & Schuster, 2004.

———. *Tarantula.* New York: St. Martin's Press, 1994. First published 1971.

Gill, Andy. *Classic Bob Dylan 1962–69: My Back Pages.* London: Carlton, 1998.

Gill, Andy, and Kevin Odegard. *A Simple Twist of Fate: Bob Dylan and the Making of* Blood on the Tracks. Cambridge, MA: Da Capo Press, 2004.

Gilmour, Michael J. "Bob Dylan's Bible." In *The Oxford Handbook of Reception History of the Bible.* Ed. Michael Lieb, Emma Mason, Christopher Rowland, and Jonathan Roberts. Oxford: Oxford University Press, forthcoming.

———. *Gods and Guitars: Seeking the Sacred in Post-1960s Popular Music.* Waco, TX: Baylor University Press, 2009.

———. *Tangled Up in the Bible: Bob Dylan and Scripture.* New York: Continuum, 2004.

Gray, Michael. *The Bob Dylan Encyclopedia.* New York: Continuum, 2006.

———. *Song and Dance Man III: The Art of Bob Dylan.* London: Continuum, 2000.

Gray, Michael, and John Bauldie, ed. *All Across the Telegraph: A Bob Dylan Handbook.* London: Sidgwick & Jackson, 1987.

Guthrie, Woody. *Bound for Glory.* New York: Plume, 1983. First published 1943.

Heine, Steven. *Bargainin' for Salvation: Bob Dylan, a Zen Master?* New York: Continuum, 2009.

Heylin, Clinton. *Bob Dylan: Behind the Shades, Take Two*. London: Penguin, 2001.

———. *Bob Dylan: The Recording Sessions 1960–1994*. New York: St. Martin's Griffin, 1995.

Kerouac, Jack. *On the Road*. Introduction by Ann Charters. London: Penguin, 1991. First published 1957.

Marcus, Greil. *Like a Rolling Stone: Bob Dylan at the Crossroads*. New York: PublicAffairs, 2005.

———. *The Old, Weird America: The World of Bob Dylan's Basement Tapes*. New York: Picador USA / Henry Holt & Co., 1997. First published with the title *Invisible Republic: Bob Dylan's Basement Tapes*. New York: Holt, 1997.

Marshall, Scott M., with Marcia Ford. *Restless Pilgrim: The Spiritual Journey of Bob Dylan*. Lake Mary, FL: Relevant Books, 2002.

Ricks, Christopher. *Dylan's Visions of Sin*. New York: HarperCollins, 2003.

Rogovoy, Seth. *Bob Dylan: Prophet, Mystic, Poet*. New York: Scribner, 2009.

Santelli, Robert. *The Bob Dylan Scrapbook: 1956–1966*. New York: Simon & Schuster, 2005.

Scobie, Stephen. *Alias Bob Dylan Revisited*. Calgary: Red Deer Press, 2003.

———. *And Forget My Name: A Speculative Biography of Bob Dylan*. Victoria, BC: Ekstasis, 1999.

Shepard, Sam. *The Rolling Thunder Logbook*. Cambridge, MA: Da Capo Press, 2004. First published 1977.

Sounes, Howard. *Down the Highway: The Life of Bob Dylan*. New York: Grove Press, 2001.

Thomson, Elizabeth, and David Gutman, eds. *The Dylan Companion*. Updated and expanded ed. Cambridge, MA: Da Capo Press, 2001.

Varesi, Anthony. *The Bob Dylan Albums: A Critical Study*. Toronto: Guernica, 2002.

Vernezze, Peter, and Carl J. Porter, eds. *Bob Dylan and Philosophy: It's Alright, Ma (I'm Only Thinking)*. Popular Culture and Philosophy 17. Chicago: Open Court, 2006.

Webb, Stephen H. *Dylan Redeemed: From Highway 61 to Saved*. New York: Continuum, 2006.

Williams, Paul. *Bob Dylan, Performing Artist: The Early Years, 1960–1973*. London: Omnibus Press, 2004.

———. *Bob Dylan Performing Artist 1974–1986: The Middle Years*. London: Omnibus Press, 1994.

———. *Bob Dylan, Performing Artist*. Vol. 3, *Mind Out of Time, 1986 and Beyond*. London: Omnibus Press, 2004.

———. *Bob Dylan: Watching the River Flow, Observations on his Art-in-Progress 1966–1995*. London: Omnibus Press, 1996.

Index

Titles of songs and albums with no songwriter designated are by Bob Dylan.

178